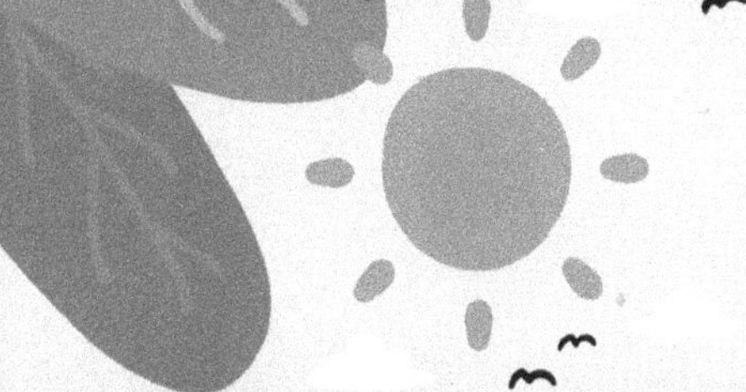

Ace Academic Publishing
ACHIEVING EXCELLENCE TOGETHER

THE ONE BIG BOOK

GRADE 3

For English, Math, and Science

- Includes Math, English, Science - all in one colorful book
- Detailed instructions to teach and learn with pictures and examples
- Best book for home schooling, practicing, and teaching
- Includes answers with detailed explanations

Detailed instructions along with interesting activities

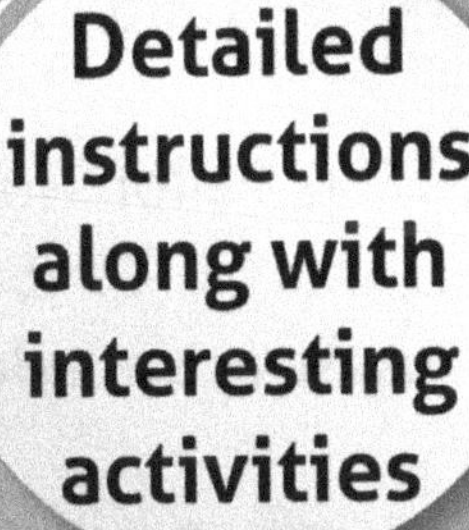

www.aceacademicpublishing.com

Author: Ace Academic Publishing

Prepaze is a sister company of Ace Academic Publishing. Intrigued by the unending possibilities of the internet and its role in education, Prepaze was created to spread the knowledge and learning across all corners of the world through an online platform. We equip ourselves with state-of-the-art technologies so that knowledge reaches the students through the quickest and the most effective channels.

The materials for our books are written by award winning teachers with several years of teaching experience. All our books are aligned with the state standards and are widely used by many schools throughout the country.

For enquiries and bulk order, contact us at the following address:

3736, Fallon Road, #403
Dublin, CA 94568
www.aceacademicpublishing.com

ISBN: 978-1-949383-37-9

Other books from Ace Academic Publishing

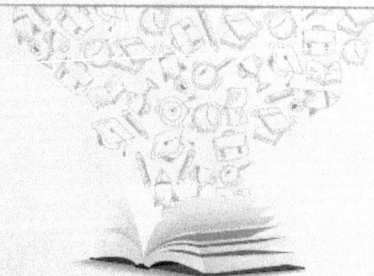

Contents

English

Math

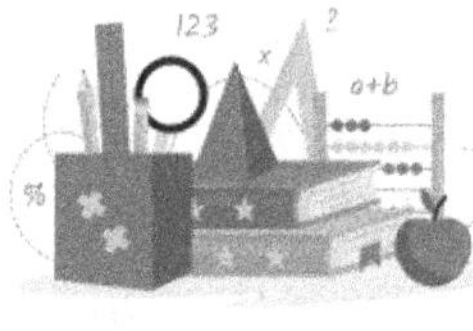

Science

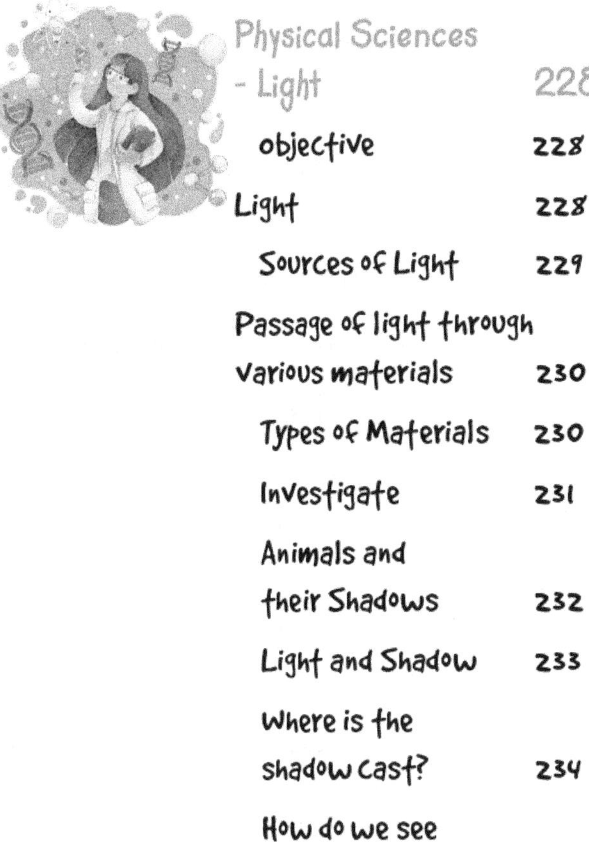

English

This book enables your children to explore the English language and develop the necessary expertise. A series of thought-provoking exercises, engaging activities, and engrossing puzzles facilitate your children with understanding the intricacies of the English language.

Language

Plural Nouns

A plural of a noun is formed by adding **s** or **es** to the end of the noun. The plural of the noun ***monkey*** is ***monkeys.***

An irregular noun is a noun that becomes plural by changing its spelling in other ways than adding an s or es to the end of the word.

Example

child - children

There are many other words that have such plural forms.

Write the plural form for the given nouns.

Singular	Plural
church	
baby	
finger	
person	
foot	
wolf	
ox	
medium	
butterfly	
sheep	

Abstract Nouns

Nouns are people, places, and things. Nouns can be either concrete or abstract.

Nouns that you can experience physically are called concrete nouns.

Example

For example: cat, pan, computer

Nouns that you cannot see, hear, smell, touch, or taste are called abstract nouns.

For example: simplicity, richness, anxiety.

Circle the Abstract Nouns

faith	silence	lie
lock	delay	pear
book	shirt	joy
nap	wisdom	chair

Underline the abstract nouns

1. Tilly told me about her childhood.

2. I wished her luck for the upcoming exams.

3. They thought of brilliant ideas for the project.

4. When you tell the truth, you don't have to remember it.

5. Carl put ice on his knee until the pain subsided.

6. Lydia fixed her printer using the internet.

7. Mona applied to colleges in Australia for higher education.

8. Mom had a scary dream last night.

9. Beauty lies in the eyes of the beholder.

10. Tina's imagination ran wild.

Fill in the abstract noun in the sentences

fear	anger	honesty	curiosity	loyalty
kindness	happiness	love	enjoyment	pleasure

1. It was a ____________ to see her performance.

2. When mom scolded me, I took out my ____________ on my pillow.

3. Mother Teresa won the Nobel Prize for her acts of ____________ .

4. Dogs wag their tails in ____________ .

5. My dad appreciates ____________ .

6. The employees showed their ____________ by working on Saturdays.

7. ____________ killed the cat.

8. I read adventure books for ____________ .

9. Her ____________ for art made her visit the Louvre Museum.

10. I have a ____________ of heights.

Pronouns are words that are used to replace a name, place, or thing in a sentence.

Example

Rebecca got a new project. **She** is working hard to complete **it** in time.

Instead of repeating the words "Rebecca" and "a new project," we replace them with the pronouns "she" and "it.'

Noun

- Elsa
- A bus
- You and Bill
- That boy
- The girls
- ______ (Your name)
- You and I

Fill in the blanks with appropriate pronouns

he	she	it	they
their	mine	both	any

1. Danny and Kate said ____________ had to leave early.

2. Jerry thought ____________ could stay up till midnight.

3. It's not your bag, it's ____________ .

4. She asked me to bring candies, but I don't have ____________ .

5. Sheila was sick, so ____________ could not go to the party.

6. Lisa and her brother asked ____________ aunt to stay longer.

7. ____________ the kittens were adopted by the same person.

8. I went to a small park with two swings in ____________ .

Regular and Irregular Verbs

Irregular verbs are verbs that do not take on the usual ***d, ed,*** or ***ied*** spelling patterns when the tense changes. Their spelling either changes with the tense or remains the same when used in a different tense.

Example

Present Tense	Past Tense
bear	bore
cut	cut

Here are a few verbs. Write their present and past tense.

Present Tense	Past Tense
sell	
	awoke
hear	
	told
take	
	scurried
wear	
	became
throw	
	saw

Subject-Verb Agreement

In a sentence, the verb should agree with the noun or subject in number.

A singular subject needs a singular verb. A plural subject needs a plural verb.

The Child is polite.

singular subject: Child

singular verb: is

both are singular

The Children of this school are polite.

plural subject: Children

plural verb: are

both are plural

Categorize the words into singular and plural nouns/verbs.

sleeps	pens	think	battery
cars	egg	am	bottle
wash	pushes	panic	rises
mirror	walls	lids	snore

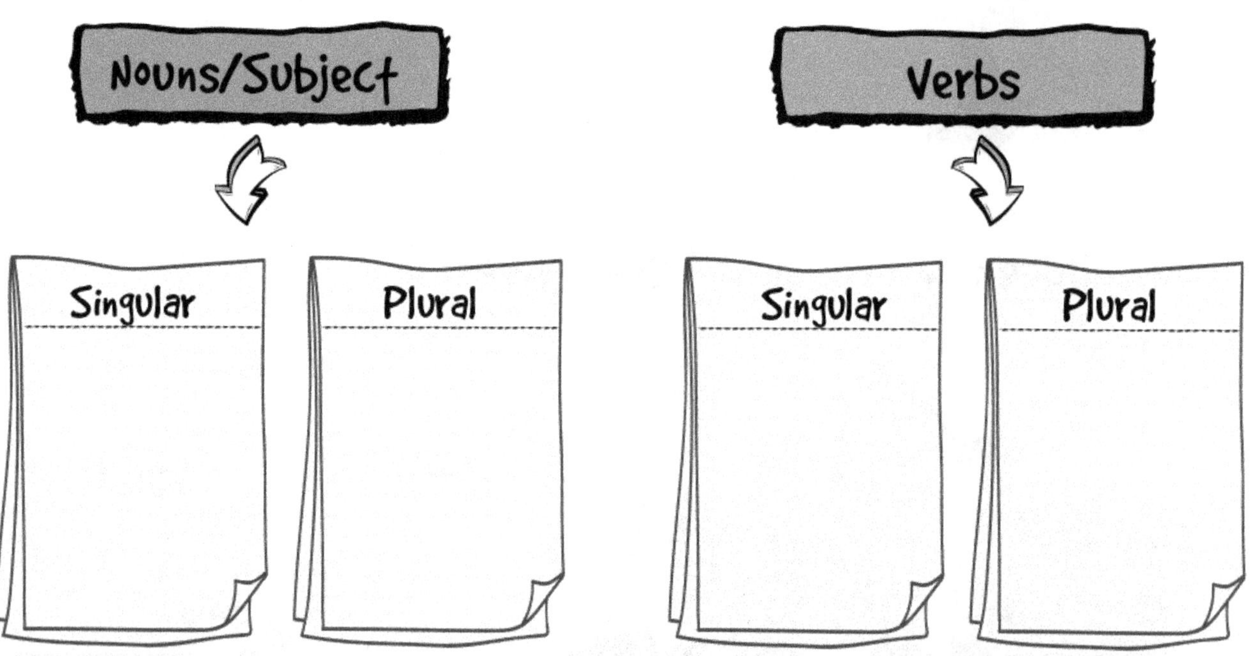

Write Y for sentences where the subject and the verb agree in number, and write N if they don't agree.

	Y	N
1) They were invited.		
2) The singer also play guitar.		
3) Where is the people?		
4) The baby with her toys are happy.		
5) The trees in the orchard look lovely.		
6) He or she are in trouble.		
7) Does the parrot talk?		
8) I were in the class.		

Pronoun-Antecedent Agreement

The pronouns in a sentence should be singular if the nouns they refer to are singular, and they should be plural if the antecedents are plural.

Rick left his keys at work.

singular antecedent: **Rick**

singular pronoun: **his**

both are singular

Students brought their tents and flasks.

plural antecedent: **students**

plural pronoun: **their**

both are plural

Choose between the two choices and fill in the blanks.

1. The dog wagged __________ tail.

 a) their

 b) its

2. Both of __________ were trapped inside.

 a) him or her

 b) them

3. This team is known for __________ loyalty.

 a) its

 b) their

4. Each child in this class has to bring __________ parents to the game.

 a) his or her

 b) their

5. The pets, adopted by her, sleep in __________ separate beds.

 a) his or her

 b) their

6. All the fruits are nutritious in __________ own way.

 a) its

 b) their

Comparative and Superlative Adjectives and Adverbs

Adjectives are words that describe nouns. Adverbs are words that describe an adjective, a verb, or an adverb.

Examples

The children are **happy.**

In this example, the adjective "happy" describes the noun "children."

The children played **happily.**

In this example, the adverb "happily" describes the verb "played."

Match the adjectives with the appropriate nouns.

Adjective	Noun
smelly	street
noisy	hot dogs
clear	neighbor
scary	pumpkin
creamy	nails
crooked	socks
friendly	glass
spicy	children
sharp	yogurt
large	costume

Circle the verb that the underlined adverb describes

1. The brothers equally divided the tasty cookies.
2. Alex needs to practice spellings regularly.
3. The thief slowly opened the door.
4. My teacher looked at me sternly.
5. The excited friends cheered loudly for the players.

File Away

Read each word and sort it into the appropriate folder.

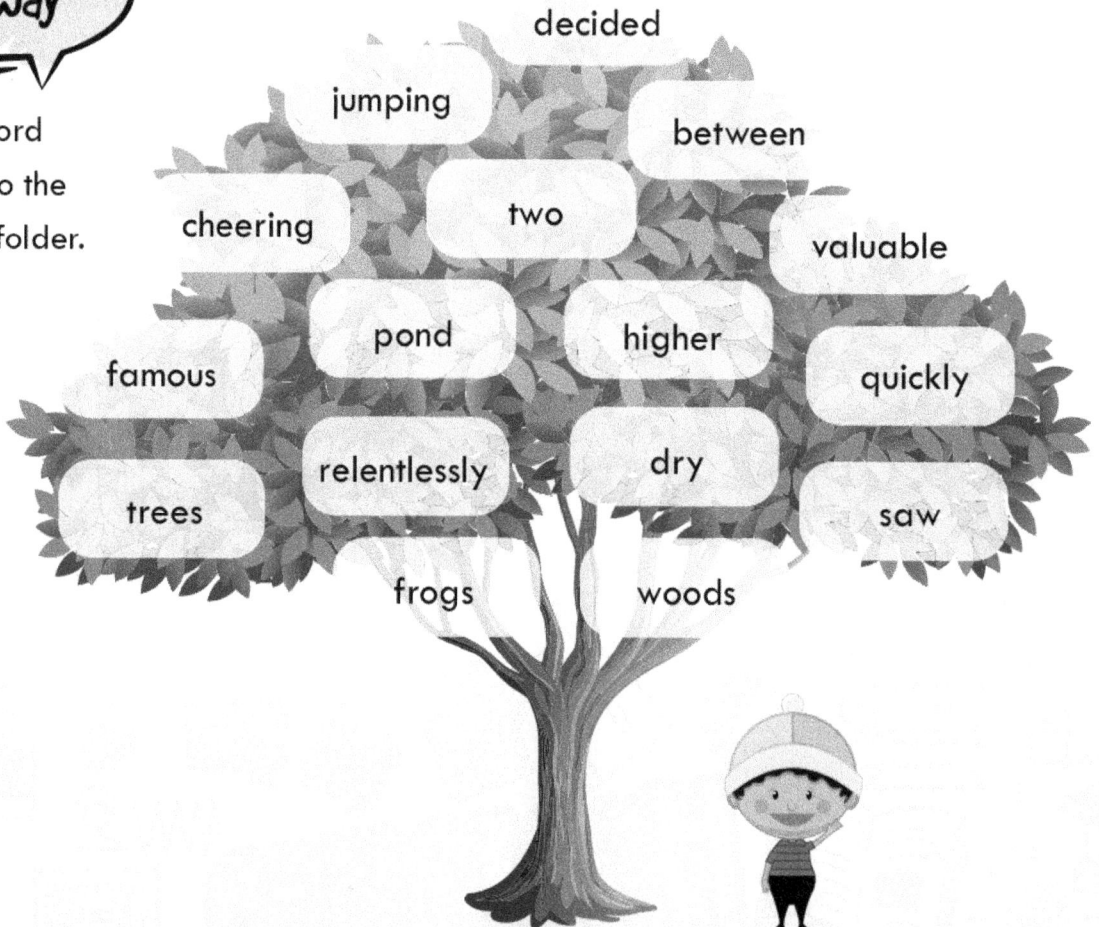

decided
jumping
between
cheering
two
valuable
pond
higher
famous
quickly
relentlessly
dry
trees
saw
frogs
woods

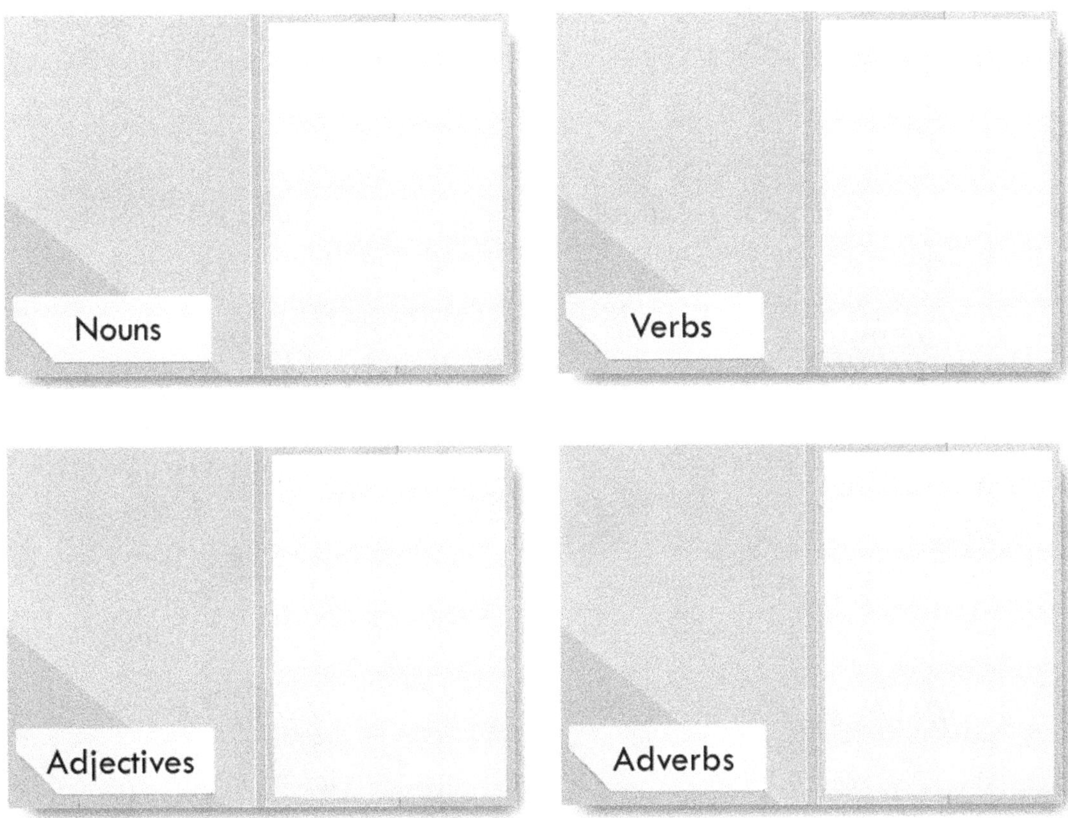

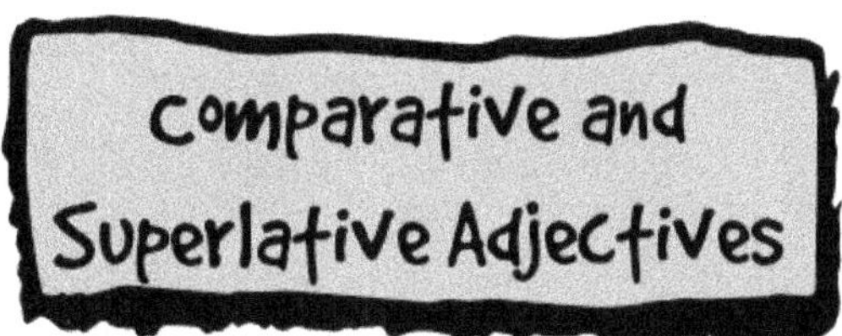

Comparative adjectives are used to compare two nouns.

Examples

Nemo was a ***fast*** swimmer.

Nemo was a ***faster*** swimmer than Pearl.

Superlative adjectives are used to compare a noun against the rest of the group.

Nemo was the ***fastest*** swimmer among his friends.

Read the sentences and mark the comparative adjective as **C** and the superlative adjective as **S.**

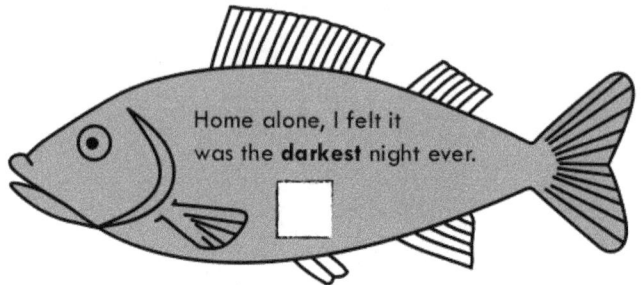

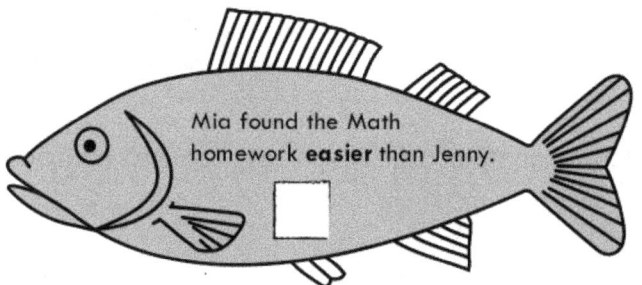

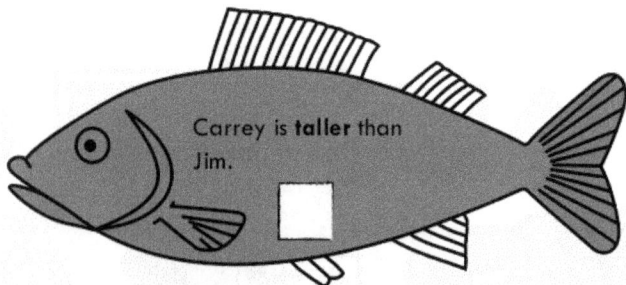

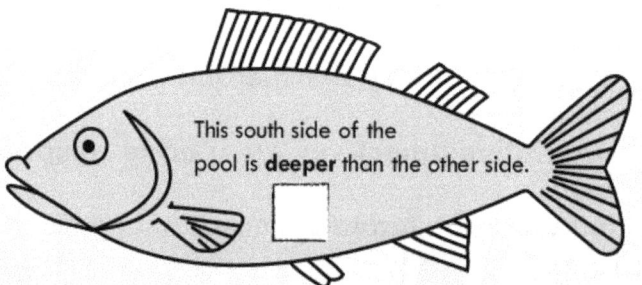

My father is **older** than yours.

Home alone, I felt it was the **darkest** night ever.

Jamie is the **prettiest** of the three sisters.

Cashews are **cheaper** than walnuts.

Owls are **wisest** of all birds.

Mia found the Math homework **easier** than Jenny.

Carrey is **taller** than Jim.

This south side of the pool is **deeper** than the other side.

Read the adjectives and fill out the comparative and superlative forms.

Adjective	Comparative form	Superlative form
angry		
bright		
good		
dull		
soft		
lovely		
quick		
easy		
heavy		
bad		

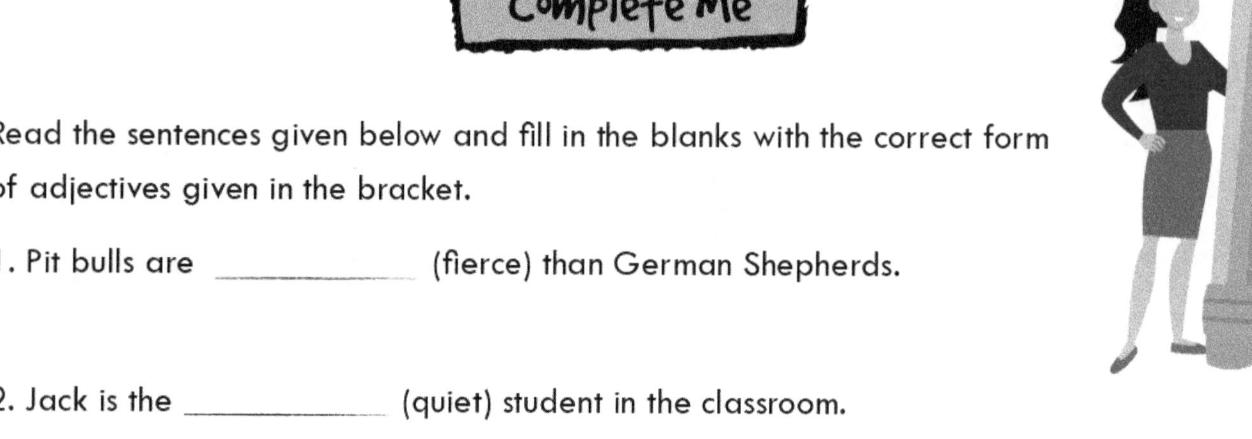

Complete Me

Read the sentences given below and fill in the blanks with the correct form of adjectives given in the bracket.

1. Pit bulls are ___________ (fierce) than German Shepherds.

2. Jack is the ___________ (quiet) student in the classroom.

3. Angel's painting was ___________ (colorful) than Heidi's.

4. Oranges are ___________ (sweet) than grapefruits.

5. Usain Bolt is the ___________ (fast) sprinter today.

6. Terry's feet are ___________ (big) than Bob's.

7. Jay was the ___________ (funny) comedian of that television channel.

8. The movie was the ___________ (long) we had ever seen.

9. My jacket is ___________ (expensive) than my sister's.

10. I made the ___________ (silly) mistake ever.

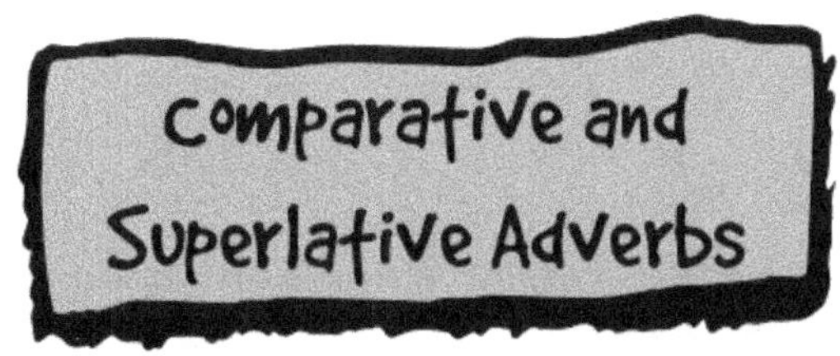

Comparative and Superlative Adverbs

Comparative adverbs and superlative adverbs are used to show the intensity of the action performed.

Examples

Nemo swam ***fast***.

Nemo swam ***faster*** than Pearl.

Nemo swam the ***fastest*** of them all.

Read the sentences given below, and fill in the blank with the correct form of adverb given in the bracket.

1. Can you speak ____________ (loud) please?

2. We had to drive ____________ (far) to reach the gas station.

3. She is having to visit her dentist ____________ (often) than she thought she had to.

4. You have to work ____________ (hard) to study in that college.

5. I learned to cook ____________ (good) than my sister.

6. My boss asked for the ____________ (late) copy of the agreement.

7. Mother went to the ____________ (near) grocery store to buy milk.

8. Please go through the list of the ____________ (frequently) asked questions.

Solve the crossword puzzle by filling in suitable adjectives and adverbs in the clue.

Across

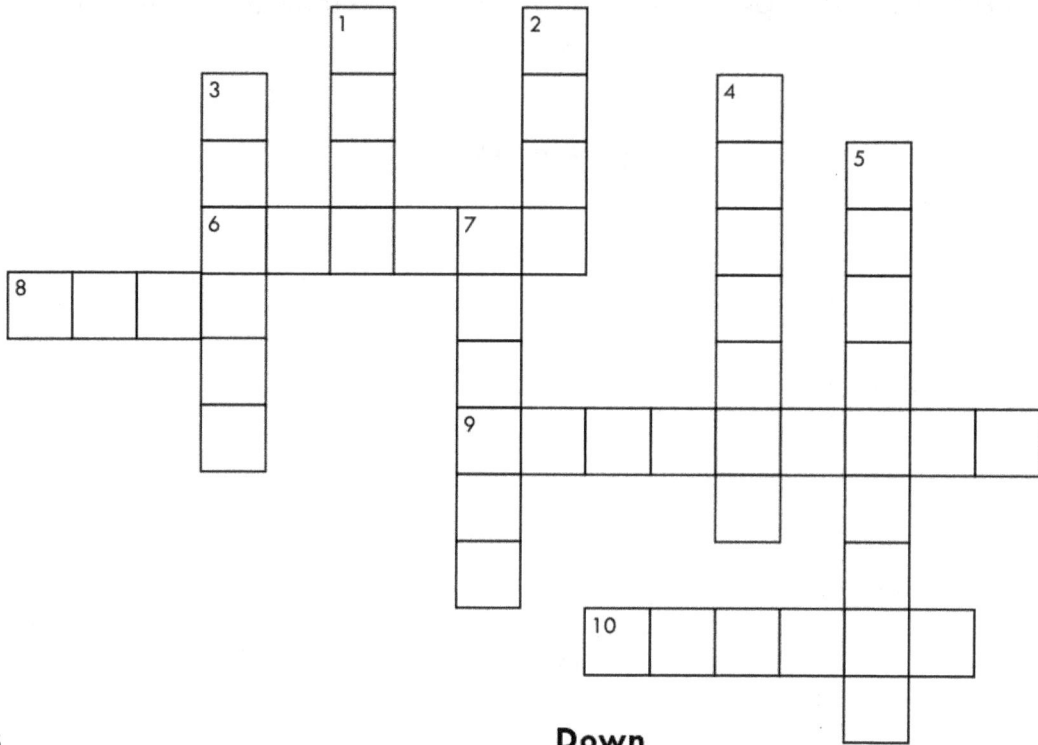

6. He ____________ (rude) turned me down.

8. Nana was a ____________ (kind) person.

9. Mountain climbing is a ____________ (danger) sport.

10. He ____________ (wise) decided to stay home.

Down

1. Michael is a ____________ (good) dancer.

2. My cat is ____________ (lazy).

3. I ____________ (hard) ever eat breakfast.

4. He was very ____________ (excite) to hear the news.

5. Mary waited for the reports ____________ (anxious).

7. He spoke ____________ (loud).

Conjunctions

Conjunctions are words that join words and other parts of a sentence together. There are different types of conjunctions such as:

Coordinating conjunctions	connect words, phrases, and clauses (and, or, so)
Subordinating conjunctions	introduce dependent clause and connect a dependent and an independent clause (while, after, as)

Examples

Coordinating conjunction

Nick **and** Erika are in the kitchen.

Subordinating conjunction

While they were in the kitchen, the doorbell rang.

Find the below words in the grid.

although	once	since
while	before	wherever
unless	after	when
because	than	till

D	S	M	U	N	U	K	J	B	E	E	E	J
F	R	P	E	L	I	H	W	W	U	D	X	H
R	Z	I	L	M	S	B	Z	L	Q	T	C	S
W	H	E	N	A	J	N	Z	A	A	Z	V	I
E	S	U	A	C	E	B	G	A	A	D	W	N
J	X	M	J	M	Y	D	Q	B	E	Y	I	C
P	G	T	R	E	V	E	R	E	H	W	T	E
Y	X	Q	O	J	E	A	D	F	G	U	R	A
R	I	B	C	C	C	Q	A	O	N	K	E	C
X	S	S	E	L	N	U	M	R	A	C	T	L
H	F	I	U	Q	O	P	H	E	H	H	F	L
V	J	D	O	H	G	U	O	H	T	L	A	I
X	G	U	G	I	B	F	J	H	J	H	H	T

Crossword Puzzle

Complete the puzzle using conjunctions.

Across

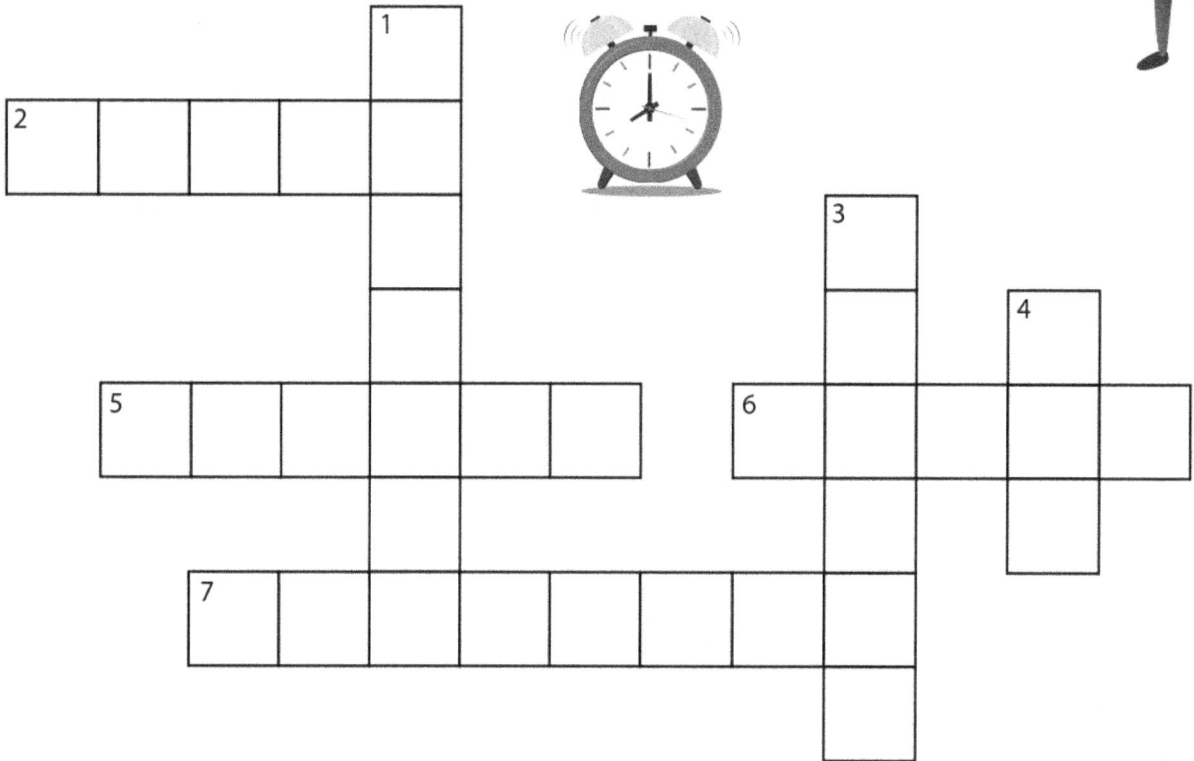

2. One of us should stay here to look after the pets __________ the other is at work.

5. __________ he reminded me to set the alarm, I forgot it.

6. __________ his movie released, he instantly gained popularity.

7. I'll always be there__________ you need help.

Down

1. I told you __________ you are my friend.

3. Preheat the oven __________ you put the pizza in.

4. The story was slow, __________ I finished the book.

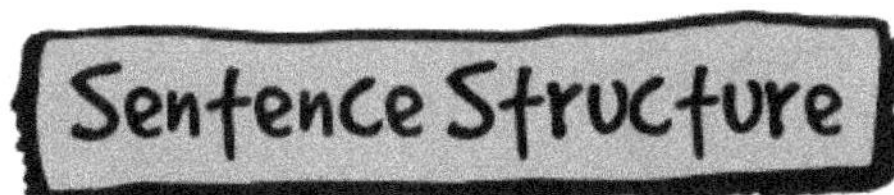

Sentence Structure

There are three main types of sentence structure: simple, compound, and complex. Using varied sentence structure brings variety to writing.

Examples

Simple Sentence = 1 Independent Clause

Example: I called them.

Compound Sentence = 1 Independent Clause + 1 Independent Clause

Example: I called them, and they showed up.

Complex Sentence = 1 Dependent Clause + 1 Independent Clause

Example: Since I called them, they showed up.

Identify the following clauses as dependent (incomplete/fragment) or independent (complete). Put a checkmark in the appropriate column.

	Dependent	Independent
I ran.		
After they arrived.		
Though she was working.		
He likes tea.		
They, in the middle of the room, made the announcement.		
Whenever I see someone sad and in need.		
The classroom is bright.		
Because she was in the house.		

Add an independent clause (before or after) to turn the simple sentences into compound sentences.

1. He was sick.

2. They were late.

3. She moved in with us.

Add a dependent clause (before or after) to turn the simple sentences into complex sentences.

1. It was a rainy day.

2. I couldn't believe my eyes.

3. They went with her.

The first word of every sentence needs to be capitalized. The pronoun 'I' should always be capitalized. The proper name of a person or a place is always capitalized. The titles such as **Mr.** and **Dr.** are also capitalized.

Example

Nicolas and I cleaned our rooms.

We have an appointment with Dr. Corey tomorrow.

Read the sentences and capitalize the necessary words.

	the museum opens at 9 am.		sydney is in australia.
	i take guitar lessons from mr. immanuel.		i have to attend manny's birthday party on sunday.

	easter usually falls in april.		uncle bernie will celebrate christmas with us this year.
	mona and mini are at the library.	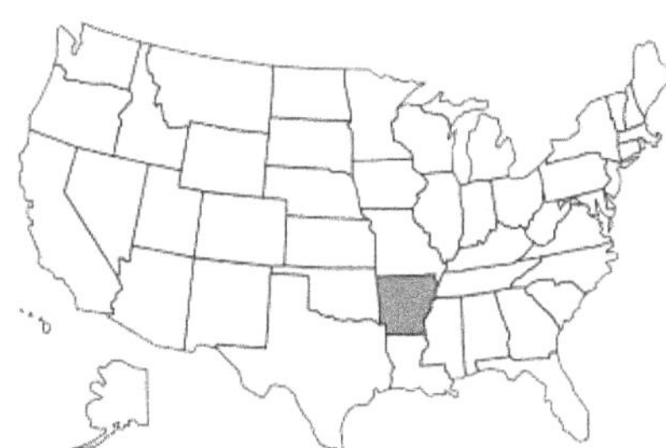	president clinton is from the state of arkansas.

Quotation marks are used when someone else's words need to be reported.

Commas are used in lists, to set apart a phrase or a clause, and in direct speech.

Example

For example: Jacob said, "It is hot outside."

In the given sentences, add commas and quotation marks where necessary.

The mother asked the doctor Will he be alright? 	Kate said quickly I know the answer. 

Sally told her friends Please be careful. 	Is dinner ready? asked Father. 
I love the gift she said. 	We need to fill gas Phil said as he got out of the car. 
Remo said I would like another piece. 	The student asked the teacher May I leave early today? 

What occurs twice in a moment, once in a lifetime, but never in a hundred years?

Spelling

English can be tricky in terms of spelling. The following are a few factors that make spelling challenging:

- different ways of spelling the same sound (there, their)
- same spelling of words with different meanings (right: correct; right: opposite of left)

Reading and writing as frequently as possible will improve spelling. Also, understanding word families can help with the spelling.

Word families are groups of words with the common spelling patterns.

Examples

eat	**ing**
beat	ring
pleat	sing
wheat	string
neat	bring

Complete the below boxes using word families.

1	own			
2	ake			
3	ight			
4	eel			
5	ink			

Unscramble the Words

I	R	C	C	S	U
F	N	U	N	Y	
O	O	F	D		
K	W	O	N		
S	K	E	P	A	
U	N	T	R		
G	U	S	T	U	A
L	A	K	W		

Write the missing letters.

G _ R A _ _ _

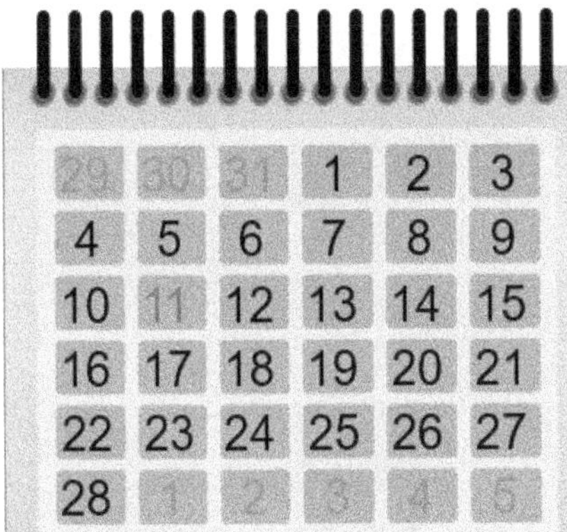

C A L _ _ _ _ R

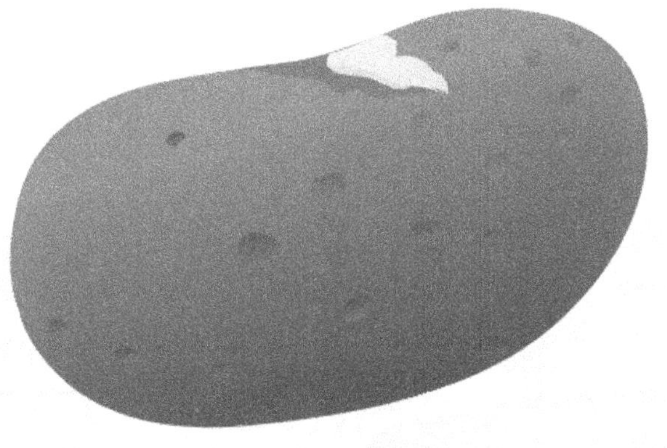

P O _ _ _ _ _ _

W R _ _ _ _ _

J _ W _ _ _ _

F U R _ _ _ _ _ _

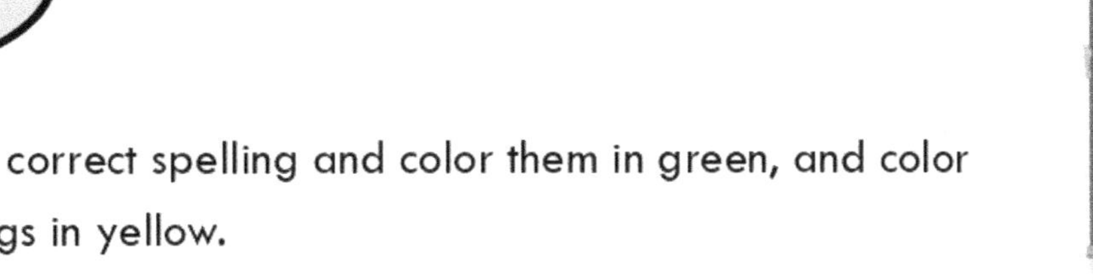

Find the boxes with correct spelling and color them in green, and color the incorrect spellings in yellow.

mend	liberary	leftuc	efect
assisst	quiet	region	ocurr
elect	culture	perpose	wanted
iritate	grammer	scar	opposite

Multiple Meaning Words

Some words have the same spelling and pronunciation but have different meanings. For example the word ***bear*** has many meanings.

The **bear** went over the mountain.

She was not able to **bear** the pain any longer.

Will this ladder **bear** my weight?

The trees in this orchard **bear** very juicy fruits.

Write down two meanings of each given word. Frame a sentence for each meaning. Feel free to use a dictionary.

rest	
rest	

saw	
saw	

trunk	
trunk	

fell	
fell	

Read the sentence and choose the picture that shows the meaning of the underlined word.

Mom rocked the baby to sleep.		
Bats are active at night.		
Students of Grade 3 will perform a play.		
I need to buy stamps.		

The bell rings loudly.		
The surfers waited for a big wave.		
Rita used glue to stick the papers.		
There were ten sheep in the pen.		

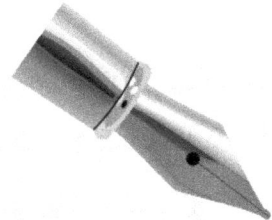

Context Clues

When we read something new, more often than not, we come across words we do not know. They may be hard to spell but not always do we have a dictionary handy. How do you then make out the meanings of these words?

The first thing to do is to circle or underline the unknown word. Then look at the surrounding words for clues.

Example

Miss Marcel is proficient in maths. She can explain even the most **abstruse** theories in a way that everyone in the class can understand.

Though the word "abstruse" may be new to some of us, we can guess the meaning of the word using the clues in the surrounding text. The words "proficient" and "everyone can understand" help us understand that abstruse means something that is difficult to comprehend.

Choose the option that gives the meaning of the underlined word. In the box below, write the words that helped you guess the meaning.

1. Even though our grandmother is old, she is vigorous. She is very active all day.

    a) weak and helpless

    b) healthy and strong

2. He never thought he would lose interest in the game, but his interest declined within weeks.

    a) increase

    b) decrease

3. The vending machine in this building <u>seldom</u> or never works.

a) rarely

b) often

4. She has a <u>coaxing</u> voice which convinces people to do what she wants.

a) persuasive

b) prevent

5. Alice gave away a <u>substantial</u> amount of money for charity, whereas Henry gave away very less.

a) small amount

b) large amount

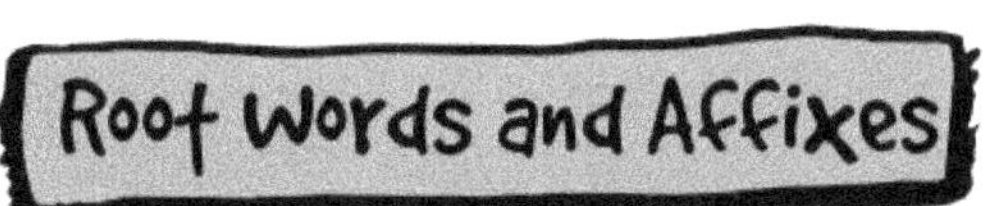

Root words are words that may or may not stand alone. When a prefix or suffix is added to the root word, the meaning or function of the word changes.

Example

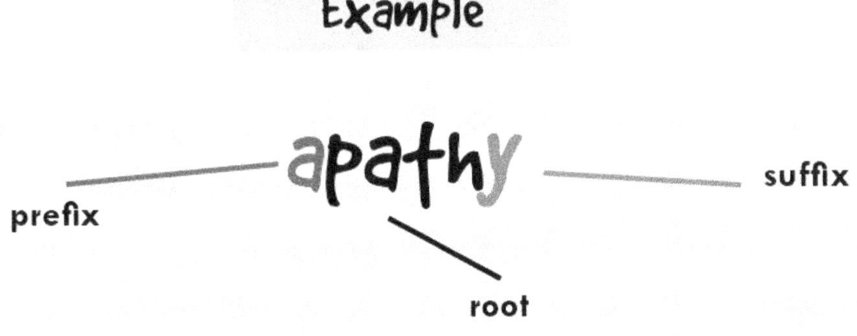

The root "path" means "feeling."

Adding the suffix "y" makes it "pathy" meaning "denoting feeling."

Adding the prefix "a" makes it the opposite meaning "lacking feeling."

A word can have a prefix, a suffix, or both.

For each of the given words, write down the prefix OR suffix, and another word with the same prefix or suffix. One is done for you.

asleep
Prefix: a
Suffix: x
ahead

grandson
Prefix: ____
Suffix: ____
____

colorful
Prefix: ____
Suffix: ____
____

leader
Prefix: ____
Suffix: ____
____

disbelief
Prefix: ____
Suffix: ____
____

return
Prefix: ____
Suffix: ____
____

Hyperbole

This is used to exaggerate for effect in poetry and writing.

Example

I am so tired. I can sleep for a year.

Now, we may feel like sleeping for a long time when we are tired, but sleeping for a year is not possible.

Yes or No?

Write Y for sentences with hyperbole, and write N for sentences without hyperbole.

	Y	N
1) Everybody in the world knows this!		
2) I think I told you that I'm turning 10 this year.		
3) They are never going to make it.		
4) This cat is as old as the hills.		
5) Could I borrow some crayons?		
6) I ate so much on vacation that I gained 3 pounds.		
7) I know! You have told me a million times already!		
8) She helps the needy.		

Write three sentences using hyperbole.

1.

2.

3.

Connotation and Denotation

In English, a few words have the same meaning but have positive or negative feelings associated with them. This is called connotation.

The words that are used with primary meaning without any association is called denotation.

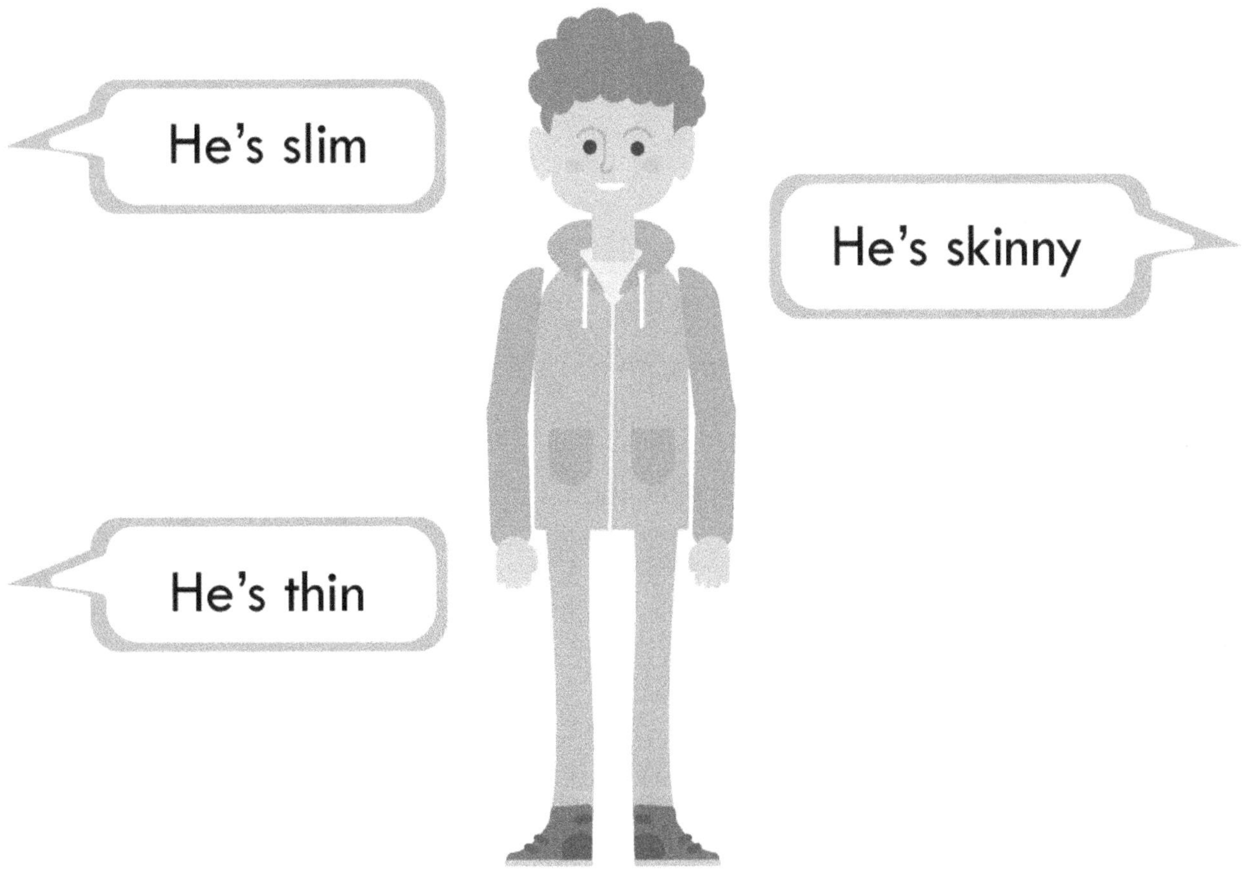
He's slim
He's skinny
He's thin

Here, the words thin, slim, and skinny all mean the same.

However, the word **slim** (appealing in a healthy way) has a **positive connotation,** and the word **skinny** (unhealthy) has a **negative connotation**.

Identify the meaning of the underlined words.

1. The speaker was **<u>nervous</u>** and kept forgetting his lines.

positive	negative	neutral

2. This puzzle is **<u>challenging</u>** and fun.

positive	negative	neutral

3. This gallery has unique and **<u>amazing</u>** collections.

positive	negative	neutral

4. She was **<u>disappointed</u>** in herself after lying to her parents.

positive	negative	neutral

5. They worry a lot about their **<u>results</u>**.

positive	negative	neutral

Color the words with positive connotations in blue, negative connotations in yellow, and neutral or denotative meaning with green.

ask	bought	help
piece	excited	thing
disappoint	project	peculiar
wheels	picky	arm

Angry and Hungry are words that end with the letters -gry. What is another word in English that ends with -gry?

Transition words are words that connect ideas and thoughts.

Examples

because, although, sometimes, meanwhile

Identify the transition words

1. We arrived a few seconds late; however, the train had left the station.

2. I like to watch the sunrise at the beach. In fact, it is my favorite place.

3. The questions given in the examination were not easy. As a result, many students failed.

4. Although the weather was bad, she went out to feed the stray dogs.

5. Tara was the last to leave class, yet she was the first on the bus.

6. Ed learned to finish his work on time. Likewise, everyone should be punctual.

7. Matt came first in the race even though he hardly practised.

8. Mom cooked dinner; meanwhile, dad and I did the laundry.

Read the given passage and fill in the transition words.

one of the	in short	in some instances	but
later	originally	whereas	hence

The goldfish, ____________ most popular fish, are the most common household pet in the United States. A goldfish kept in a fishbowl grows just a few inches long, ____________ some goldfish can grow up to two feet. Many are orange-gold in color, ____________ some are grayish-white and have orange spots.

There are many varieties of goldfish. For example, the bubble eye goldfish have big bulging eyes. The comet goldfish have long slim bodies with trailing tails.

Goldfish are a freshwater fish, ____________ live in slow moving rivers, lakes, and ponds. They like to eat plants and insects in the water. ____________ from China, goldfish were bred for their golden color. ____________ , they became popular in Japan. They were brought to the United States in the 1800s.

Goldfish can recognize the person who feeds them each day.

____________ , goldfish have been trained to swim through mazes and hoops and even push a ball into a net. ____________ , goldfish are smarter than you think!

Mark the transition words that can be found.

P	U	G	V	P	H	D	B	A	S
S	S	E	L	E	U	L	C	P	O
D	E	S	I	R	P	R	U	S	T
I	G	P	Z	O	F	H	H	V	H
E	L	I	H	W	N	A	E	M	E
T	M	T	Z	G	W	C	E	V	R
Z	T	C	G	W	P	R	D	U	W
K	Y	L	L	A	N	I	F	W	I
G	F	A	M	C	T	J	R	K	S
V	S	O	O	N	W	J	S	O	E

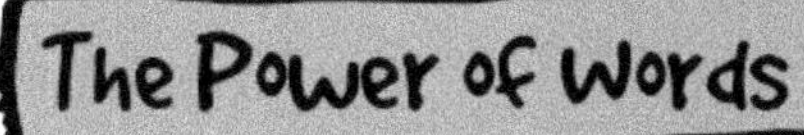

The Power of Words

Once upon a time, the ponds in a village were drying up. A drought[1] had hit the village. An army of frogs decided to leave the pond in search of another home. They travelled through dry fields and the woods in search of water.

Just as they were hopping along, two frogs, Glen and Gina, fell into a deep pit. They tried to get out, jumping again and again, each time a bit higher, but in vain[2].

The other frogs saw them trying hard. They could see how deep the pit was. So, they shouted into the pit, "The pit is very deep. No matter how much you try, you are as good as dead. So, stop trying and save yourself the pain!"

Soon, Glen believed what the frogs said. He lost hope and decided there was no point in trying. He fell deeper into the pit and died.

Meanwhile, Gina tried relentlessly[3], jumping higher each time.

The frogs outside were crying and begging her to stop.

Finally, Gina held her breath and jumped as high as she could go. To everyone's surprise, she landed right in between them!

The other frogs asked Gina, "Did you not hear us?" Clueless[4], she said, "Sorry friends, I can't hear you. I was born deaf. But, hey! Thanks for all the cheering. Otherwise, I would have given up long ago!"

Surprised, the other frogs learned a valuable lesson: Never give up, whatever the odds may be!

[1]drought: period of no rainfall leading to shortage of water	[2]vain: useless or pointless
[3]relentlessly: continuously	[4]clueless: having no idea

1. Why were the frogs looking for a new home?

2. What places did they have to travel while searching for water?

3. What happened to Glen and Gina?

4. Why did Glen die?

5. What did the other frogs learn from Gina?

6. Is there another moral you learned from this story? If so, mention it here.

Have you heard people say, "A picture is worth a thousand words"? Pages with pictures attract readers more than a page full of text. The pictures are usually included to support the information in the text.

Complete the given story.

Mom always read bedtime stories to Ronnie, Betty, and Jake.

She read the story of Aladdin and the Magic Lamp. The children were awed by the genie, the magic carpet, and the adventure!

That night Jake had a dream. He dreamt that on his way to school next morning, he found a lamp in the bushes. He picked it up. Was he supposed to rub it? Would a genie appear if he did?

He took a chance and rubbed the lamp with the palm of his hands.

Continue the story from here. Use pictures and words to convey the story in the best possible way.

Moral:

My Lost Puppy

One warm morning, I took my puppy, Cookie, for a walk. She was excited to be outside. She started chasing dragonflies. Not able to control her, I said, "Slow down, Cookie. You are tugging[2] at the leash," but, she insisted[1] on having fun!

She continued to tug at the leash and I lost my grip. Set free, she bounded[3] off into the woods chasing the dragonfly. I ran after her crying, "Cookie, get back here!"

She did not pay heed to my words. She ran fast and was out of sight soon.

I ran home and narrated what happened to my parents. They followed me into the woods. We took different trails and searched for Cookie, but couldn't find her.

We went back home and made 'Missing dog' flyers to distribute to our neighbors and to stick on electric poles and mailboxes.

Two days went by. There was no news about Cookie. I was worried about her.

MISSING
Please help me find my puppy!
Answers to the name: COOKIE
If you find her please call : (234) (987-6543)
Lost near: Green wood Avenue, Ladue Road, MO 63141
On: Sunday, 5th May 2019

Just then, Mrs. James, the librarian called. She said she had a surprise for me and asked me to come over to the library quickly.

I walked two streets up to the library, wondering what it could be.

To my surprise, I saw Cookie sitting beside her at the counter! Thrilled to see me, Cookie pounced on me, wagging her tail and licking me.

Mrs. James explained that her cat Smokey had wandered off into the woods as usual, this morning. When he returned, Cookie had followed him home. Having seen the flyer on the notice board of the library, she had called us immediately.

I thanked Mrs. James for taking care of her and calling me. As we walked home, I realized, Cookie was calmly walking by my side, without even a leash!

[1]insisted: demanding	[2]tugging: pulling hard	[3]bounded: run with big strides

1. What was the name of the puppy?

2. How did she get lost?

____

____

3. What did the author do as soon as the puppy was lost?

____

____

4. Who found the puppy?

____

5. Was there a change in the puppy after being lost and found?

____

____

6. Would you have done anything different to find your puppy if you lost him/her?

____

____

____

____

____

Write the summary of the story from the dog's point of view.

Read the two passages written by an author. In each passage, the writer shares her experiences.

I learned building robots using a kit my mom bought me for my 10th birthday. I remember the day I received it; I was excited and couldn't wait to build my own robot. I worked on it for 2 days, but the robot did not make any movement.

Frustrated[1] and disappointed, I put the kit away. My mom said, "You can always ask for help. You know?" I asked her to help me with it. We disassembled[2] the whole thing and started to rebuild from the scratch.

We followed the instruction[3] closely this time. We were nervous when it was time to test the pick and place robot arm. I took the remote and I remember I was not able to bring myself to do it.

Then, mom and I together turned the control stick. It felt amazing seeing it work.

Since then, whenever I find time, I build robots from the things I find around me. I recently built a robot with wheels to follow me around the house.

I enjoy woodworking classes in my school. Mr. Carmen made me fall in love with creating marvelous things with pieces of wood.

The first thing I made was a pallet shelf. It was uneven and peculiar, but Mr. Carmen said that it's not about getting it perfect. He was right. I painted it to accentuate its imperfections and it looked like a weird piece of art. The entire experience was funny, but it taught me to never give up and make most of what I have.

I practised regularly and got better at woodworking. As Mr. Carmen and I are picky, we take projects that are challenging and unique.

[1]frustrated: annoyed or ready to give up	[2]disassembled: to separate into pieces	[3]Instruction to the design team: a manual with directions

1. What is the common theme of both the passages?

2. Where did the author develop her hobbies and who helped her?

	where	who
robotics		
woodworking		

3. How did the author get good at robotics and woodworking?

4. What kind of hobbies interests the author?

5. Why did the author write these passages?

List two of your hobbies here.

1. ______________________________

2. ______________________________

How did you start these hobbies? Who inspired you?

1. ______________________________

2. ______________________________

Did you try to develop a hobby and almost quit it like the author? What did you do to keep going?

____

____

What do you think about getting help when you feel like quitting a hobby?

____

____

What other hobby would you like to have when you grow up?

____

Do you prefer educational gifts? Why?

____

Just like the way we compared two texts above, compare the two pictures below and circle the differences.

Match the pictures with their names.

cooking

music

fishing

painting

In the space below draw a hobby that you enjoy doing and color it.

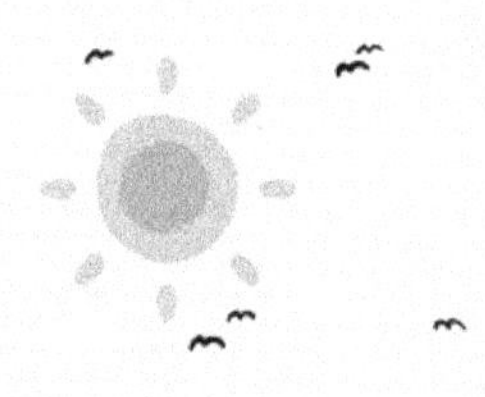

Evening Ditty

Girls and boys come out to play,

The moon doth[1] shine as bright as day:

Come with a hoop, come with a call,

Come with a good will, or not at all:

Leave your supper[2] and leave your sleep,

Come to your playfellows[3] in the street:

Up the ladder and down the wall,

A penny loaf will serve us all.

by

Joseph Ritson

[1]doth: do	[2]supper: evening meal	[3]playfellows: friends

1. What does the title "Evening Ditty" mean?

a) an evening story

b) an evening song

2. Who is the narrator?

a) the children

b) the author

3. What is the point of view used in this poem?

a) first person

b) third person

4. Pick out two pairs of rhyming words.

__________ __________

__________ __________

5. Write a line from the poem that has a hyperbole or shows exaggeration. Why is it a hyperbole?

Line: ____

Explain: ____

What question can you never answer as 'Yes'?

Reading: Informational Text

Popular Sport

A survey was conducted in Los Angeles County to find out the most popular sport in the area. A total of 250 students participated. The students were allowed to choose only one sport as their favorite.

Favorite Sport of Students in Los Angeles County

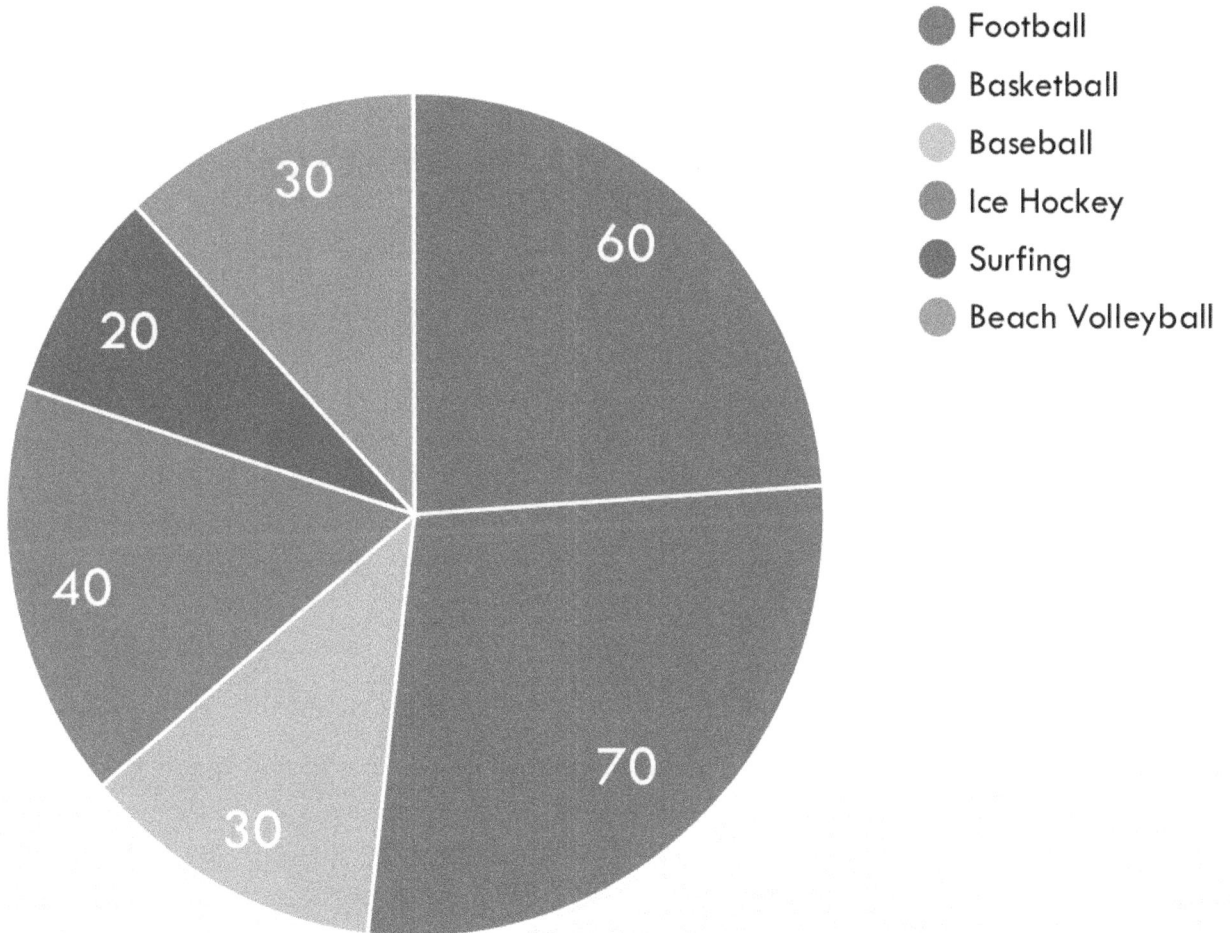

Study the graph and answer these questions.

1. Which sport was the least favorite?

____

2. Which sport was preferred the most?

____

3. Which two sports earned the same number of votes?

____

4. Does this chart make it easier to answer the questions? Why/Why not?

____

____

Gathering information from pictures is far easier than reading text. Don't you agree?

Let us take a look at a map, which is a different kind of picture that helps us a lot in our everyday lives.

A map is an image of an area on Earth or part of the Earth itself.

Read the given map and fill in the blanks with correct answers.

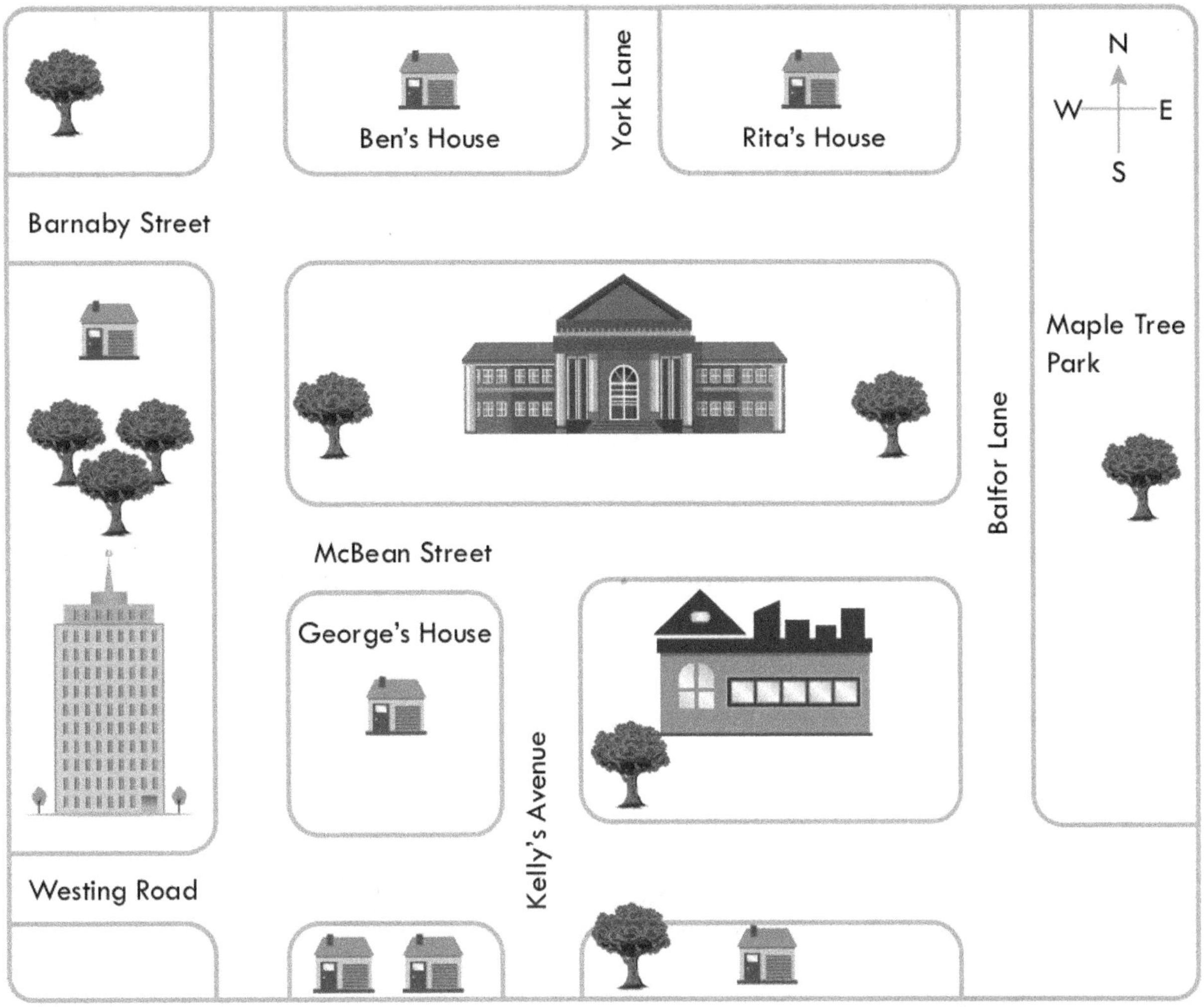

Ben's House

York Lane

Rita's House

N

W

E

S

Barnaby Street

Maple Tree Park

Balfor Lane

McBean Street

George's House

Kelly's Avenue

Westing Road

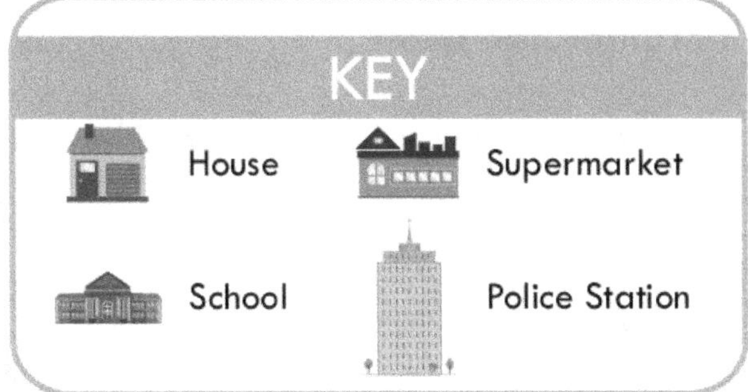

1. George heads __________ to go to school.

2. Rita goes __________ to go to Ben's house.

3. Ben heads __________ to go to the supermarket.

4. A police officer leaving the police station would go __________ to the supermarket.

5. The supermarket is to the __________ of the park.

6. Students at school head __________ to have a picnic at the park.

7. Ben's dad is a police officer. He heads __________ to go to work.

8. The school is __________ of the supermarket.

Things You Need

- An origami paper of any color
- A scissor
- Markers

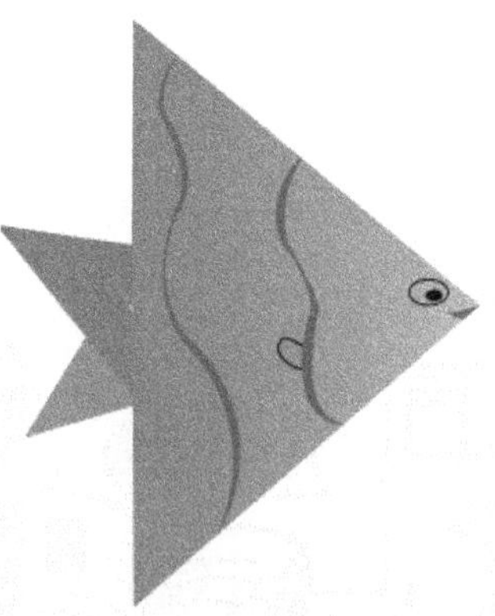

Steps in the Process

Take a square piece of an origami paper.

To crease the paper diagonally, fold the upper right corner to meet the lower left corner and then unfold.

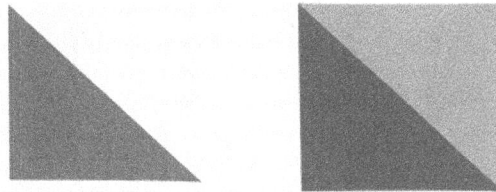

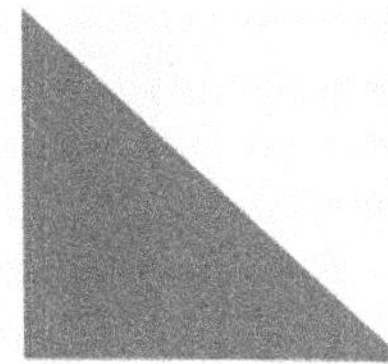

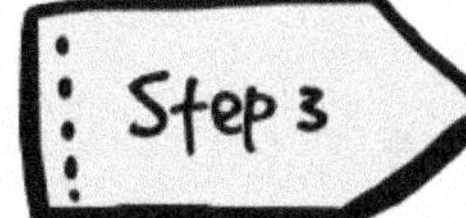

Fold the upper left corner to meet the lower right corner and then unfold.

Fold the paper in half.

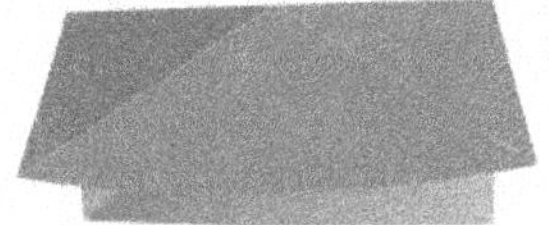

Hold the center of the folded paper and push the right and left ends inward along the crease as shown in the picture.

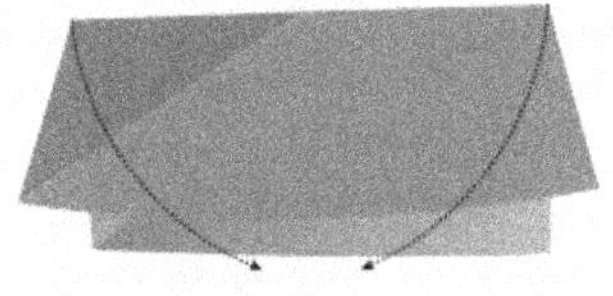

The ends of right and left corners will meet at the center forming a triangle.

Step 7

There will be two flaps on the front triangle and two on the flip side of the triangle. On the front triangle, fold both the flaps as shown in the picture.

Step 8

Flip the triangle. Draw and color patterns to make the fish colorful.

Your paper fish is ready! You can put a hole on top and hang the fish with a yarn or you can stick it with an adhesive tape.

1. What are the things required to do the paper fish?

2. What are the headings of the two sections?

3. How are the pictures helpful in the process?

4. How many steps are given?

5. Which step was difficult? Did the pictures help?

Find the meaning of the verbs from the glossary/dictionary and frame sentences using those verbs.

amused

Meaning: ______

Sentence: ______

scurried

Meaning: ____

Sentence: ____

mimic

Meaning: ____

Sentence: ____

exasperated

Meaning: ____

Sentence: ____

Use any reference material such as an atlas or a map to find the places marked on this map.

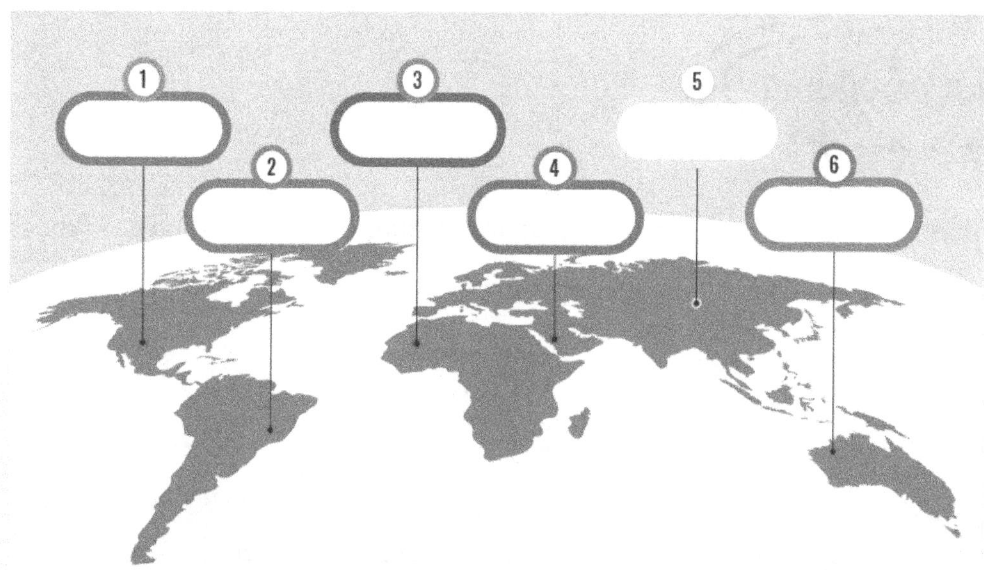

Text 1

Text 2

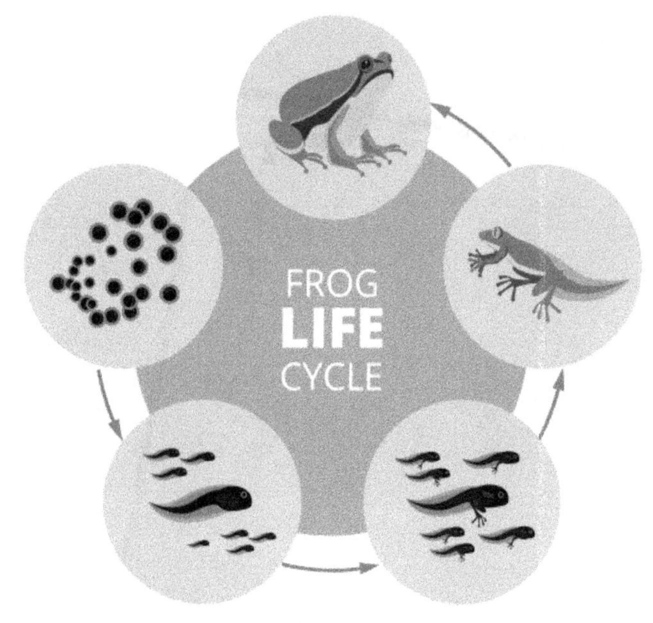

Life Cycle of a frog is a perfect example of metamorphosis.

Text 3

frustrated: annoyed or ready to give up

disassembled: to separate into pieces

instruction: a manual with directions

Find the right answer and color it.

1. Text 1 is an example of ________

Glossary	Illustration
Index	Table of contents

2. Text 2 is an example of ________

Glossary	Illustration
Index	Table of contents

3. Text 3 is an example of ________

Glossary	Illustration
Index	Table of contents

1. How many sections are there under lessons 1 and 2?

   Lesson 1 ________ Lesson 2 ________

2. What is there on page 18 of Text 1?

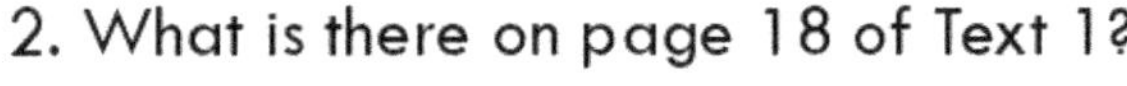

3. What is there on page 38 of Text 1?

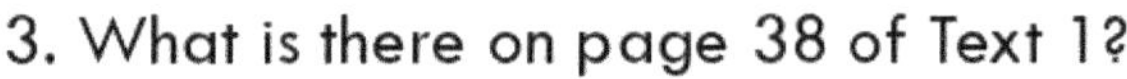

4. Which section under lesson 2 has more number of pages?

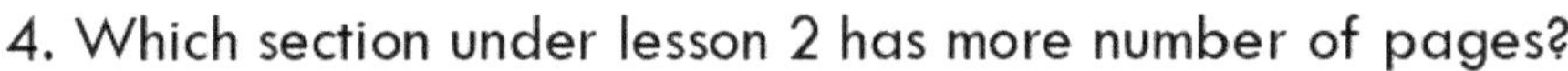

5. Why is the picture in Text 2 important?

6. Where are you likely to find something like Text 3 in your textbook?

Which is the odd one?

pin, can, mad, tar, war

How did you know where the maze begins and where it ends?

Were the pictures of the animals important to solve the puzzle?

Writing

Informational Writing

Time for you to describe a process. Use headings for each section and illustrations wherever possible.

Choose one of these topics:

Recipe: Help your friends cook one of your favorite dishes. The sections could include "Ingredients" and "Method."

OR

DIY: Help your friends make something creative. The sections could include "Things Required" and "Method."

Write a four-line poetry with rhyming words and hyperbole.

Decide the theme, characters, place, or things about which the poem will be.

First Draft

Make corrections in terms of punctuation, word choice, and ideas, and write the revised draft below with a suitable title.

Title ______________________________

____

____

____

____

____

Opinion Writing

Here are some common opinions on qualities of a good friend.

A friend should be reliable.

A friend should be fun.

A friend should be honest.

A friend should be caring and loving.

What in your opinion is the most important quality of a friend? Give your opinion backed up with proper reasons.

Do a research with 3 of your family members (each member will be a subject). Observe them for 10 days and take notes.

Subject 1

Name of the subject

Your relationship with the subject

What is his/her hobby?

Why does the subject like it?

How many days in a week does the subject practise the hobby?

When did the subject start the hobby?

Has the subject improved with practise?

How is the hobby helping the subject in life?

What are the secondary hobbies? If any.

Is there any common factor in primary and secondary hobbies?

Subject 2

Name of the subject

Your relationship with the subject

What is his/her hobby?

Why does the subject like it?

How many days in a week does the subject practise the hobby?

When did the subject start the hobby?

Has the subject improved with practise?

How is the hobby helping the subject in life?

What are the secondary hobbies? If any.

Is there any common factor in primary and secondary hobbies?

Subject 3

Name of the subject

Your relationship with the subject

What is his/her hobby?

Why does the subject like it?

How many days in a week does the subject practise the hobby?

When did the subject start the hobby?

Has the subject improved with practise?

How is the hobby helping the subject in life?

What are the secondary hobbies? If any.

Is there any common factor in primary and secondary hobbies?

Write a brief summary of the observation telling the readers why hobbies are important and how they can develop healthy hobbies.

Narrative Writing

A narrative is a written account of a story from one's point of view.

Here are certain rules to write a narrative.

1. Use temporal words or time-related words such as ***long ago, once upon a time, last night, tomorrow.*** These will show the order of events in the story.

2. Introduce the situation, characters, and the narrator.

3. Write the sequence of events using interesting dialogs and exclamations.

4. Provide a conclusion.

Write a story with a clear setting, characters, theme, and point of view.

Write a report on two of your family members. They will be the subject of this research.

Follow them around for a day and list their activities. Then compare the details and find out who needs your help more and how you can be of help.

Subject 1 ________

Subject 2 ________

Math

Use this book to enable your children to explore numbers by solving interesting puzzles and real-life problems. Engage your children with fun, colorful activities and let them fall in love with Math.

Arithmetic Operations

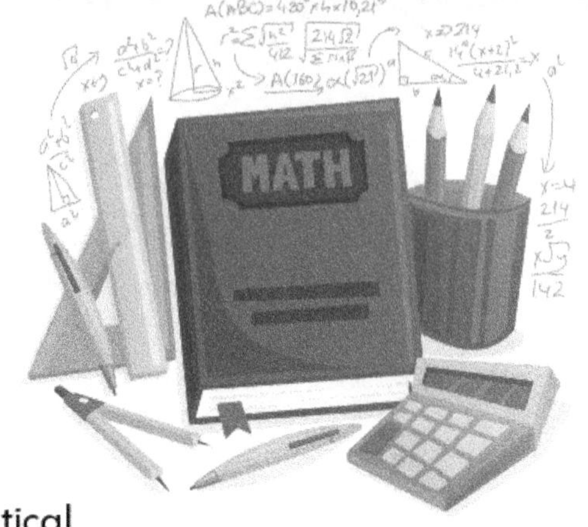

When a number is added to itself repeatedly, the mathematical process is called **multiplication.**

Example

Here each group has 5 ice creams, and there are three such groups.

So, there are 3 times 5 or 5 + 5 + 5 or 15 ice creams in total. In other words, multiplication is repeated addition.

Multiplication is represented by the symbol '×'. When two numbers are multiplied, the answer is called **'product'**. The number of objects in each group is called **'multiplicand'**, and the number of such equal groups is called **'multiplier'**.

Division is a mathematical process of splitting a group of things into equal parts.

Example

There are 12 easter eggs and 4 boxes, how to put 12 easter eggs into four equal-sized boxes?

Let's practice

1. Fill in the blanks to make the statements true.

a.

4 + 4 + 4 = ____

Three groups of four = ____

3 x 4 = ____

b.

5 + 5 = ____

Two groups of five = ____

2 x 5 = ____

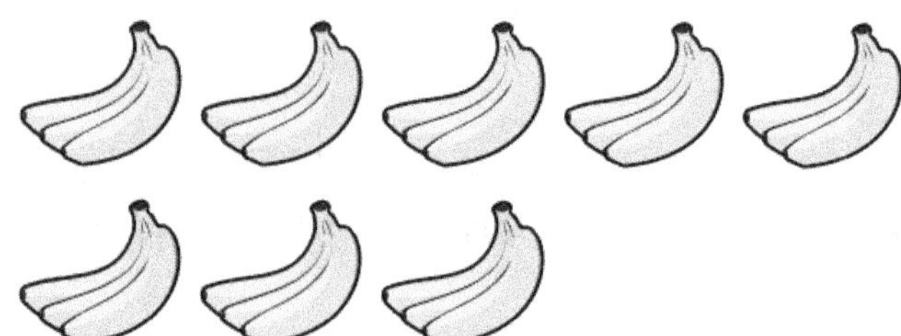

c.

3 + 3 + 3 + 3 + 3 + 3 + 3 + 3 = ____

Eight groups of three = ____

8 x 3 = ____

2. Does the picture show 3 × 4? Explain why or why not.

Explain your thinking:

____

____

3. Olivia, Emma, Sophia and Rachel share a box of oranges. Circle the oranges such that they each get the same number of oranges. Then, write a repeated addition sentence and a multiplication sentence to represent the picture.

(Hint: 4 groups of 4)

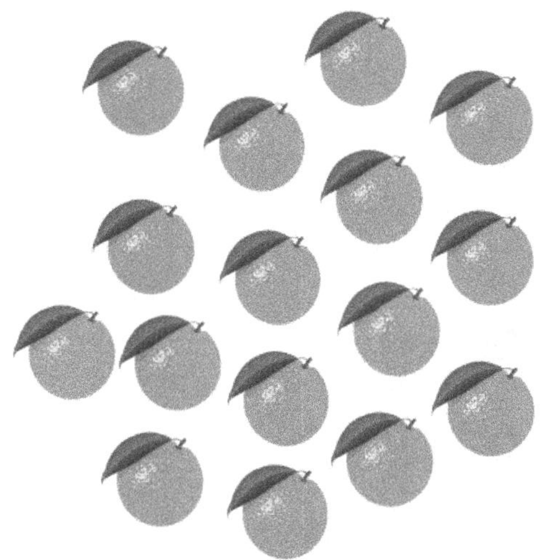

Addition statement:

____

____

Multiplication statement:

____

____

4. Draw a picture to show $5 + 5 + 5 + 5 = 20$ and represent it as a multiplication sentence.

Your drawing:

Multiplication statement:

____

5. Use the arrays to complete the sentences.

a.

i) Number of rows ____

ii) Number of objects in each row ____

b.

i) Number of rows ____

ii) Number of objects in each row ____

c.

i) Number of rows ____

ii) Number of objects in each row ____

d.

i) Number of rows ____

ii) Number of objects in each row ____

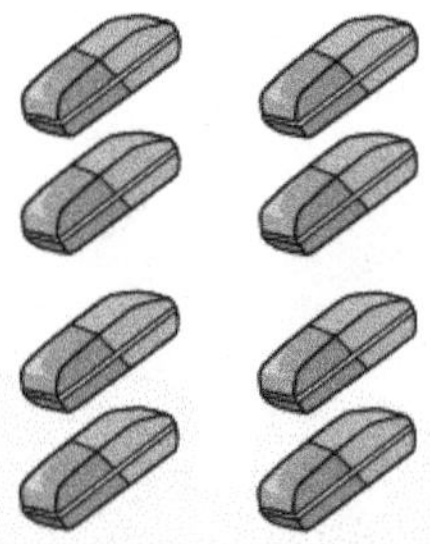

6. Look at the image. There are 4 groups of 3 dots.

a. Redraw the dots to make an array with 4 rows of 3 dots.

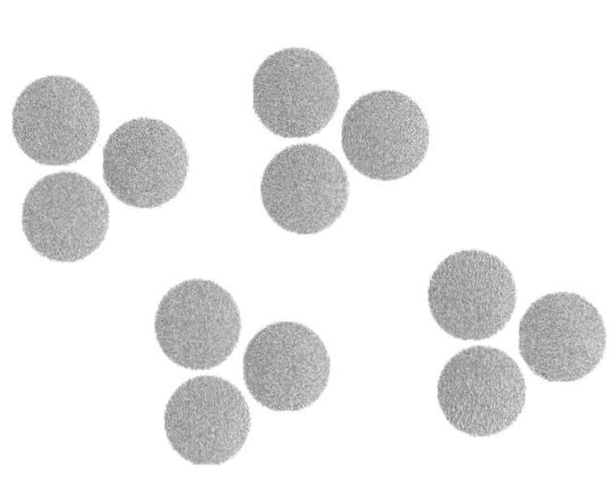

b. Compare the image to your array. Write at least 1 reason why they are the same and 1 reason why they are different.

Why are they the same?

____

____

____

Why are they different?

____

____

____

7. Amelia has a collection of coins. She arranges the coins into five rows of six. Draw an array to represent Amelia's coins. Write a multiplication sentence to describe the array.

Array:

Multiplication sentence:

8. Fill in the blanks.

a. 3 sixes = ____ threes

b. ____ × 7 = 7 threes
= ____

c. 7 × 8 = ____ × 7

d. 8 × ____ = ____ × 8

e. 3 twos = ____ × ____

9. Write multiplication statements for each array arrangement.

a.

20 = ____ x ____

20 = ____ x ____

b.

____ = ____ x ____

____ = ____ x ____

c.

____ = ____ x ____

____ = ____ x ____

d.

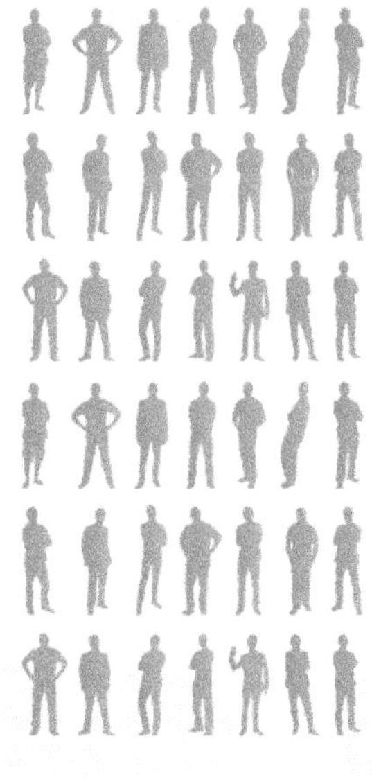

____ = ____ x ____

____ = ____ x ____

10. Complete the equations.

a. Each  has a value of 9.

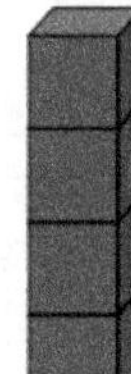

Unit form: 4 nines

4 x ____ = ____ x 4

Total : ____

b. Each  has a value of 8.

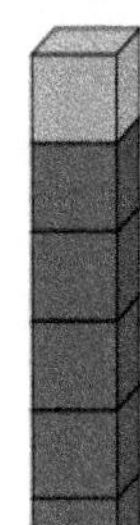

Unit form:

____ eights + ____ eight

= 40 + ____

= ____

Facts: ____ x ____ = 48

____ x ____ = 48

c. Each  has a value of 6.

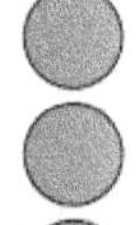

Unit form: 5 ____

5 x ____ = ____ x 5

Total : ____

d. Each 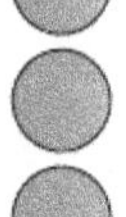 has a value of 7.

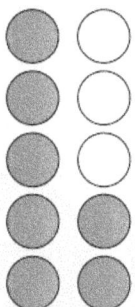

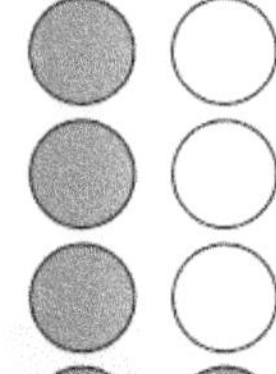

Unit form:

____ sevens + ____ sevens

= 42 + ____

= ____

Facts: ____ x ____ = 70

____ x ____ = 70

11. Skip count by 9. Then match each multiplication problem with its value.

9, 18, ____, ____, ____, ____, ____, ____, ____

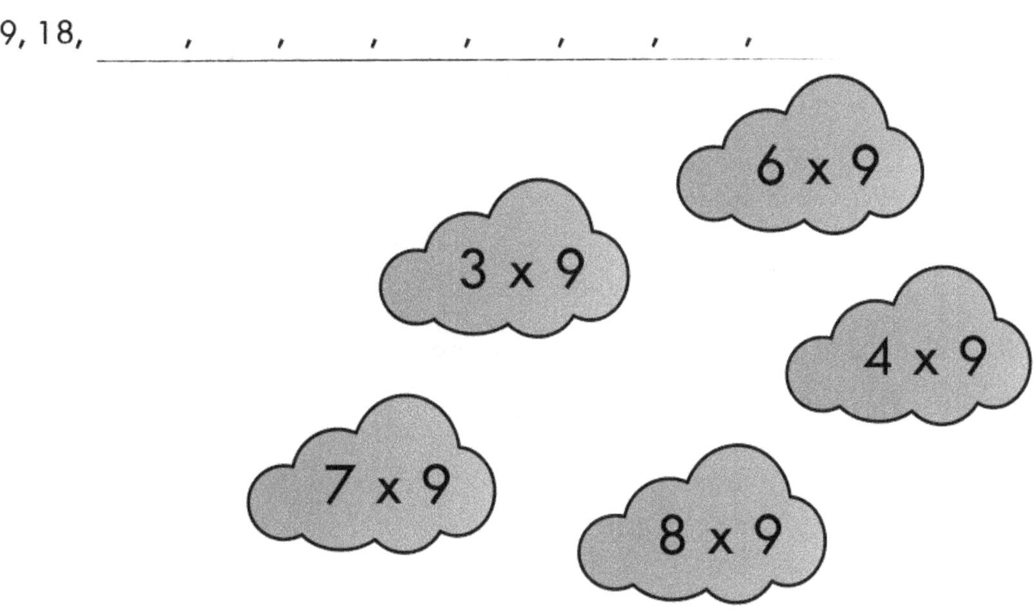

12. Each  has a value of 5.

Use this fact to find 9 x 5. Show your work using pictures, numbers or words.

Picture:

Words:

Numbers:

13. Solve the word problems.

a. Grace spends $32 on buying plants. Each plant costs $8. How many plants does she buy?

b. Victoria organizes her magazines into 5 equal piles. She has a total of 35 magazines. How many magazines are there in each pile?

c. Hazel buys 30 strawberries to make smoothies. Each smoothie needs 5 strawberries. How many smoothies can she make?

14. Draw tape diagrams to solve the word problems. One is done for you.

a. Ms.Isabella divides 35 students into 7 equal groups for a field trip. Draw a tape diagram, and label the number of students in each group as n. Write an equation, and solve for n.

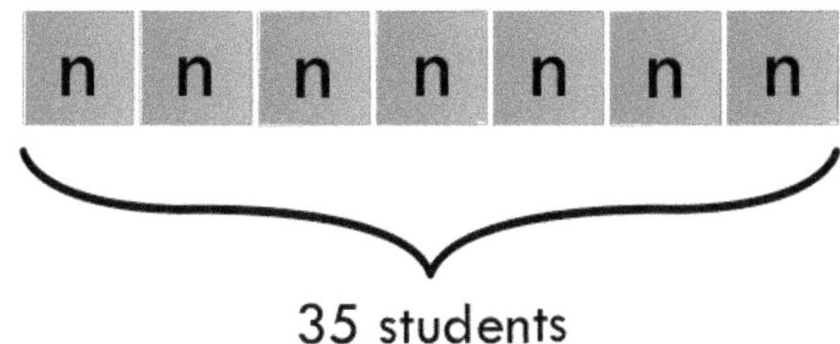

$35 \div 7 = n$

$n = 5$

There are 5 students in each group.

b. Mia buys 5 packs of chocolates. Each pack of chocolates costs $7. Draw a tape diagram, and label the total amount she spends as m. Write an equation, and solve for m.

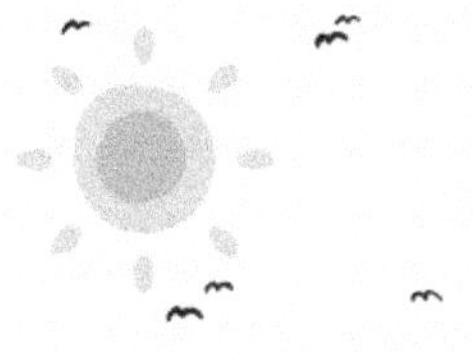

c. Mr. Micheal spends $32 on buying wheat on looking at the poster. How many kilograms of wheat does he buy? Draw a tape diagram, and label the total amount of wheat he buys as c. Write an equation, and solve for c.

$8 for 1kg

d. Six boys equally share 4 packs of football cards. Each pack contains 3 cards. How many cards does each boy get? Draw a tape diagram to represent. Write an equation, and solve for c i.e unknown number. (Hint: Find out the number of cards in 4 packs first)

15. Break apart and distribute to solve. One is done for you.

a. 35 ÷ 5

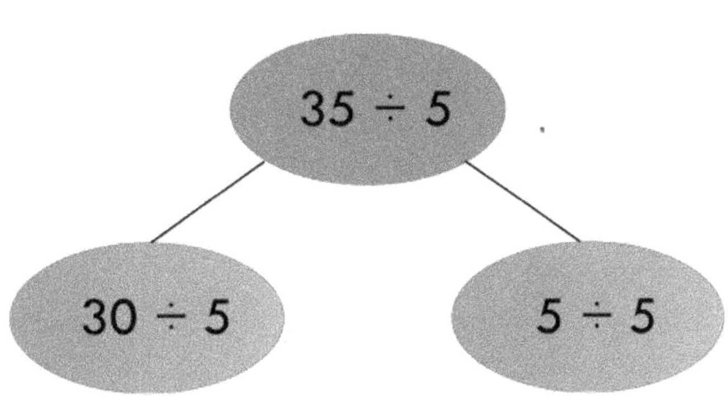

$$35 \div 5 = (30 \div 5) + (5 \div 5)$$
$$= 6 + 1$$
$$= 7$$

b. 28 ÷ 4

c. 54 ÷ 6

d. 99 ÷ 9

The order of numbers while multiplying does not change the product.

Example

4 x 5 = 20 is same as 5 x 4 = 20

Product of numbers can be found using fact families of that number.

Example

$4 \times 6 \times 2$ can be found by $4 \times 6 = 24$, then $24 \times 2 = 48$, or by $6 \times 2 = 12$, then $4 \times 12 = 48$.

Let's practice

1. Fill in the blanks with the missing numbers.

a.

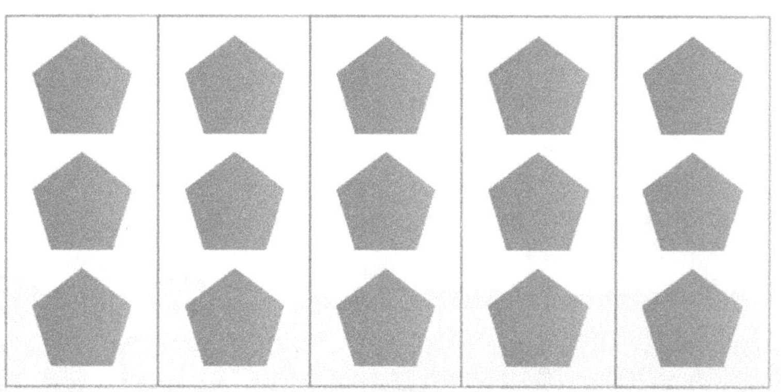

5 x _____ = 15

15 ÷ 3 = _____

b.

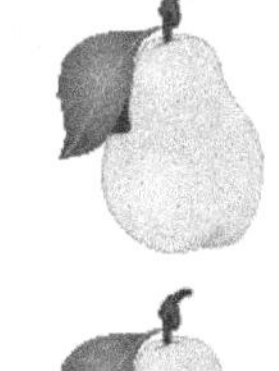

_____ x 4 = 16

16 ÷ _____ = 4

c.

2 x 4 = _____

8 ÷ _____ = _____

d.

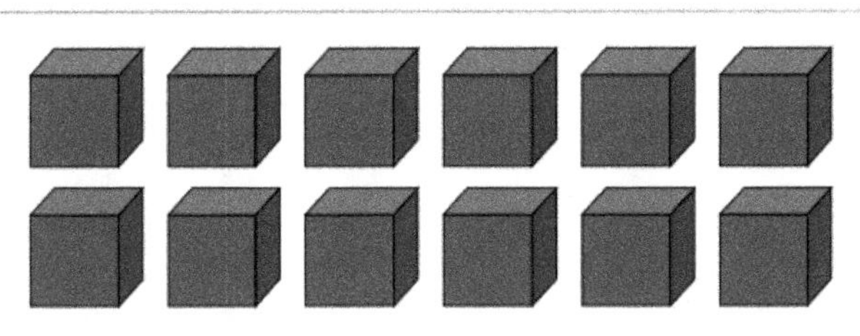

2 x _____ = _____

24 ÷ _____ = 2

Relationship between division and Multiplication

2. Match the division fact with the respective multiplication fact.

49 ÷ 7 = 7	7 x 8 = 56
56 ÷ 7 = 8	9 x 8 = 72
72 ÷ 8 = 9	6 x 8 = 48
32 ÷ 8 = 4	7 x 7 = 49
48 ÷ 6 = 8	4 x 8 = 32

3. Draw a picture array for the division facts.

a. $36 \div 4 = 9$

b. $54 \div 9 = 6$

c. $18 \div 6 = 3$

d. $45 \div 5 = 9$

Arrays and division

4. Solve the word problems.

a. Leo has fifteen strawberries. If he packs them such that there are three strawberries in each packet. Circle to show the number of packets.

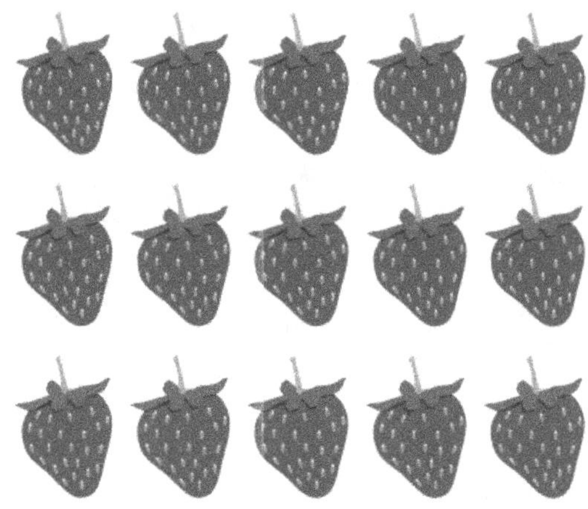

15 ÷ 3 = ____

There are ____ packets of strawberries.

b. There are twenty-four fish in an aquarium. Olivia wanted to keep six fish in each bowl. Circle to show how many bowls are there.

24 ÷ 6 = ____

There are ____ bowls of fish.

5. Complete the number bonds.

Write four different number sentences for each fact family.

One is done for you.

a.

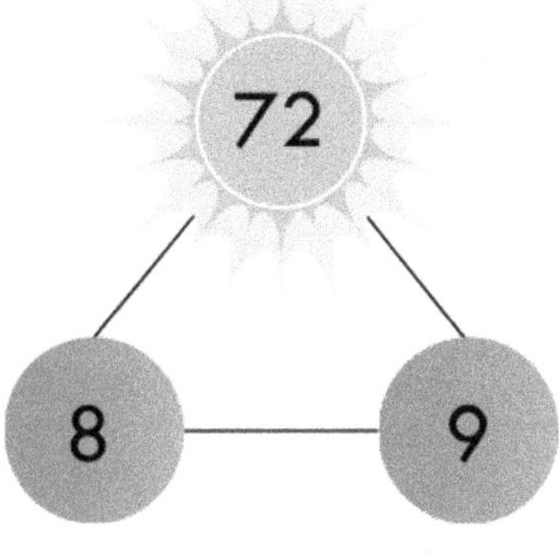

____ x ____ =

____ x ____ =

____ ÷ ____ =

____ ÷ ____ =

b.

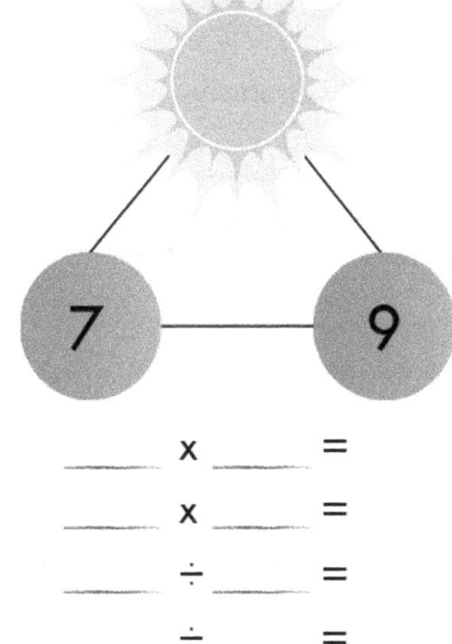

____ x ____ =

____ x ____ =

____ ÷ ____ =

____ ÷ ____ =

c.

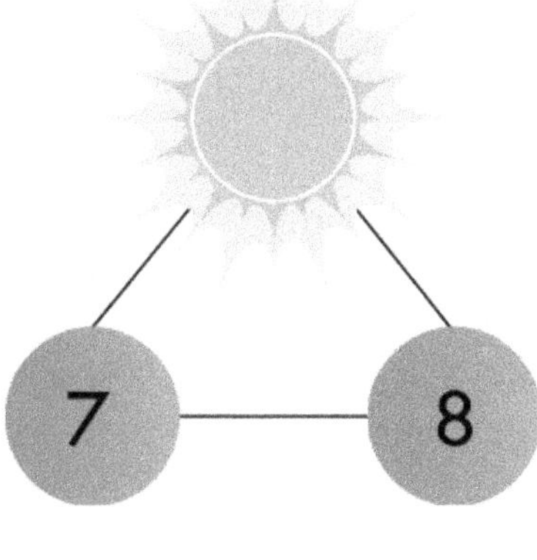

____ x ____ =

____ x ____ =

____ ÷ ____ =

____ ÷ ____ =

d.

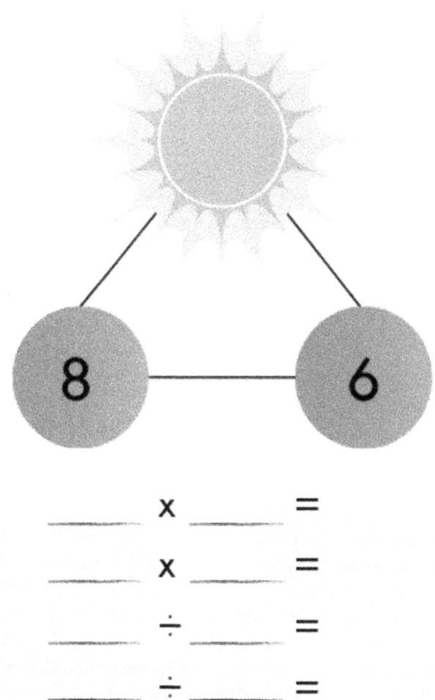

____ x ____ =

____ x ____ =

____ ÷ ____ =

____ ÷ ____ =

6. Mary arranges 15 shirts in her cupboard. If she puts an equal number of shirts on 3 racks, how many shirts are on each rack? Represent and solve the problem using a tape diagram.

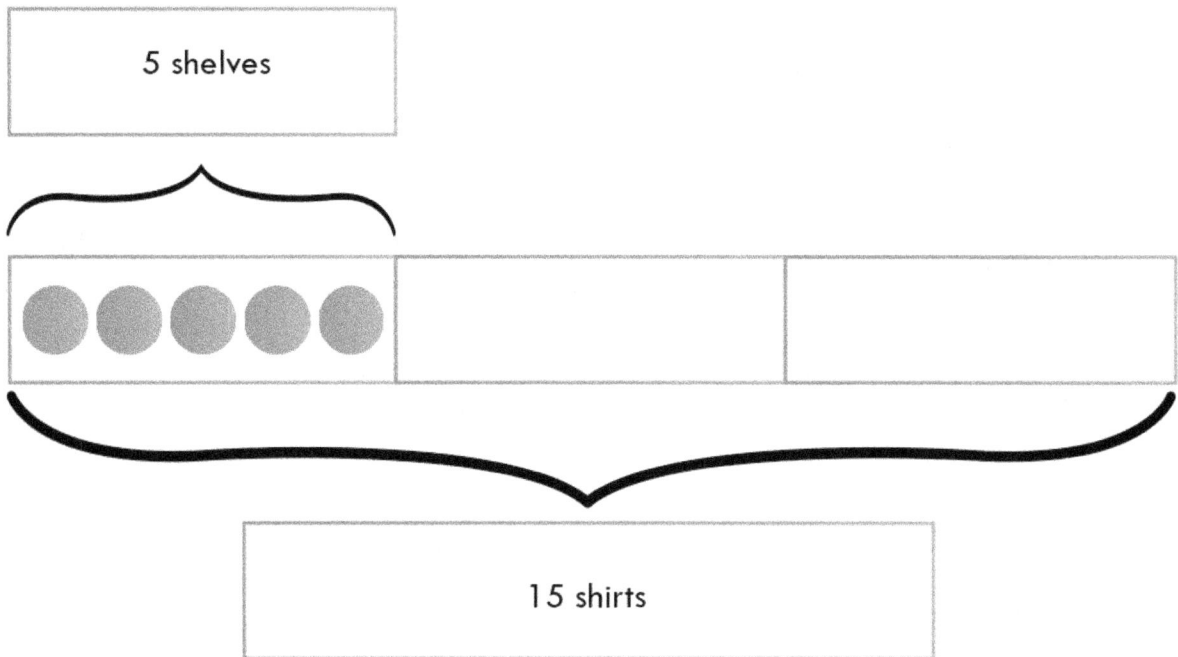

5 shelves

15 shirts

15 ÷ 3 = ____

There are ____ shirts on each rack.

7. Mr. Daniel buys a rope of length 21 meters. He cuts the rope into 7 equal pieces. How long is each piece? Represent and solve the problem using a tape diagram.

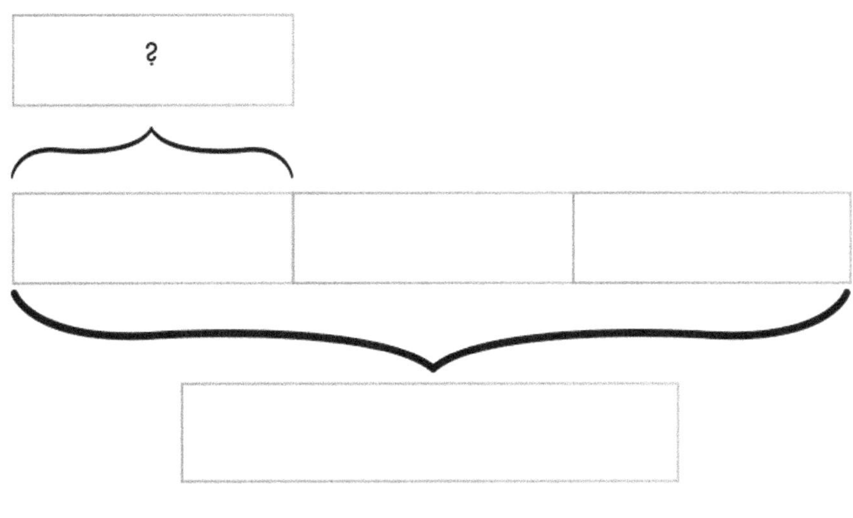

$21 \div 7 =$ ____

Each piece is ____ metre long.

8. Stella buys 30 eggs. She puts 5 eggs in each box. How many boxes are there? Represent and solve the problem using a tape diagram.

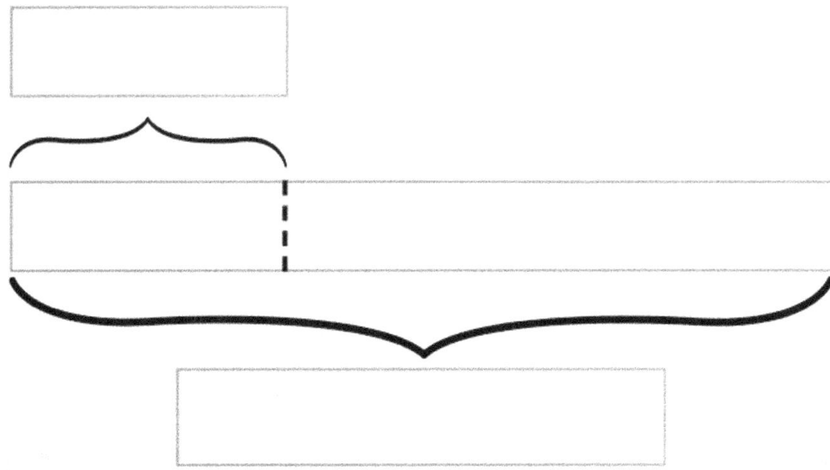

$30 \div 5 =$ ____

There are ____ boxes.

9. Roselyn has 10 apples. She puts 2 apples in each basket. How many baskets does she have?

a. Draw an array where each column shows a basket of apples.

10 ÷ 2 = ____

There are ____ baskets.

b. Redraw the apples in each basket as a unit in the tape diagram. As you draw label the diagram with known and unknown information from the problem.

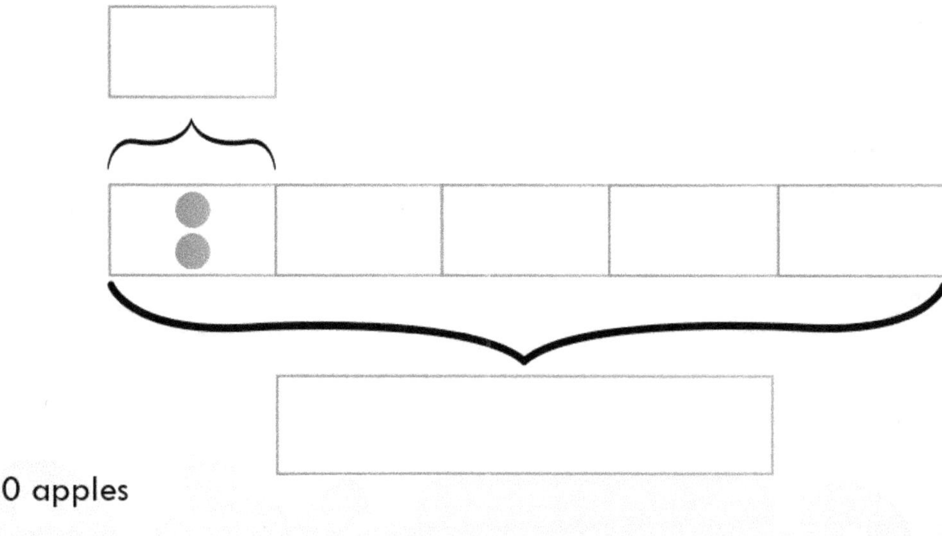

10 apples

____ baskets

10. Alexander arranges 72 stamps in 6 pages of his collection book. How many stamps can be arranged equally on each page?

Model the problem with both an array and a labeled tape diagram. Show each column as the number of stamps on each page.

11. Look at the number search below. Circle or highlight groups of three numbers that belong together in the fact family. There are 10 fact families hidden horizontally and vertically together. One is done for you

2	3	8	24	12	5
6	11	9	4	28	7
23	33	72	13	9	5
1	8	6	48	7	6
4	7	5	35	8	30
16	36	4	9	56	8
4	11	20	8	32	4

4 x 7 = 28; 28 ÷ 7 = 4; 28 ÷ 4 = 7

Did you find all the families?

Pick any two sets and write the fact family.

a. Fact family numbers

____, ____, ____

Fact family equations

____

b. Fact family numbers

____, ____, ____

Fact family equations

____

12. Solve the word problems.

a. Ricky and Micheal buy a gift worth $18 for their friend. The boys share the cost equally. How much does Ricky pay?

b. James plants 30 tomato plants in rows of 6. How many rows will he plant? If he adds six more tomato plants in rows of 6, how many rows will be there? Label the tape diagram to represent the problem, including the unknown.

c. Mrs. Angelina has 14 precious stones. Her father gifted her two more. She arranges the stones in a box, placing 4 stones in each row. How many rows will be there in the box? Model the problem with both an array and a labeled tape diagram.

d. Daniel worked for $48. He got $6 for an hour. How many hours did he work?

Understanding Place Value

Multi-Digit Arithmetic

1. Write the halfway point.

a. 30 ____ 40	f. 60 ____ 70
b. 290 ____ 300	g.1280 ____ 1290
c. 1130 ____ 1120	h. 200 ____ 210
d. 270 ____ 280	i. 1450 ____ 1460
e. 1390 ____ 1380	j. 530 ____ 520

2. Measurements of few things are given. Complete the chart below.

object	Measurement (in cm)	The object measures between (which two tens)	Length rounded to the nearest 10 cm
Length of a shorter side of an A4 sheet	21 cm	____ cm to ____ cm	
Length of a cable	98 cm	____ cm to ____ cm	
Length of my ribbon	15 cm	____ cm to ____ cm	
Length of a new pencil	18 cm	____ cm to ____ cm	
Length of longer side of a teapoy table	91 cm	____ cm to ____ cm	

3. Draw an arrow to match each number to its nearest 10.

4. Read the statements and fill in the blanks.

a. Measure the liquid to the nearest 10 milliliters.

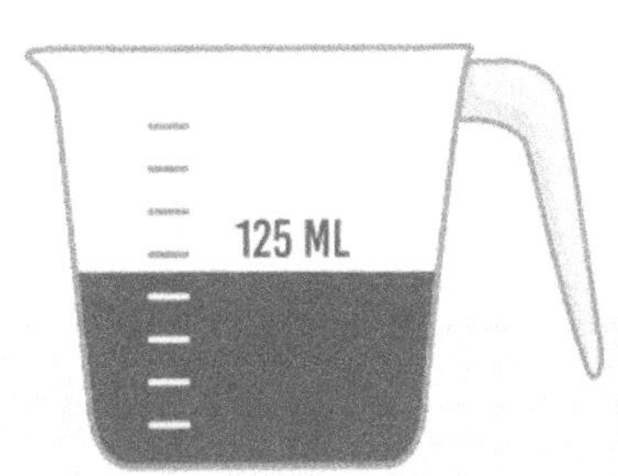

There are about _____ milliliters.

b. Ovia has only 296-gram sugar left at home. Round the weight to the nearest hundred.

She has about ____ gram of sugar left.

c. Aria wanted to bake a cake. She has 192 grams of butter. Round the weight to the nearest hundreds.

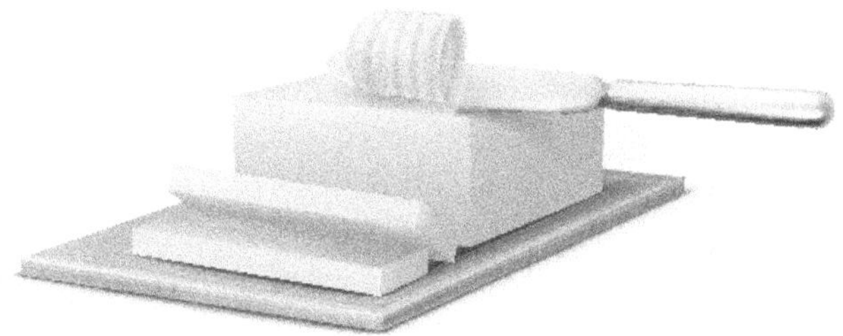

She has about ____ gram of butter.

d. Richard's football class starts at 8:09 in the morning. Round the time to the nearest tens.

Football class starts at about ____ a.m.

e. Ema finished her homework by 5:56 in the evening. Round the time to the nearest tens.

She finished her homework at about _____ p.m.

f. The drive between a city and Zürich is shown below. Round the distance to the nearest hundreds.

The distance is about _____ km.

5. The weight of the vegetable sacks is shown below.

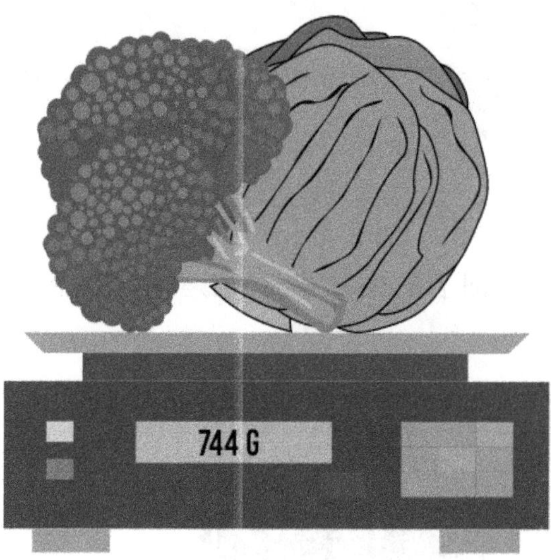

a. The weight of vegetable sacks is ____________ .

b. The weight of the vegetable sacks is about ____________ . (Round the weight to the nearest tens)

c. Round the weight of the vegetable sacks to the nearest hundreds. Model your thinking on the vertical number line.

d. Explain how you use the halfway point on the number line to round to the nearest hundred grams.

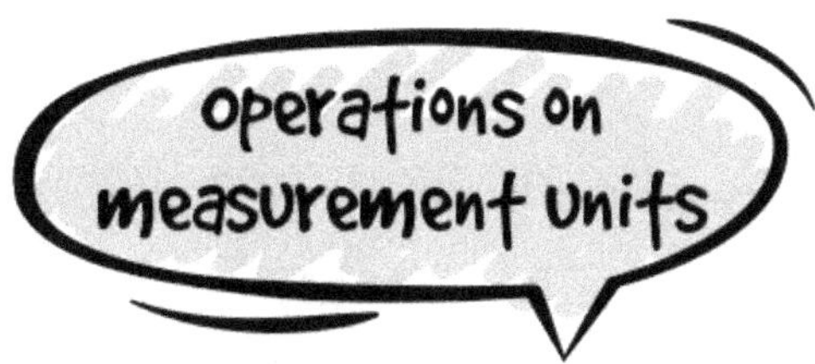

6. Find the sums below. One is done for you.

a. 46 cm + 7 cm 4 + 3 46 + 4 = 50 cm 50 + 3 = 53 cm	b. 78 m + 12 m
c. 123 mL + 34 mL	d. 158 g + 121 g
e. 3 kg 153 g + 1 kg 312 g	f. 2 L 361 mL + 4 L 321 mL

7. Solve the word problems.

a. Boonie found 56 rocks on her sidewalk and 74 rocks in her backyard. Draw and label a tape diagram to find the total number of rocks found in all?

b. The capacity of the bucket is 330 mL more than the bottle. The capacity of the bottle is 220 mL. What is the total capacity of the bucket and the bottle?

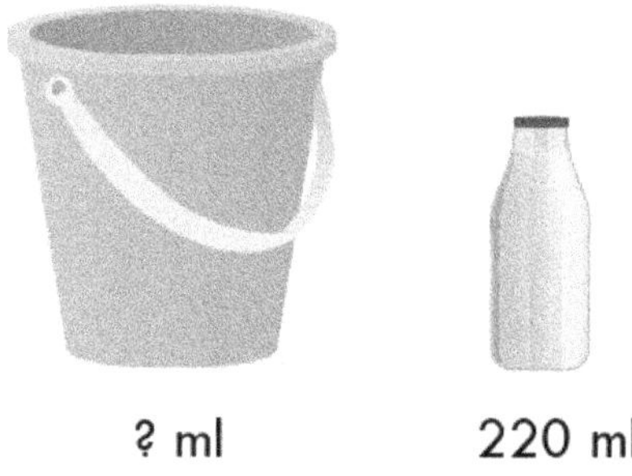

c. Mrs. Rachel bakes a cake for 28 minutes. She takes another 12 minutes to decorate the cake. Draw a tape diagram to find the total minutes Mrs.Rachel took to prepare the cake?

d. It takes George 22 minutes to mow the back lawn and 13 minutes more to mow the front lawn. What is the total amount of time George spends mowing the lawn?

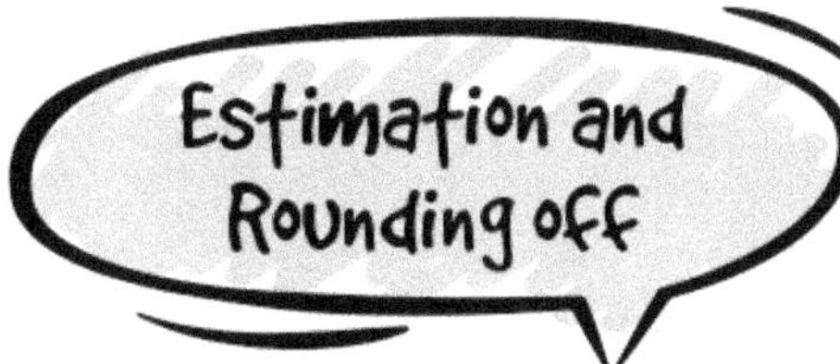

8. Find the actual sum. Round each addend to the nearest hundred, and find the estimated sum.

a. 132 + 146 = ____

____ + ____ = ____

b. 453 + 157 = ____

____ + ____ = ____

c. 256 + 144 = ____

____ + ____ = ____

Circle the estimated sum that is the closest to its actual sum.

a. 687 + 143 = ____

____ + ____ = ____

b. 765 + 155 = ____

____ + ____ = ____

c. 553 + 237 = ____

____ + ____ = ____

Circle the estimated sum that is the closest to its actual sum.

9. Jenelle went for a long drive on three consecutive days. Which two days distance covered by Jenelle will give 450 km. Round the distances to nearest 10 and find out.

Saturday	Sunday	Monday
243 km	245 km	203 km

10. Solve the subtraction problems below.

a. 260 g - 16 g	b. 432 cm - 115 cm
c. 750 km - 75 km	d. 654 kg - 249 kg
e. 6 L 538 mL - 3 L 379 mL	f. 7 L 643 mL - 2 L 197 mL

11. The total weight of the three apples is shown below. If two apples weigh 550 grams, how much does the third apple weigh? Use a tape diagram to model the problem.

12. Use the chart to complete the blanks in the equations.

a. Tens | Ones: 9 dots in Ones 3 x 3 ones = ________ ones 3 x 3 = ________	b. Tens | Ones: 6 dots in Tens 2 x 3 tens = ________ tens 2 x 30 = ________
c. Tens | Ones: 12 dots in Ones 4 x 3 ones = ________ ones 4 x 3 = ________	d. Tens | Ones: 12 dots in Tens 3 x 4 tens = ________ tens 3 x 40 = ________

13. Solve the word problems.

a. A minibus can carry 20 passengers. How many passengers can 4 such minibus carry? Model with a tape diagram.

b. In a school there are 9 classrooms. Each classroom has 30 desks. How many desks are there in all? Model with a tape diagram.

c. In a general ward of a hospital, there are 20 beds. How many beds can be placed in 5 such general wards?

d. In one minute there are 60 seconds. How many seconds will be there in 6 minutes 10 seconds? Model with a tape diagram.

14. Samantha saves $ 20 each month for 6 months. Does she have enough money to buy the sewing kit box? Explain why or why not.

Sewing kit box $135

15. Lucas earns $10 an hour working at a restaurant. He works for 8 hours each day on Mondays and Thursdays. How much does Lucas earn each week?

16. Angel's nursery sells radish seed packets weighing 32 grams. Round the total weight of two seed packets to the nearest 10. Model your thinking using a number line.

17. Write four numbers that round to 100.

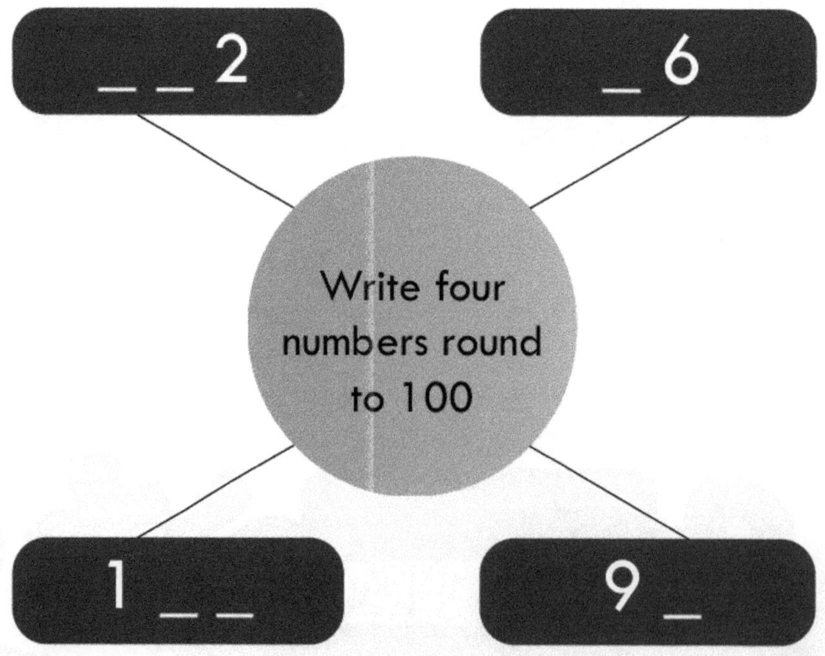

18. Jason has 73 marbles more than Rocky. Rocky has 137 marbles. Draw and label the tape diagram to find the total number of marbles they have?

19. Few boys went to a juice shop. They found the liquid volume of five drinks as shown below.

Drink	Liquid volume
Watermelon juice	285 mL
Apple juice	248 mL
Mango juice	135 mL
Lemonade	242 mL
Strawberry milkshake	196 mL

a. Daniel drinks strawberry milkshake and lemonade. How many milliliters does he drink in all? ______________________

b. Jacob drinks apple juice and watermelon juice. How many milliliters does he drink in all? ______________________

c. What is the volume of mango juice and apple juice in all? ______________

20. The chart below shows the sale of different breeds of dogs in a month.

Name of the breed	Number of dogs sold
Pug	246
Labrador Retriever	423
Pomeranian	?

a. The number of Pomeranians sold was 34 less than Labrador Retrievers. How many Pomeranians were sold? ________________

b. How many more Pomeranians were sold than the Pugs? __________

Fractions

When an object is divided into a number of equal parts then each part is called a **fraction.** A whole is divided into equal parts and each part is a fraction.

Example

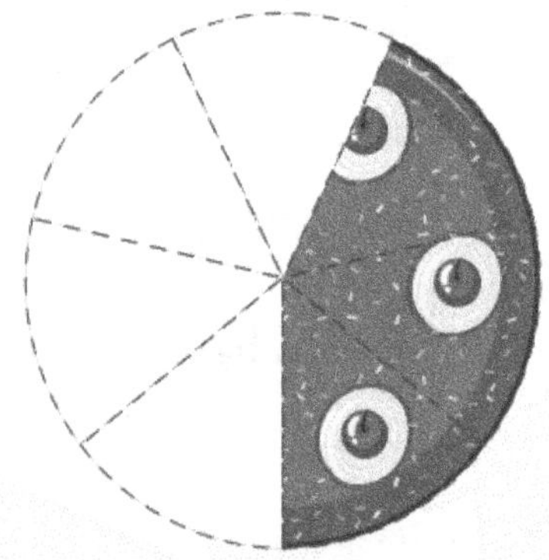

The whole chocolate cake is divided into 7 equal parts. Four parts have been eaten and 3 parts are remaining.

A fraction is represented as :

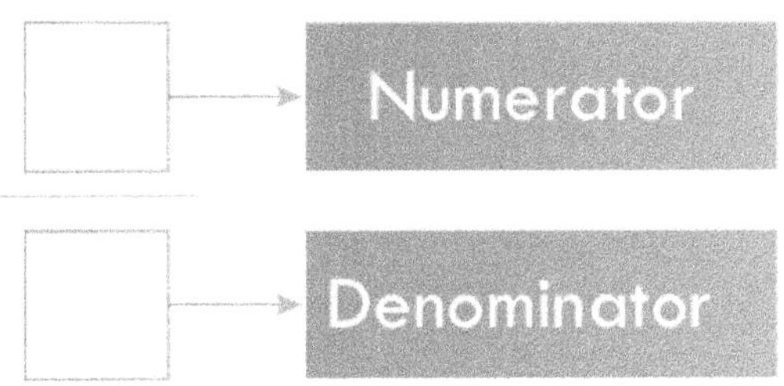

The total number of parts is written in the denominator and the part taken is written in the numerator.

In the above example, $^4/_7$ represents 4 out of 7 slices of cake eaten.

Let's practice

1. Which shapes have $^1/_8$th of their shapes shaded?

a.

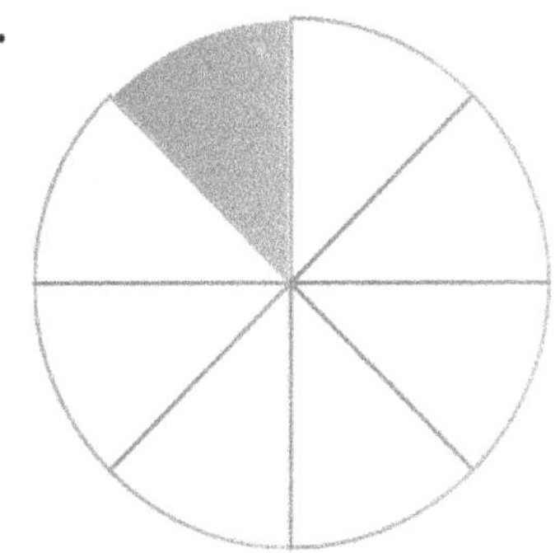

b.

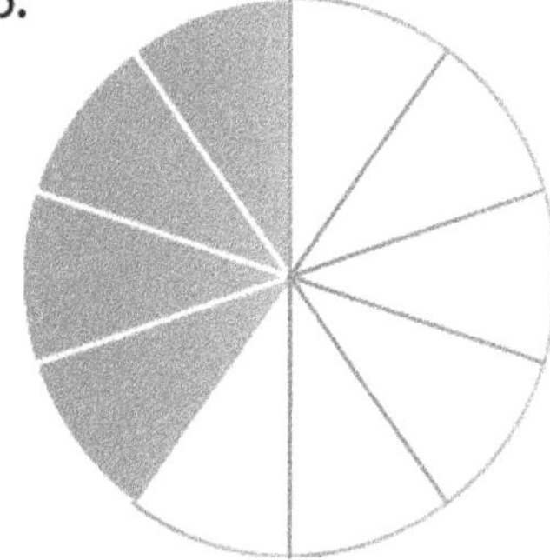

c.

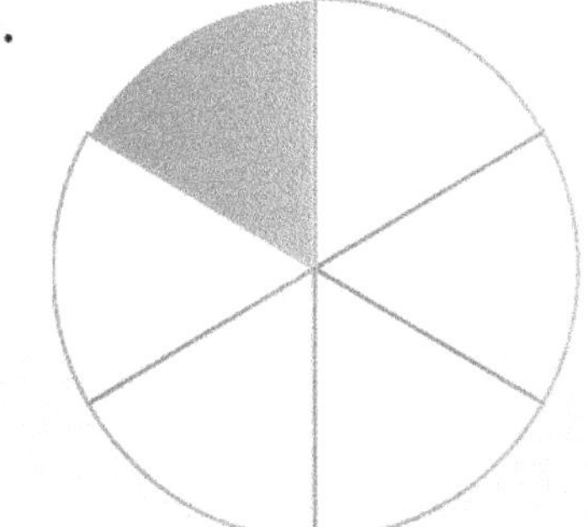

d.

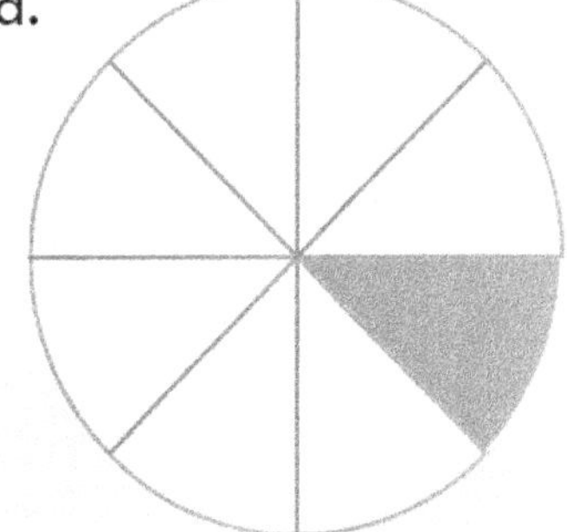

2. Which figures have been divided into equal parts?

a.

b.

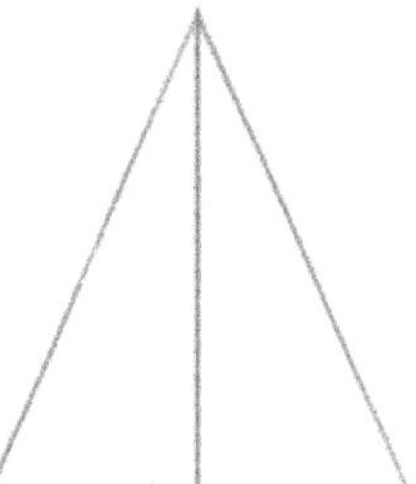

c.

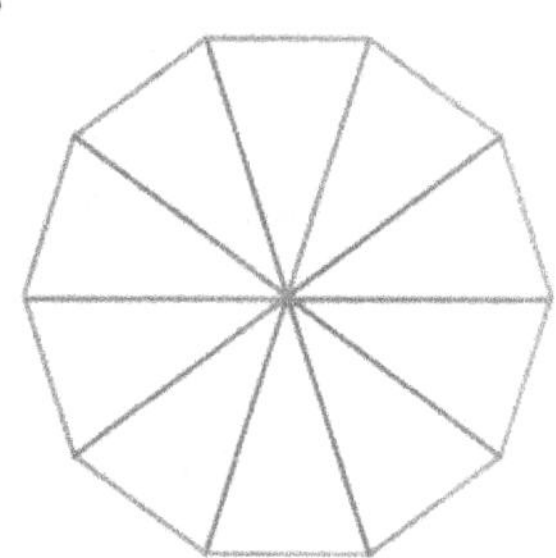

d.

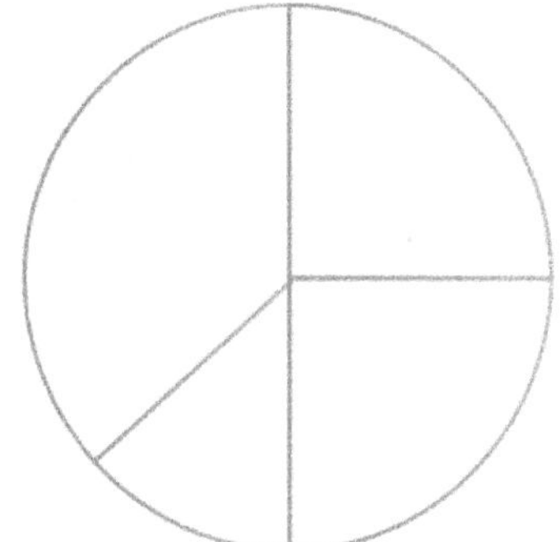

e.

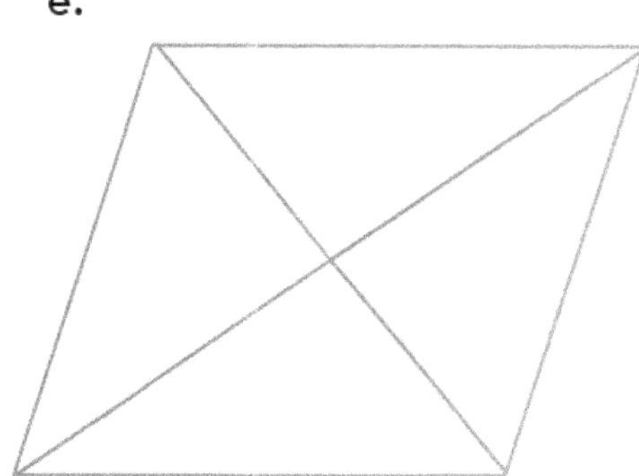

f.

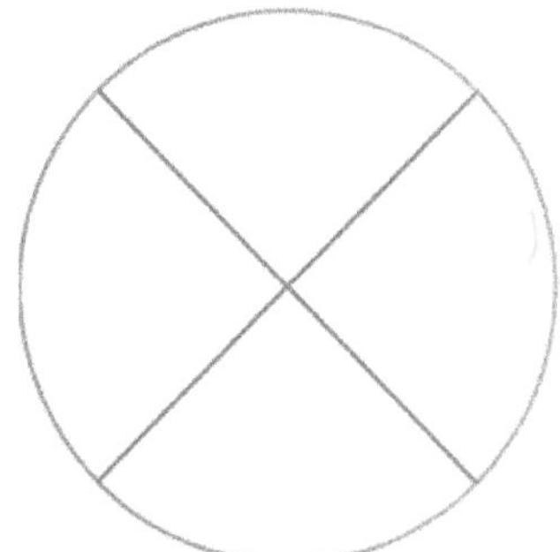

3. Solve the following problems:

a. John's dinner plate is divided into 3 equal parts. He puts all his carrots into one part. What fraction of John's plate has carrots?

____

____

b. Steve has a square box with four equal compartments. He fills in two of the compartments with marbles. What fraction of Steve's box is empty?

____

____

4. Match the fractions

	Two - fifths
	Two - fourths
	One - fifths
	Four - fifths
	Three - fourths

5. a. Which number line is divided into one-thirds? Colour it.

i.

ii.

b. Which fraction is represented by the length of the red line on the number line?

6. Label all the fractional parts of the number line from 0 to 1.

a.

b.

c.

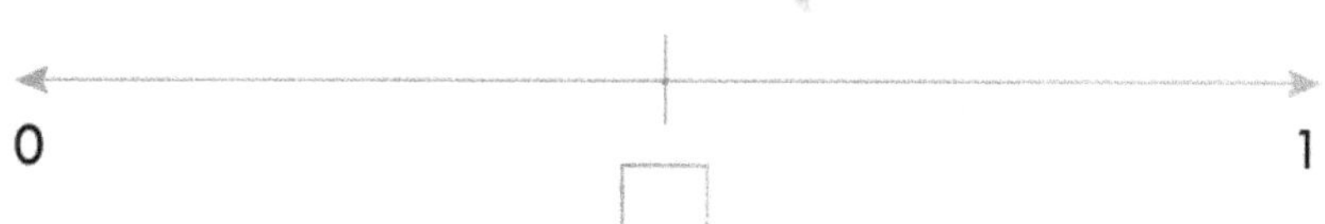

7. A big rectangle has been divided into equal parts

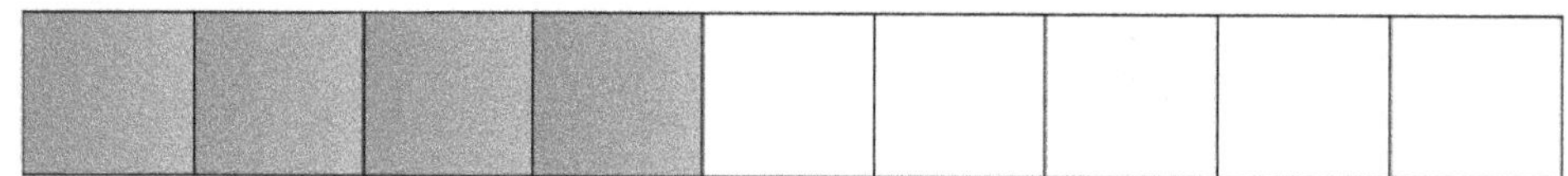

a. How many equal parts has the rectangle been divided into? __________

b. Label each part with a unit fraction.

c. What is the fraction of the strip that has been shaded? __________

d. What is the fraction of the strip that has not been shaded? __________

8. Solve the following:

a. There were two pizzas, cheese and pepperoni, at a party. Both the pizzas were of equal size. Ron ate 1/3rd of the cheese pizza and Sam ate 1/4th of the pepperoni pizza. Who ate a larger piece of pizza? Explain your answer.

b. The brothers George and Mark had a candy bar each. The candy bars were of the same size. George ate 1/8th of the bar and Mark ate 1/5th of the bar. Who is left with more candy now? Explain your answer.

9. Solve the following:

a. Ava says 1/3rd is the same as 2/6th. Is she right? Explain your answer.

b. Bret says 3/4th of the cake is more than 3/6th of the cake. Is he right? Explain your answer.

10. In Mrs. Smith's class, the coat hanger has seven pegs that are placed at an equal distance.

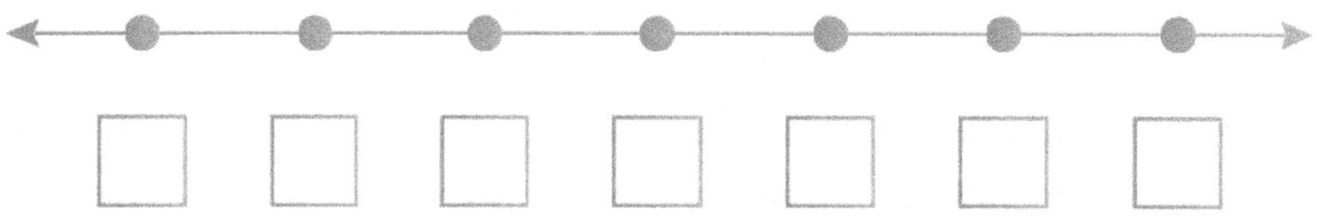

a. Label each hook with its corresponding fraction.

b. If Zoe hangs her coat in the peg that is placed at the half-way point, what is the corresponding fraction?

____

c. If Nicole hangs her coat at the third peg, what fraction is the peg at?

____

11. Compare the following using the symbols > < or =.

a.

3/8 ☐ 3/4

b.

1/3 ☐ 1/6

c.

4/8 ☐ 6/8

d.

1/2 ☐ 1/4

e.

9/6 ☐ 3/6

12. Solve the following:

a. Emma's wardrobe is taller than her study table. Emma's school bag is one-third the height of her study table. Emma's sports kit is one-third the height of her wardrobe. Which is taller, the school bag or the sports kit? Why?

____

____

b. Steve is four-sixth the height of his dad. His sister is five-sixth the height of his dad. Who is the tallest, Steve or his sister?

____

____

13. Solve the following.

a. What fraction does the triangle represent?

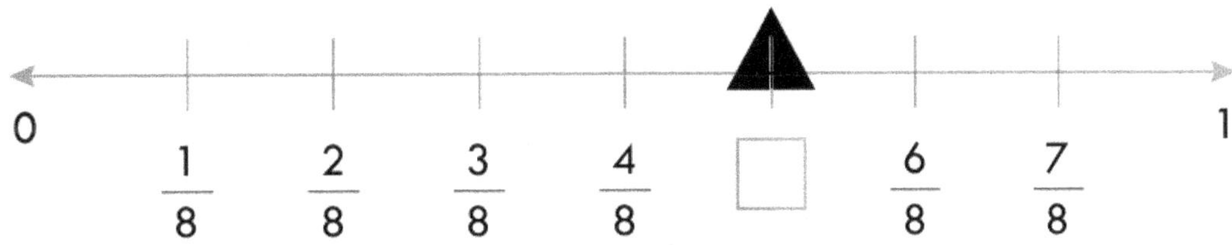

b. What fraction does the square represent?

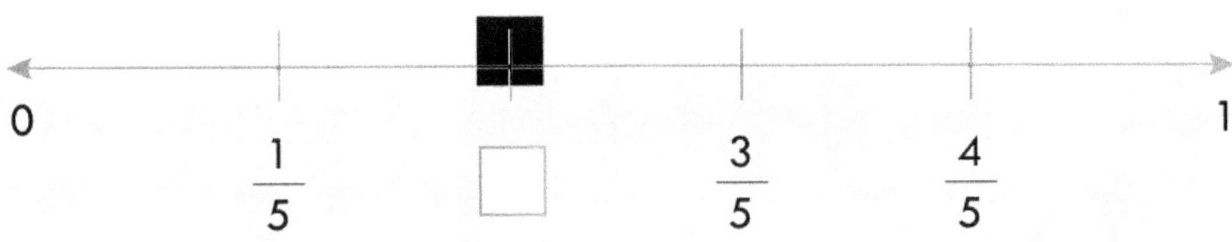

14. Answer the following

a. What part of the group of triangles is shaded?

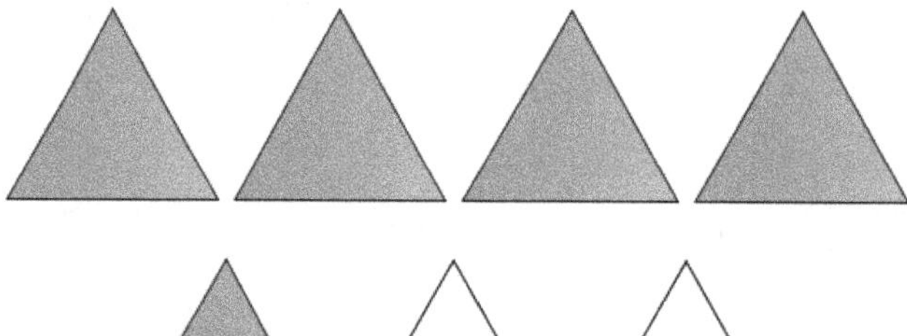

____

b. What part of the group of stars is not shaded?

____

c. What part of the group of circles are shaded?

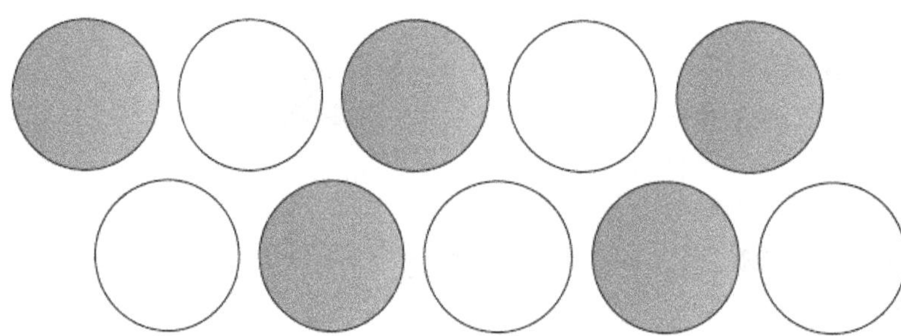

____

15. Select all the fractions that are equivalent to a whole number

a. 3/3

b. 8/4

c. 2/3

d. 1/6

e. 6/3

16. In each of the following questions, write the appropriate fractions

a.

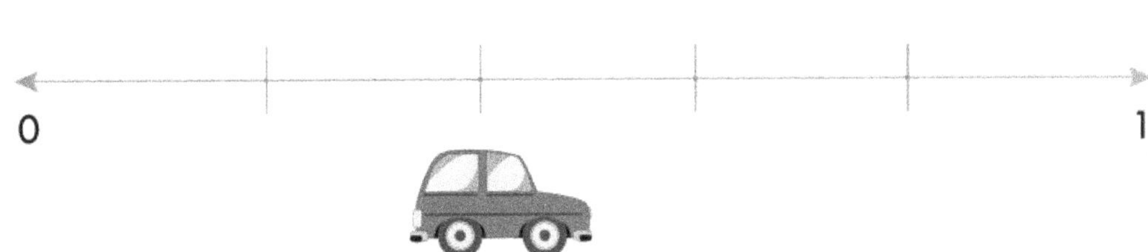

i. How far has the car travelled on the number line?

____

ii. How far should the car travel to reach 1 on the number line?

____

b.

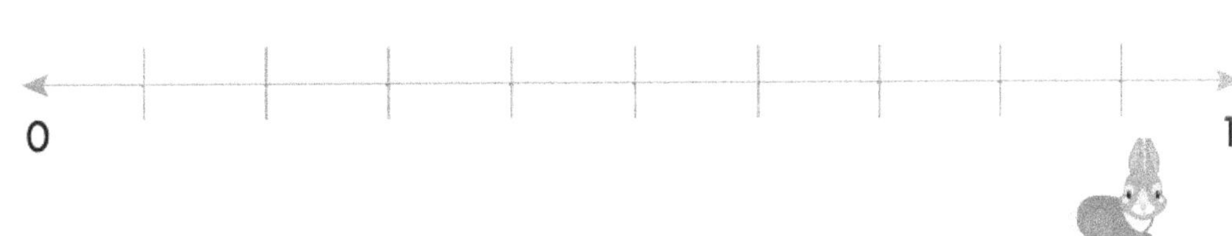

i. How far has the rabbit hopped on the number line?

____

ii. How far should the rabbit hop to reach 1 on the number line?

____

17. Solve the following

a. Trent has a steel rod of length 15 feet. He has cut it into pieces that are of 3 feet each. What fraction of the steel rod does one piece represent? Explain.

____

____

b. Maggie has a ribbon of length 24 centimeters. She cuts it into equal pieces of 4 centimeters each. What fraction does each piece represent? If she loses 2 of the pieces of the ribbons, what fraction of the ribbon is she left with?

____

____

____

18. Matt baked a cake and cut it into fourths.

a. What fraction of the original cake does each piece represent?

____

b. Matt ate 1 piece of the cake in the evening and his sister ate 1 piece. What fraction of the original cake is still not eaten?

____

____

c. Matt divides 1 piece of the cake between 2 of his friends. What fraction of the original cake did each friend get?

____

19. Each shape represents 1 whole. Equally partition the shapes and shade to show the given fraction.

a. one- fourth

b. one-half

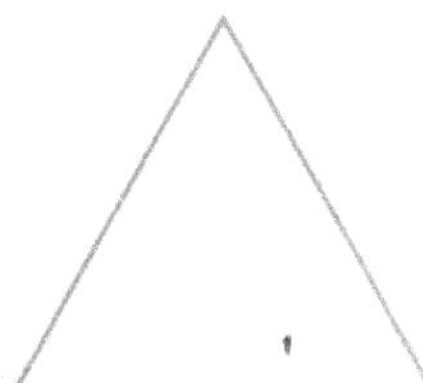

c. one- fifth

d. one-fourth

e. two-sixths

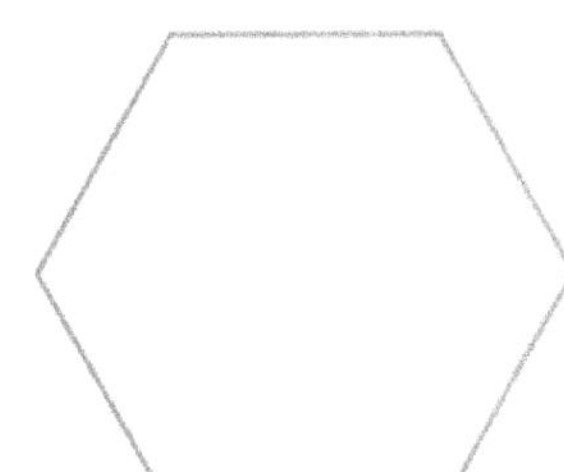

f. three-fourths

20. Ella had two bars of chocolate that are of the same size.

a. She divided Bar A into 4 parts. Are they each one-fourth? Explain.

Bar A

b. How can she divide Bar B between her 3 friends and herself so that everyone gets an equal share?

Bar B

c. What fraction of the Bar B did each of the friends get?

Measurement

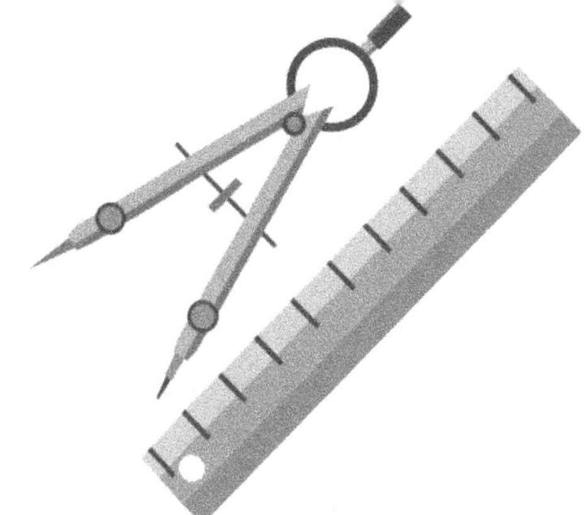

Time

Time is a continuous measurement, stopwatches and clocks are used to measure its movement. Hour, Minute and Seconds are units of time. Seconds are smaller than minutes, so we can use them to measure short amounts of time. Minutes are longer than seconds. 60 seconds make a minute. 60 minutes make an hour.

Let's practice

1. Solve the following with the help of a number line.

a. Ava completed a lego model at 3.15 pm. If she took 35 minutes to build it, what time did she start building it?

____

b. Steve went for a walk at 6.12 am and returned home at 7.10 am. How long did he walk?

____

c. Mary started her homework at 3.12 pm and took 45 minutes to finish it. What time did she finish it?

____

____

2. Answer the questions.

a. How much time has elapsed from the first clock to the second clock?

---

b. Look at the time in the Clock A. Color the correct clock which shows an elapsed time of 32 minutes.

Clock A

3. What time is shown in the number line?

a.

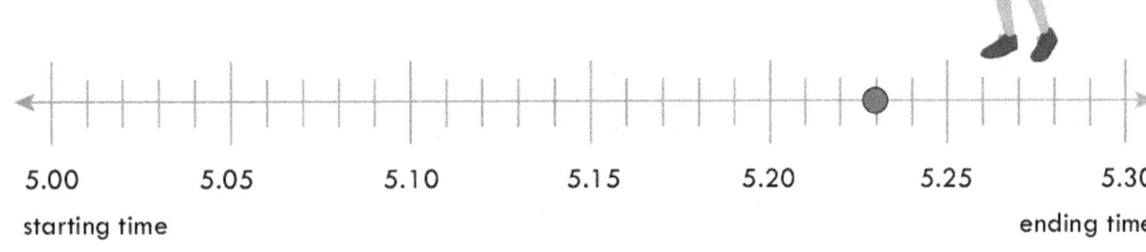

____

b.

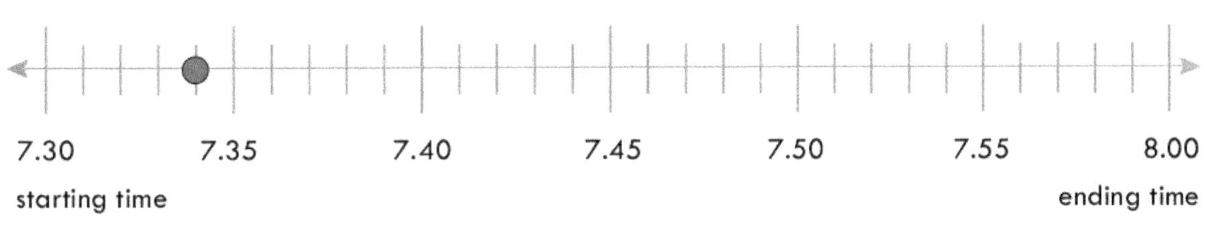

____

c.

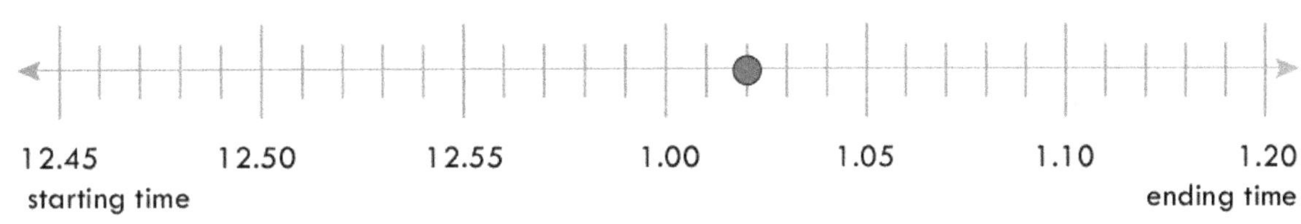

____

4. Dave gets up at 7.00 am. He has to leave for school at 8.00 am.

7.00 am and 8.00 am are marked in the number line below. Do the following.

a. Each interval represents 5 minutes. Count by 5s, starting at 7.00 a.m.
Label each 5-minute interval between 7.00 am and 8.00 am.

b. He brushes his teeth at 7.10 am. Mark this time on the number line.

c. He gets dressed up at 7.25 am. Mark this time on the number line.

d. He finishes his breakfast at 7.40 am. Mark this time on the number line.

e. He takes the bus at 7.50 am. Mark this time on the number line.

5. The number line shows the time Joe and his friends attended Soccer practice. Look at the number line below and answer the questions.

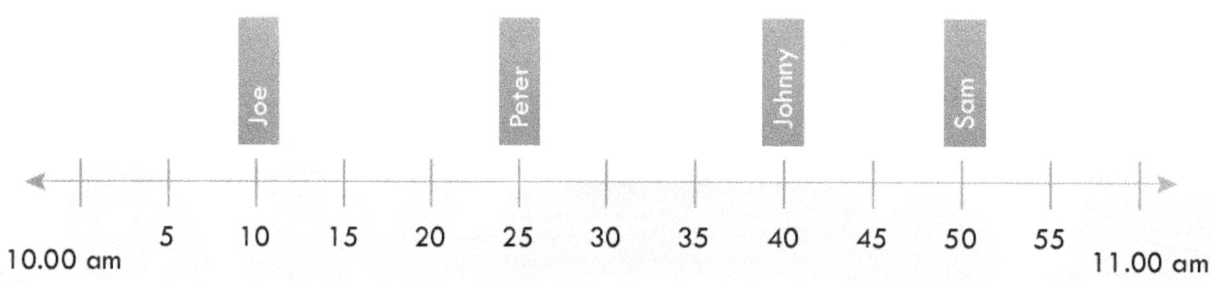

a. Complete the table.

Player's name	Time arrived for practice
Joe	
Peter	
Johnny	
Sam	

b. Who was last to come for the practice?

____

c. What is the difference in minutes between the arrival of Johnny and Peter?

____

6. Plot points on the number line for each time shown on the clock below. Then, match the clocks to the points.

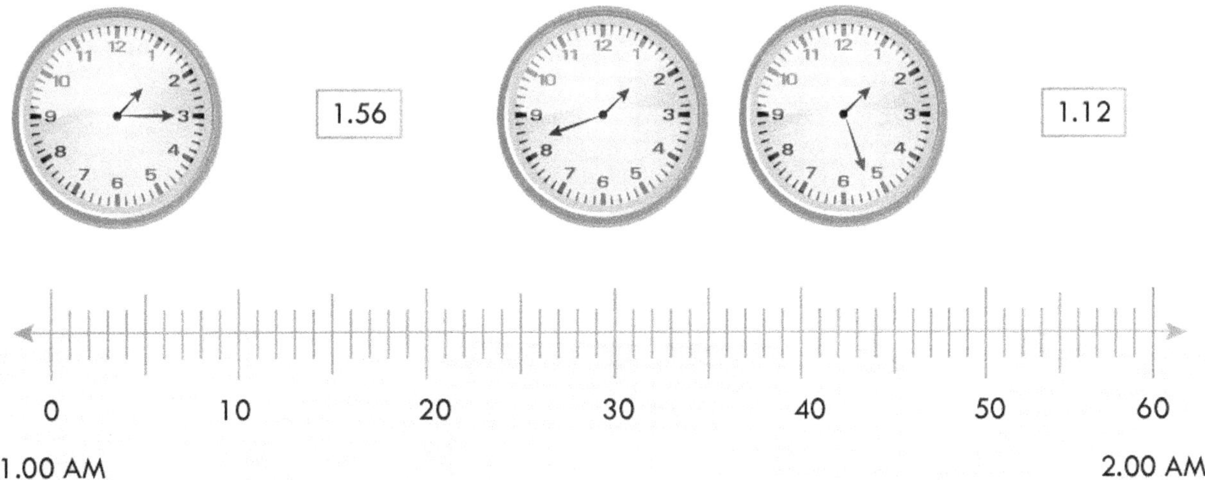

7. Find the duration of time between the two clocks.

8. Estimate the amount of liquid in each of the following objects:

a. A cup of coffee	3 milliliters	300 milliliters
b. A bucket of water	5 milliliters	5 liters
c. A small pond	20 liters	20 milliliters
d. A bottle of water	1 liter	1 milliliter
e. A glass of lemonade	500 liters	500 milliliters

9. Solve the following problems:

a. If one pitcher holds 5 liters of orange juice and the other pitcher holds 7 liters, how many liters of juice are in total?

____

b. There are 5 cartons of milk in the rack. Each carton has 2 liters of milk. How many liters of milk are there in the rack?

____

c. There are 48 milliliters of syrup left. If Ana takes out 4 milliliters each time, for how many times will the syrup last?

____

d. There was 320 milliliters of water in the bucket. After Steve added some more, there was 525 milliliters of water. How much water did Steve add?

____

10. Adam is making a science experiment using a sugar and salt solution. Look at both the solutions below and answer the questions.

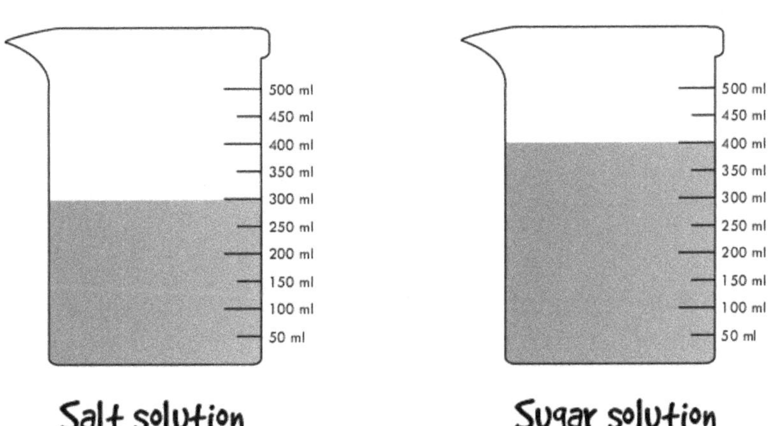

a. What quantity of salt solution is there? ____________________

b. What quantity of sugar solution is there? ____________________

c. What is more in quantity? Sugar solution or Salt solution? ____________

d. If he mixes the salt solution in 323 milliliters of water, how much liquid will the quantity be?

____

11. Look at the chart below. Mark the number line to show the capacity of each tank.

Tank A	63 liters
Tank B	55 liters
Tank C	24 liters
Tank D	61 liters

a. Which tank has the most capacity?

____

____

b. Which tank has the least capacity?

____

____

c. What is the combined capacity of Tank A and C?

____

____

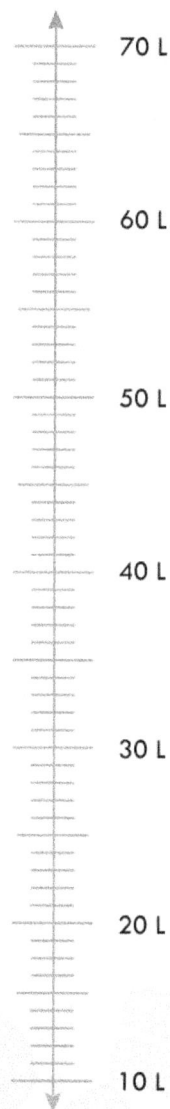

70 L

60 L

50 L

40 L

30 L

20 L

10 L

12. Solve the following problems:

a. If the weight of a carton is 3 kilograms, how much do 12 cartons weigh?

b. A box can hold 900 grams of chocolate. If each pack of chocolate weighs 10 grams, how many packets can fit into the box?

c. The weight of a puppy is 800 grams. After two months, it has increased by 243 grams. How much does the puppy weigh now?

d. Stella is making a cake. If Stella mixes 630 grams of flour, 200 grams of sugar and 150 grams of chocolate powder, what will be the weight of the mix?

13. Circle the odd one out. Explain your thinking.

Explain your thinking.

Explain your thinking.

14. Solve the following:

a. David finds out that 1 kilogram of rice is the same as 1 bottle of oil. He then says, "My bike weighs the same as 9 bottles of oil". Explain his reasoning and find out the weight of his bike in kilograms?

b. Drake's father says that 1 kilogram of beans is the same as 10 bags containing 100 grams of rice each. Do you agree? Explain your reasoning.

15. The table below shows how long it takes each student to finish packing their bags.

Student	Time Taken
Ava	56 seconds
Emma	45 seconds
John	33 seconds
Joshua	28 seconds
Mary	52 seconds

a. Who packs the bag fastest?

____

b. Who is the slowest in packing his/her bag?

____

c. How much slower is Ava in packing her bag than John?

____

d. What is the combined time taken by Emma, John, and Ava?

____

e. Emma says she is 6 seconds faster than Ava. Is she right? Explain your reasoning.

____

Data

1. Ron has prepared a graph to show what snack every kid in third grade prefers. Use the bar graph to answer the questions that follow.

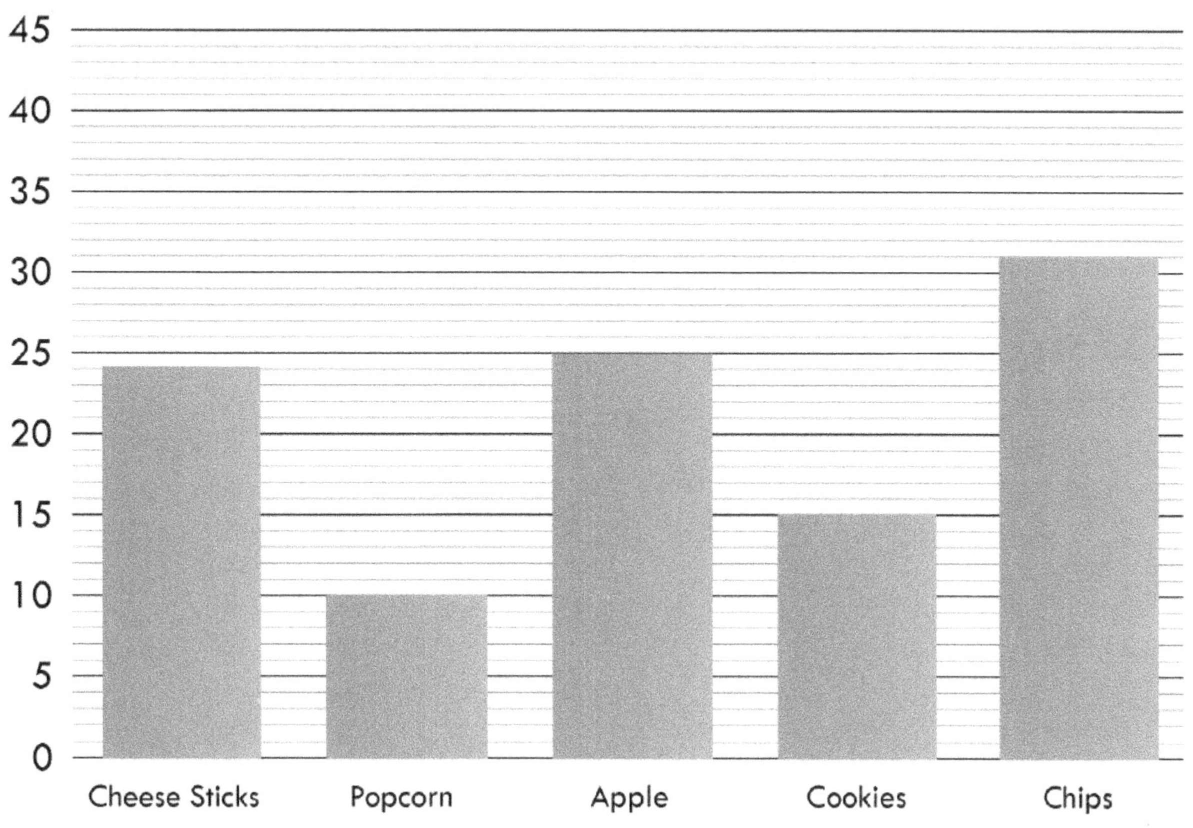

a. How many kids participated in the survey? ____________________

b. Which was the most favorite snack? ____________________

c. Which was the least favorite snack? ____________________

d. How many of them preferred chips more than popcorn? ____________________

e. Do more students prefer cheese sticks or apples? ____________________

All about cupcakes

2. Stella, George, and Jack were selling cupcakes in the school fair. The graph below shows how many cupcakes each of them sold.

Stella	
George	
Jack	

Key:  = 2 cupcakes

a. How many cupcakes did Jack sell?

____

b. How many cupcakes did George sell?

____

c. Who sold 12 cupcakes?

____

d. Who sold more cupcakes, Jack or Stella and by how much?

____

e. Who sold the least number of cupcakes?

____

3. Ann wanted to find out how many students played soccer, tennis and basketball. She recorded her findings in a table. Draw a bar graph to represent the data

Sports	Number of students
Soccer	40
Tennis	15
Basketball	25

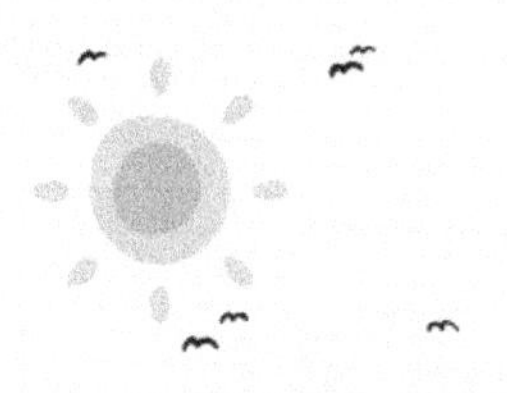

4. For the class party for 3rd grade, the students opted for the following flavors of icecreams.

Vanilla - 9 Chocolate - 15 Strawberry - 12

Mango - 5 Mint - 8

Use the information from the list to complete the pictograph below:

Key

= 2 votes

a. How many students prefer Strawberry or Mango?

____

b. What two flavors are least liked?

____

c. How many votes were there in all?

____

Icecream Flavor	Number of Votes
Vanilla	
Chocolate	
Strawberry	
Mango	
Mint	

5. Peter is preparing for his English test. The number of pages he reads each day is shown as below:

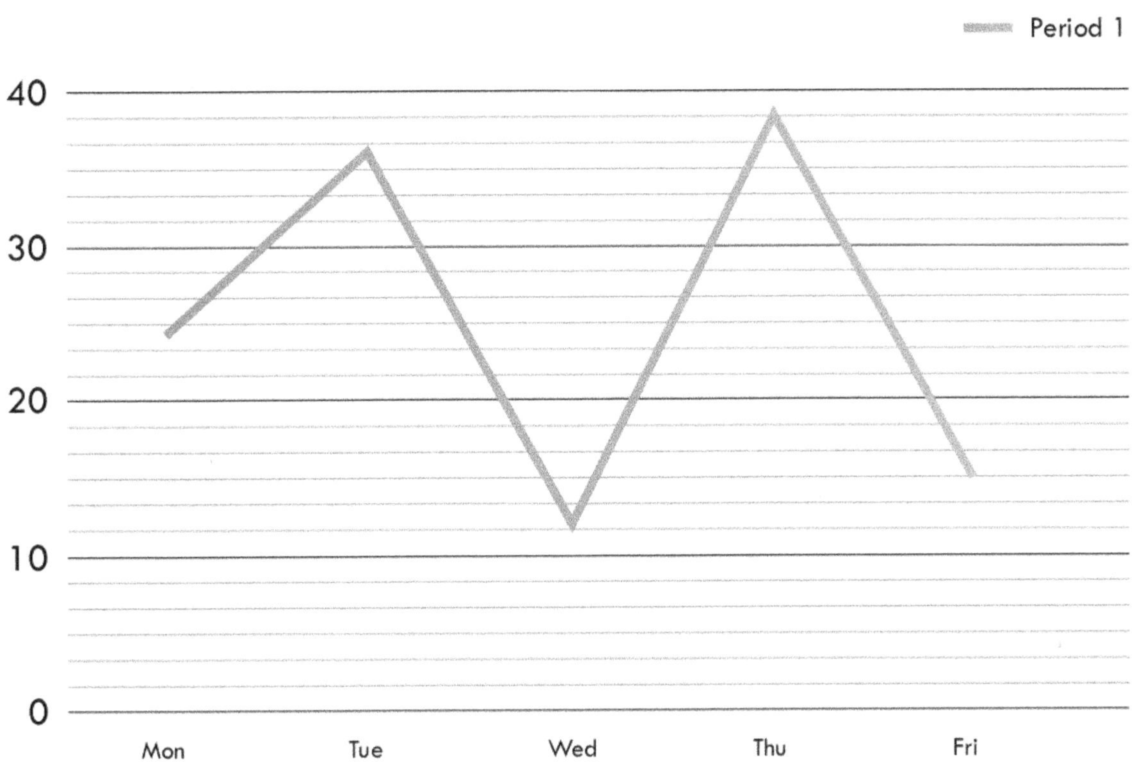

a. How many pages did he read each day:

Mon: ___________

Tue: ___________

Wed: ___________

Thu: ___________

Fri: ___________

b. On which day did he read the most? ___________________________

c. On which day did he read the least? ___________________________

6. The class was asked to pick their favorite color. Below is the tally chart for the same. Construct a bar graph for the recordings (use a scale of 1).

Favorite color	Tally Marks
Red	𝍸 ||
Blue	𝍸 ||||
Green	|||
Yellow	𝍸 𝍸
Pink	𝍸

7. In 3rd grade, the average marks the students got in the last examination is as recorded below. Study the bar graph and answer the following questions.

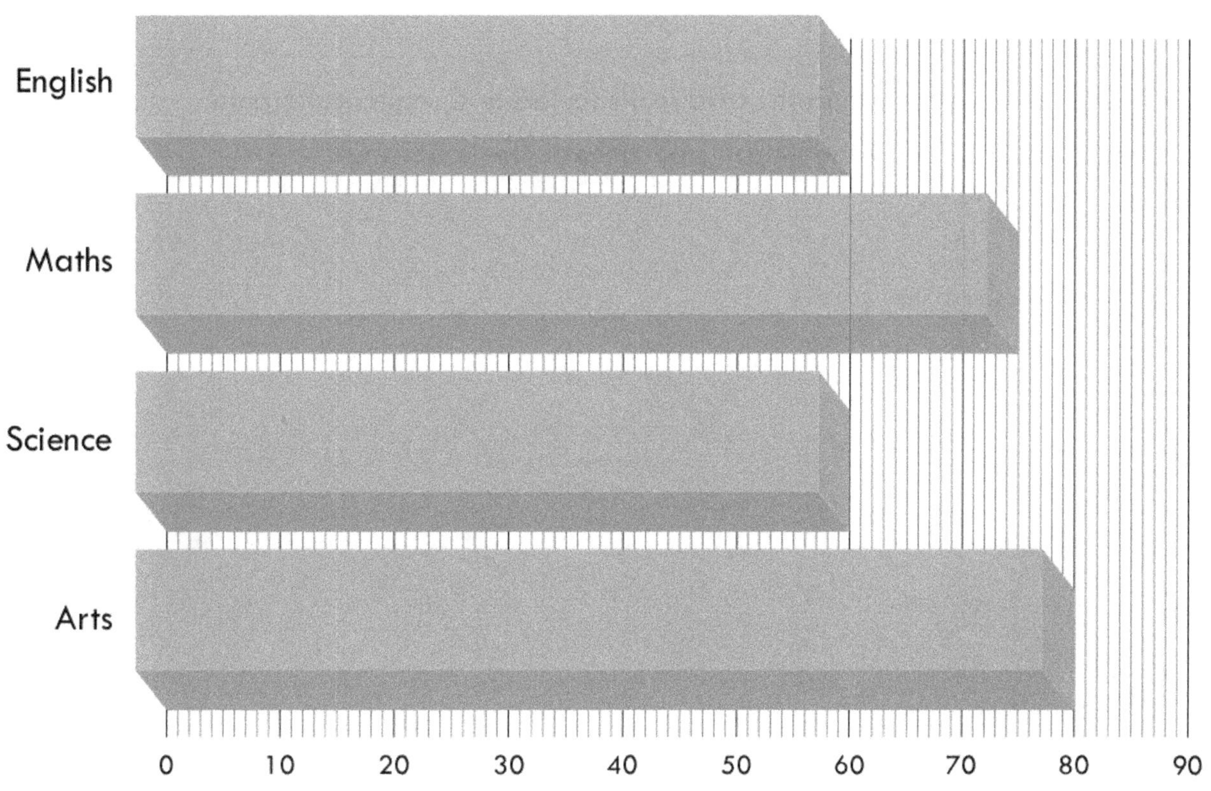

a. What is the total marks scored by all the students in all the subjects?

____

b. Which subject did the students do best?

____

c. In which two subjects did the average marks be the same?

____

d. On which subject do the students need more practice?

____

8. The line plot shows the number of days it snowed in Connecticut from December to March. Study the graph and answer the following.

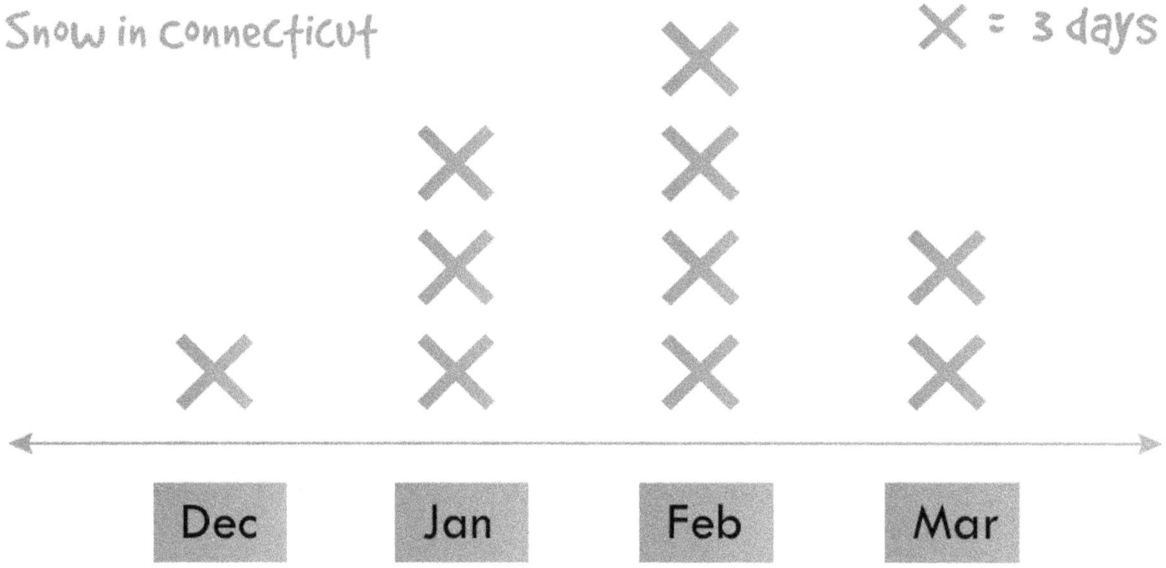

Snow in connecticut

X = 3 days

Dec	Jan	Feb	Mar
X	X X X	X X X X	X X

a. How many days did it snow in January?

____

b. Which month did it snow the least?

____

c. How many more days did it snow in February than in March?

____

d. How many days did it snow after January?

____

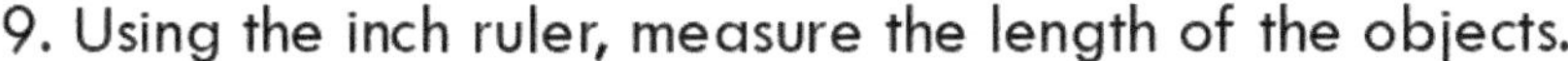

9. Using the inch ruler, measure the length of the objects.

a. What is the length of the caterpillar to the nearest whole inch?

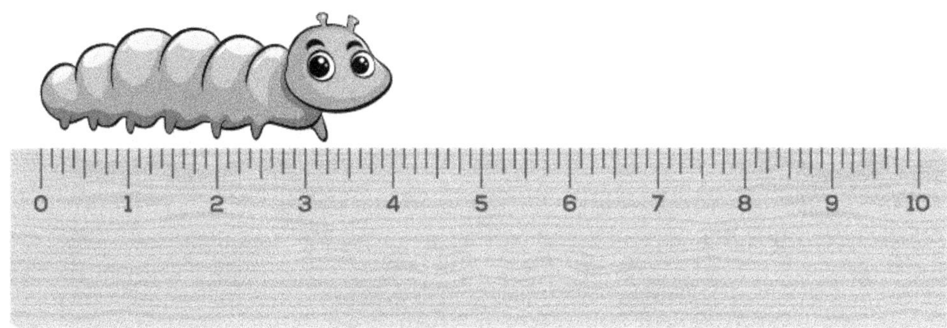

b. What is the length of the paperclip to the nearest half-inch?

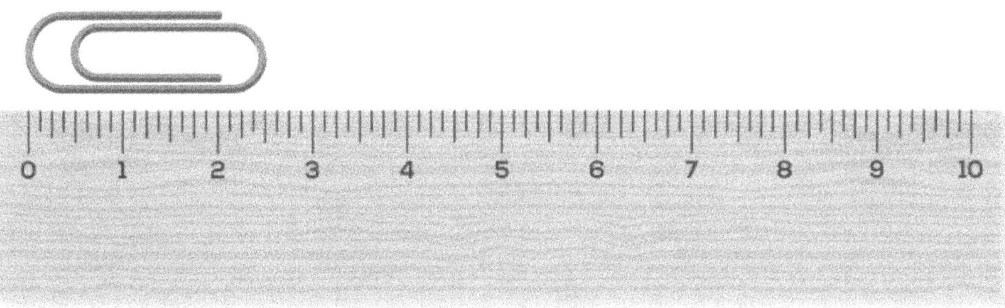

c. What is the length of the key to the nearest quarter inch?

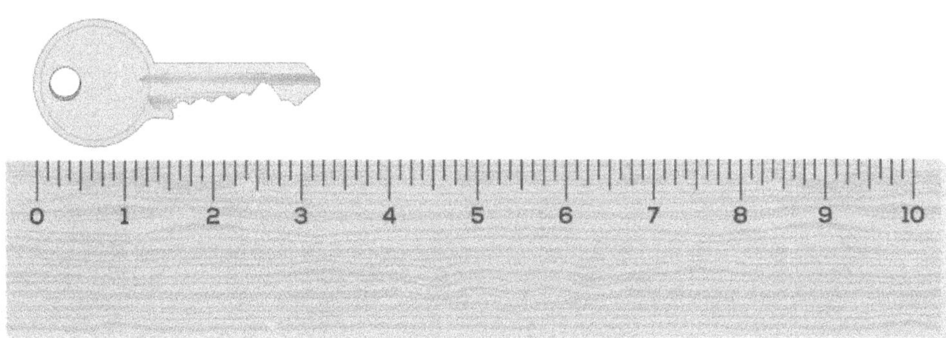

10. Dave has measured the length of all the pencils he has and made a line plot as shown below:

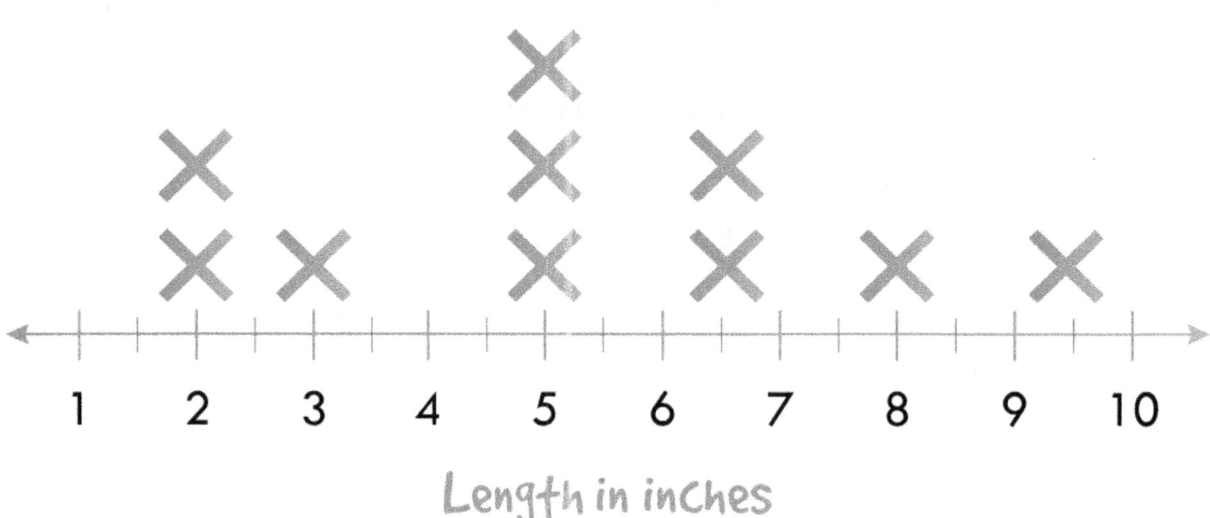

Which could be one of the pencils that Dave measured?

a. 3.5 inches

b. 4 inches

c. 9.5 inches

d. 10 inches

11. The image shows how high few frogs jumped in a pond (in feet).

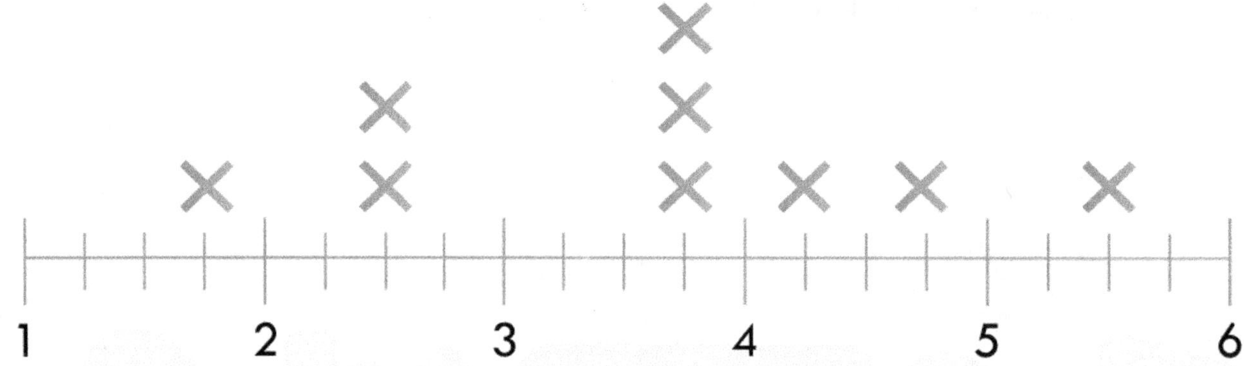

a. How many frogs jumped 3 ¾ feet? ____________________

b. How many frogs jumped 4 ¾ feet? ____________________

12. The length of each crayon is measured in centimeters and displayed as shown below:

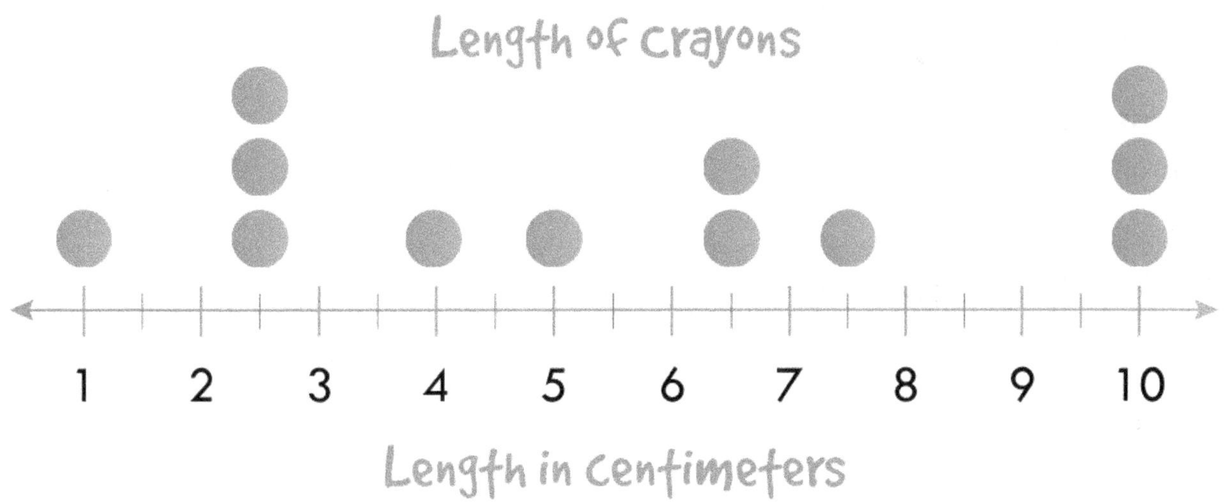

a. How many crayons measured less than 6 ½ centimeters? ________________

b. How many crayons measured 2 ½ inches? ________________

13. Look at the graph below and answer the questions that follow

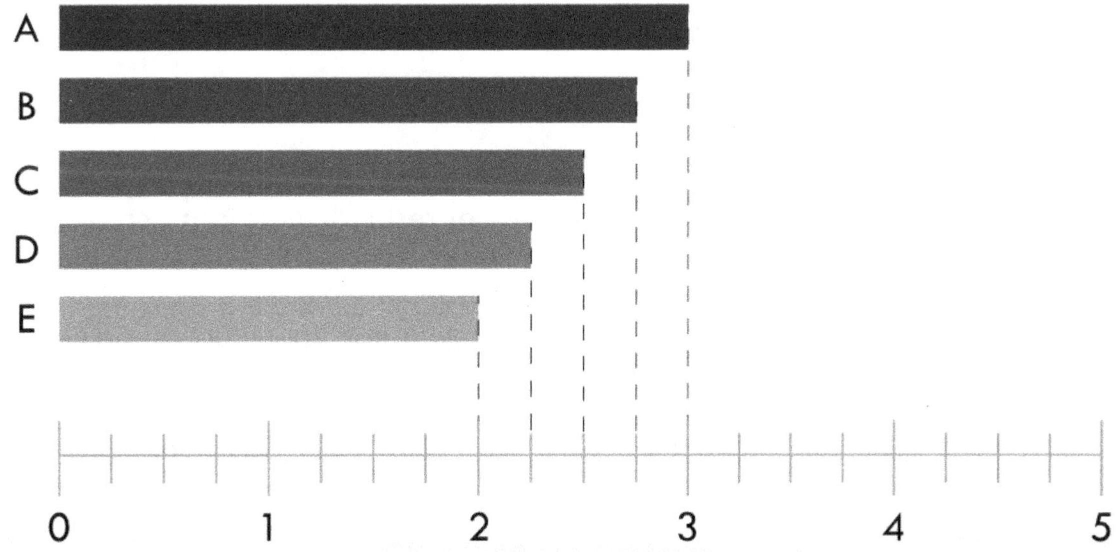

a. Which rod measures 2 ¼ inches? ________________

b. What is the length of the rod B? ________________

The season of apples

14. It was apple picking season. Adam, Mark, Joe and Sam picked apples and the chart below shows how many apples each kid picked.

Kid's name	Number of apples picked
Adam	12
Mark	15
Joe	
Sam	21

Total: 61

a. How many apples did Joe pick? ____________________

b. Create a picture graph using the data above.

Let's play a math game.

15. Measure the commonly used objects to their nearest inch, half-inch and quarter-inch

objects	Nearest Inch	Nearest Half-Inch	Nearest Quarter-Inch
Spoon			
Clothes peg			
Glue stick			
Stick			

16. Eva sold tickets for her school's play. The table below shows the number of tickets sold each day. Using the information, complete the graph below and answer the given questions:

Monday	Tuesday	Wednesday	Thursday	Friday	Saturday
55	30	25	40	50	65

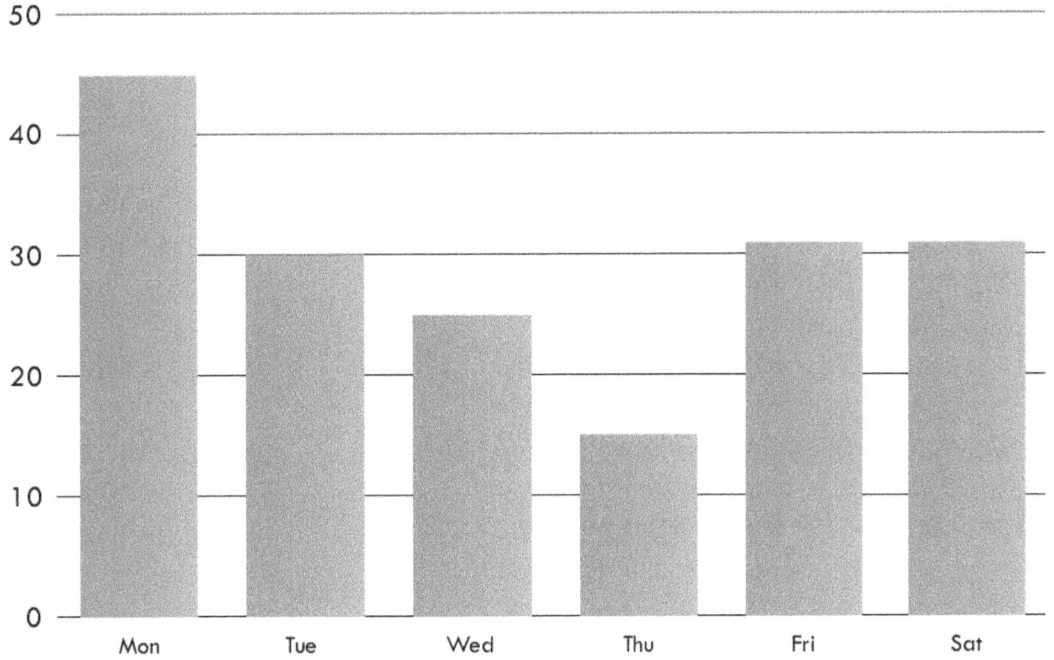

a. How many tickets were sold on Tuesday? ____________________

b. On which day were the ticket sales lowest? ____________________

c. How many tickets were sold after Thursday? ____________________

d. How many tickets were sold before Wednesday? ____________________

e. How many fewer tickets were sold on Thursday than Friday? __________

f. How many tickets were sold in all? ____________________

17. Mr. Adams gave a Math test to his class. The test contained ten 1-mark questions. The marks scored by the students in the class are listed below. Use the list to make a line plot.

1, 10, 8, 2, 1, 8, 8, 8, 9, 10, 10, 1, 2, 2, 4, 10, 10, 9, 7,

4, 4, 2, 4, 7, 7, 10, 10, 8, 9, 1, 4, 7

a. How many students took the test? __________

b. How many students scored 5 and more? __________

c. What score did the highest number of students receive? __________

d. How many students scored less than 4? __________

18. The table shows the number of trees that were available in the park.

a. Complete the table by filling in the number of oak trees.

Type of Tree	Number of Trees
Birch	12
Maple	24
Oak	
Pine	20
Total Number of Trees	72

b. Use the lines below to create and label a picture graph using the data in the table. Use a scale of 4 trees per key.

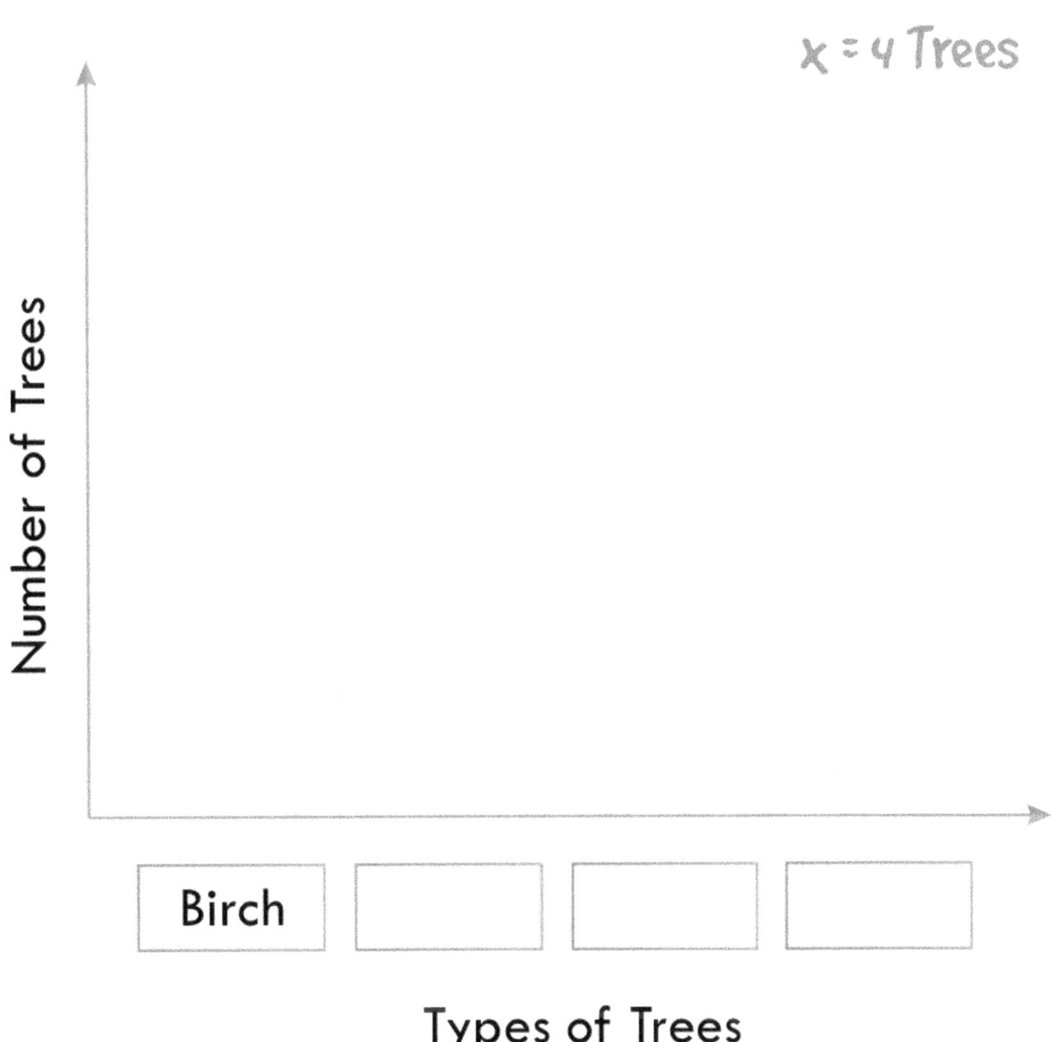

19. Ava says " The ribbon measures 6 half inches".
Jack says, "The ribbon measures 3 inches".

Explain how both of them are right using pictures, words and numbers.

20. The height of the students in 3rd grade in inches have been measured and plotted as below:

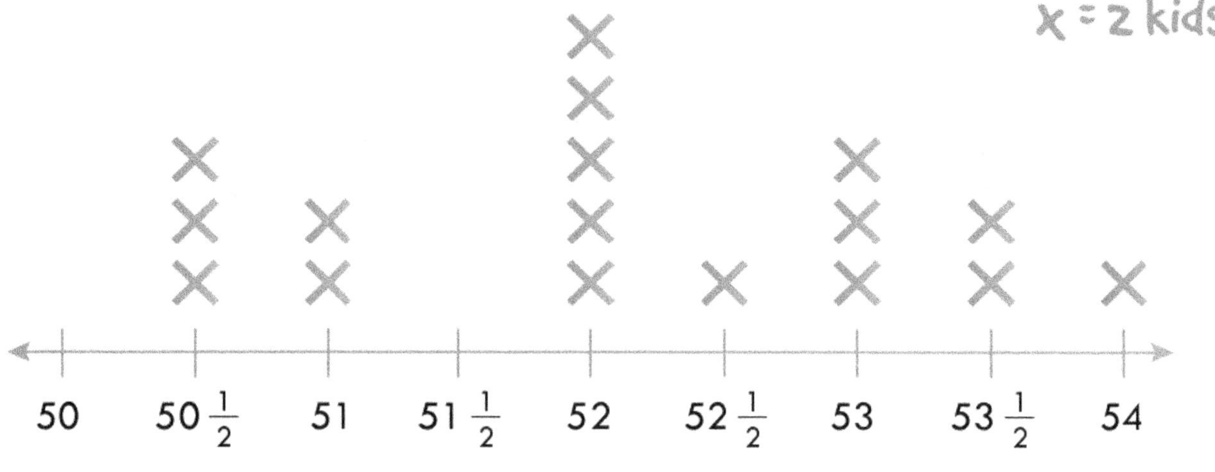

a. How many students are there in grade 3?

b. How many children are less than 52 inches?

c. The most common height for the children in grade 3 is 52 inches. Explain how.

d. To participate in the basketball team, the kids should be 53 inches or above. How many students will be eligible?

Geometric Measurement - Area

The area is the amount of space inside a plane shape. The area is an important attribute of plane shapes.

Example

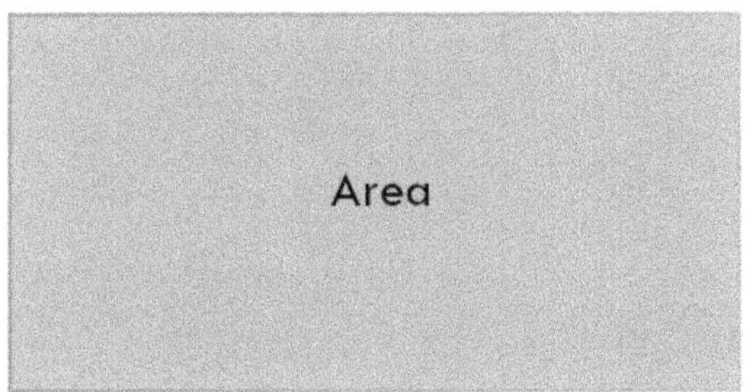

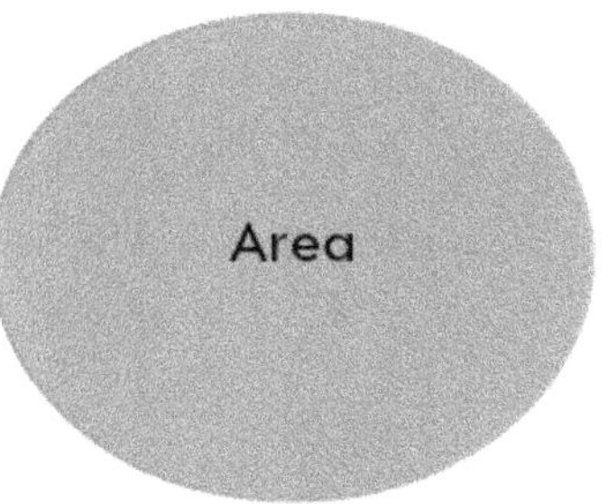

Let's practice

1. Colour the area for each of these shapes.

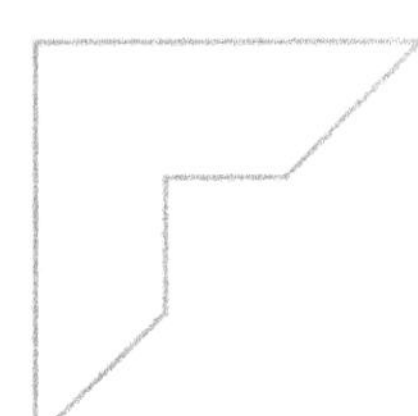

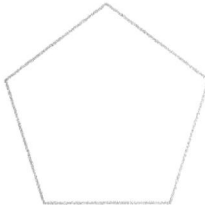

2. Use triangle pattern blocks of the same size to cover each shape. Count the number of triangles used to fill the shape. A few triangles are drawn for you.

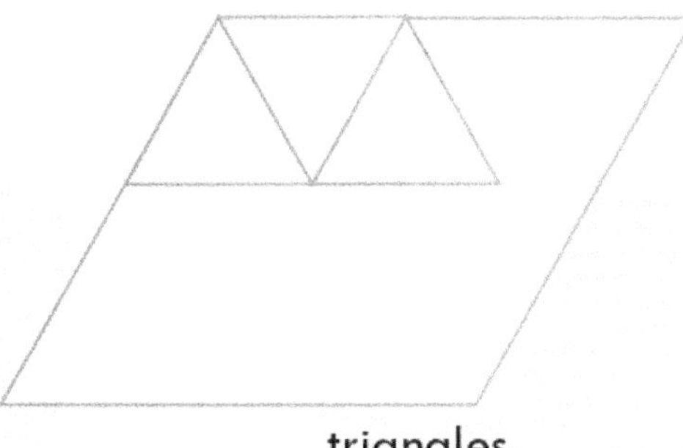

triangles

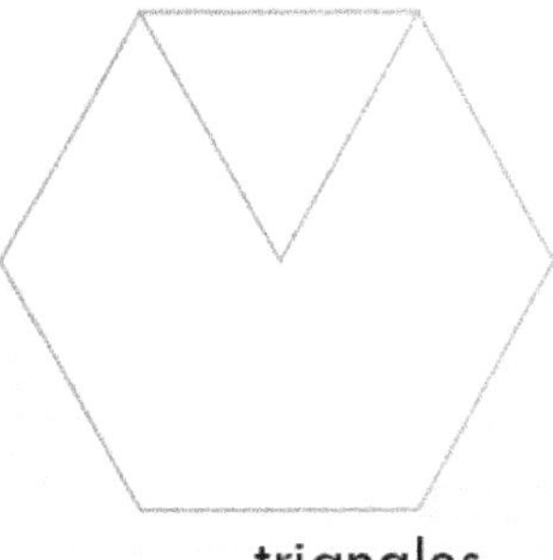

triangles

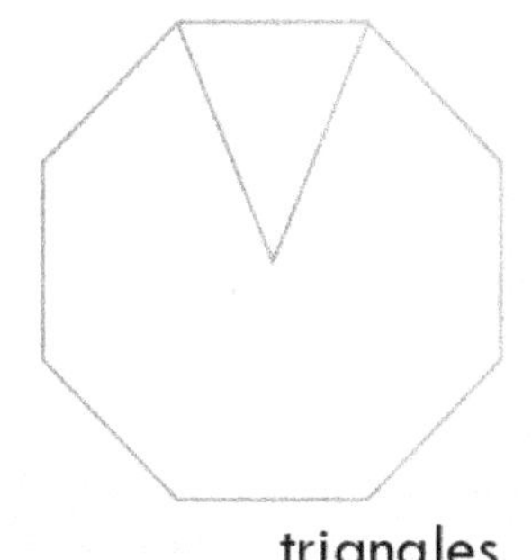

triangles

3. Fisher uses square units to create two rectangles. Do both these shapes have the same area? How do you know?

Shape A

Shape B

4. Find the area of each of these shapes. Each ☐ is 1 square unit.

a.

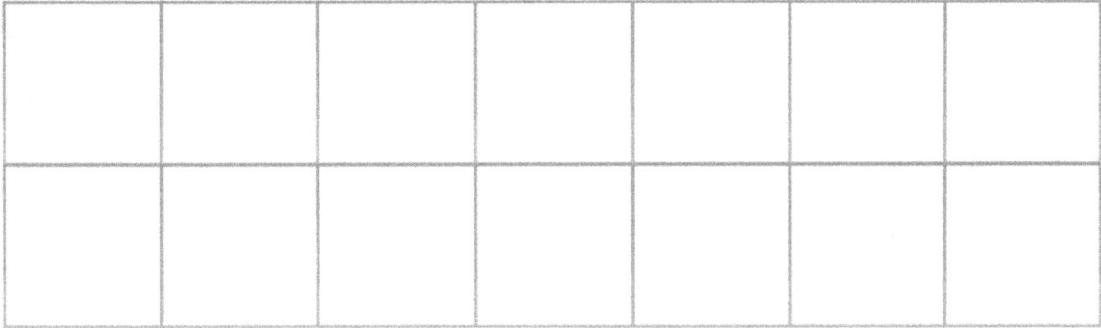

_____ square units

b.

_____ square units

c.

_____ square units

d.

_____ square units

5. Each ☐ is 1 square unit. Circle the shape that has the largest area.

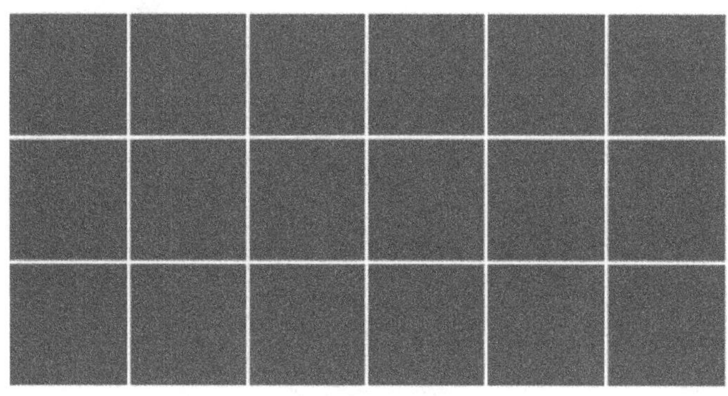

Rectangle A

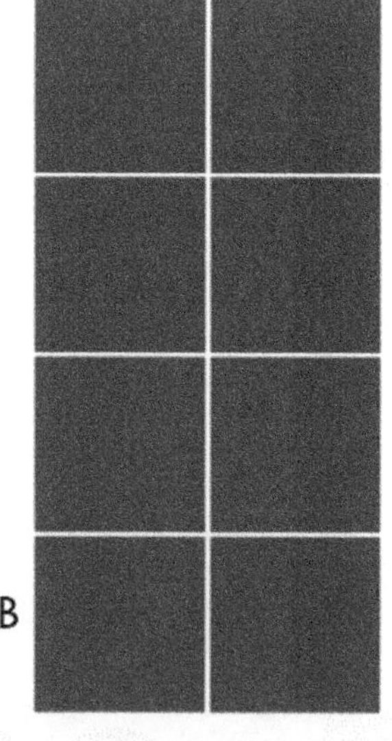

Rectangle B

Rectangle C

6. Count to find the area of this rectangle. Each ☐ is 1 square unit.

_____ square units

a. Draw a different rectangle that has the same area.

b. Draw a rectangle by increasing the area by 2 square units.

7. Hilda draws a square with an area of 3 square inches and Derek draws a square with an area of 3 square centimeters. Will both the squares have the same area? Why or why not?

Draw here:

Explain your thinking:

8. Each □ is 1 square unit. Find the area of each shape.

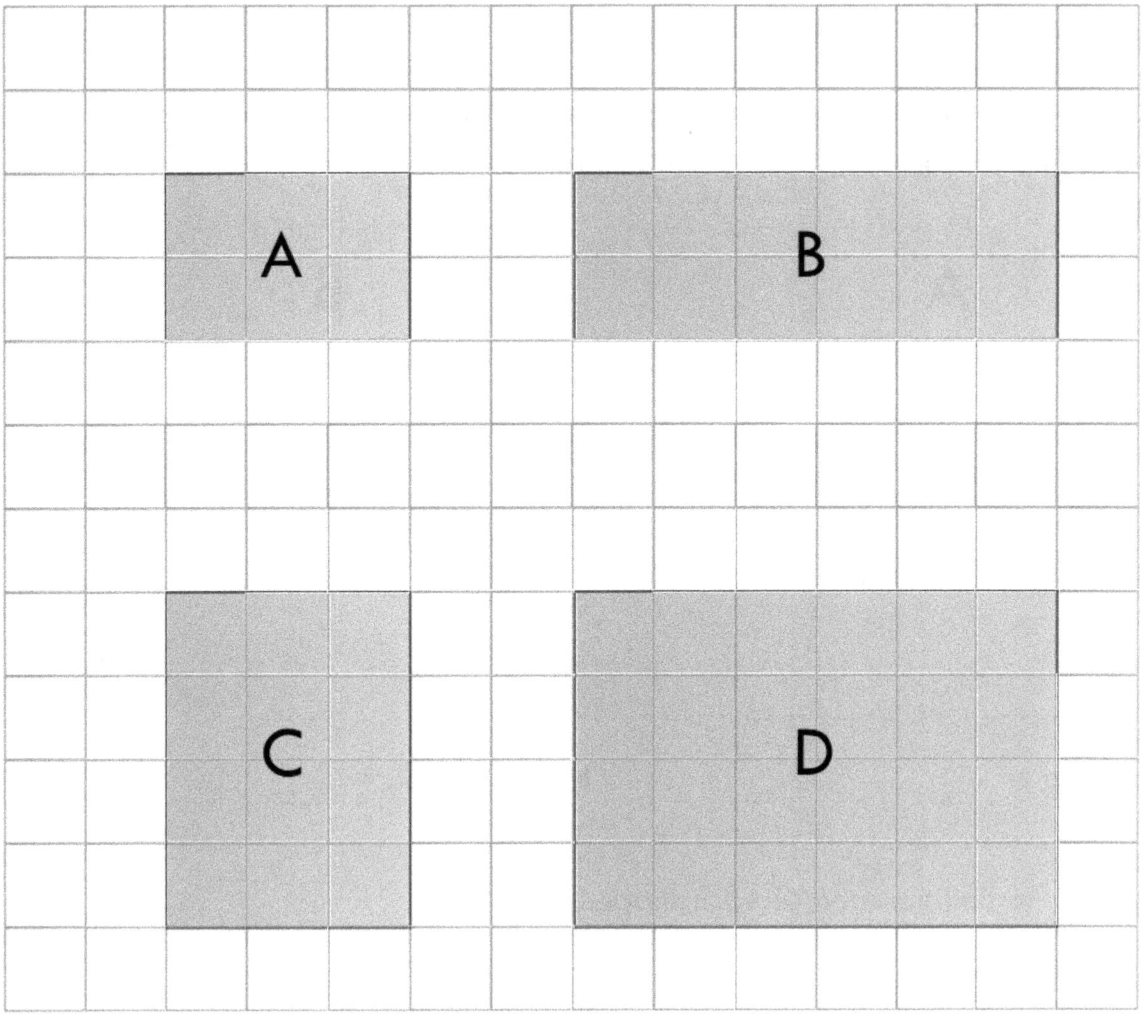

A

B

C

D

A - ____________

B - ____________

C - ____________

D - ____________

9. Use a ruler to measure the sides of these shapes. Mark each centimeter with a point and connect the points to show square units. Then, find the area of the shape.

A

B

a. Total area = ____

b. Total area = ____

10. Skip count to find the area of each shape.

a.

b.

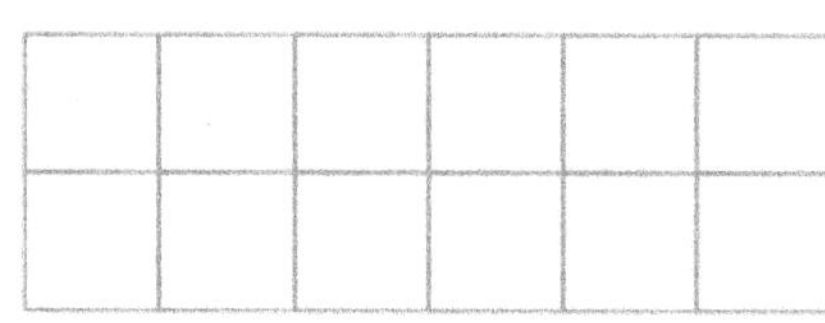

c.

d.

11. Use the centimeter side of a ruler to draw the squares. Write a multiplication statement for each shape to show how the area can be calculated.

a. Area = 18 square centimeters

3cm

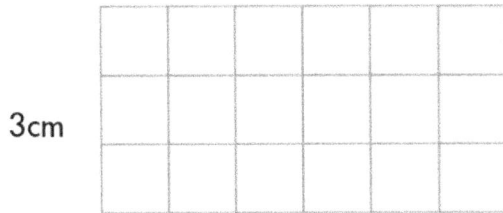

3 x ____ = 18

b. Area = 24 square centimeters

3cm

____ x ____ = 24

c. Area = 15 square centimeters

5 cm

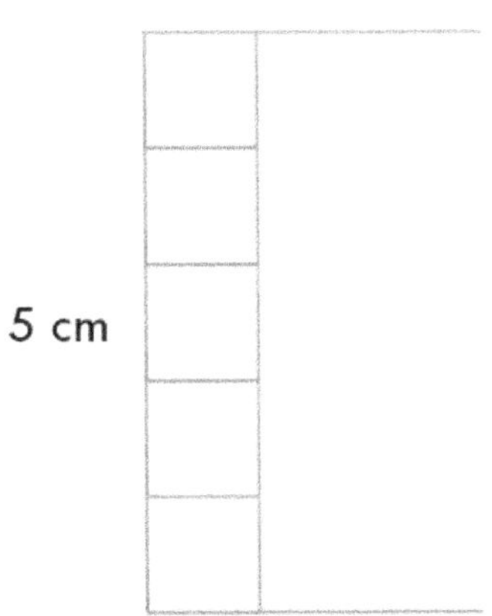

____ x ____ = 15

d. Area = ____ square centimeters

3 cm

3 cm

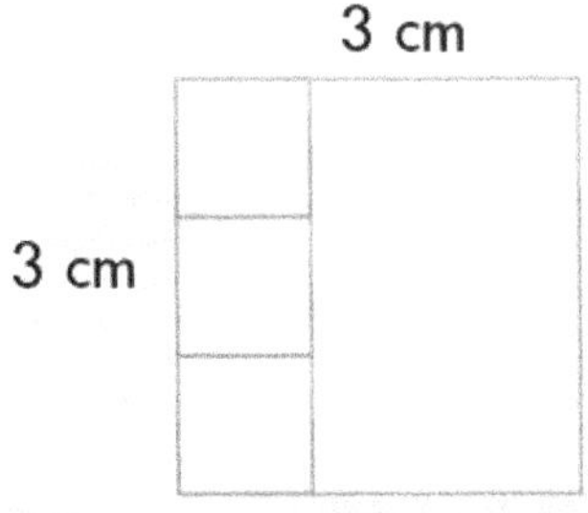

____ x ____ = ____

12. Mark draws a rectangle. Find the area of the rectangle.

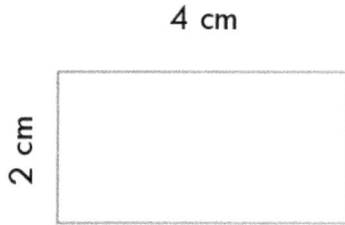

4 cm

2 cm

Total area = ____

Explain how you calculated the area.

____

____

The problem of tiles

13. Linda makes a rectangle with 36 square inch tiles. She has 6 tiles in each row. Calculate the area of the rectangle. Use a drawing to arrive at your answer.

14. April has 27 square centimeter tiles with her. She uses 18 tiles to make one rectangle and the remaining to make another square. Draw two arrays to show what April made. Write a multiplication statement for each.

a.

b.

15. Nish marks her bedroom floor as 6 feet by 7 feet and her brother's bedroom as 5 feet by 9 feet. Nish says both bedrooms are of the same size. Is she correct? Why or why not?

16. Use the centimeter and inch grid to draw a square with an area of 12 square units.

Centimeter grid

Inch grid

17. Label the sides of the shaded and unshaded sides where ever needed. Then, find the total area of the large rectangle by adding the areas of both the smaller rectangles.

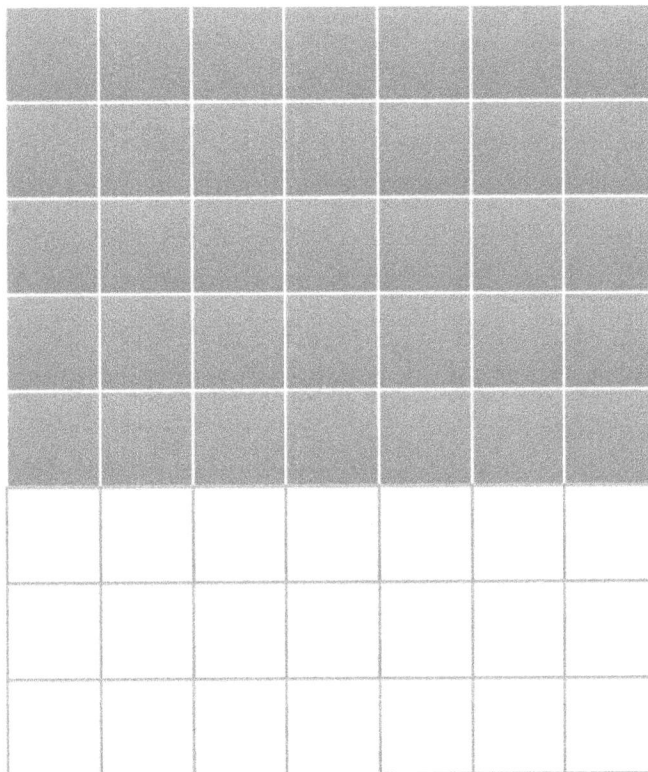

a.

8 x 7 = (5 + 3) x 7

_____ = (5 x 7) +(3 x 7)

_____ = _____ + _____

_____ = _____

Area = _____ square units.

b.

_____ x 4 = (_____ + _____) x 4

_____ = (_____ x 4) +(_____ x 4)

_____ = _____ + _____

_____ = _____

Area = _____ square units.

c.

8 x 7 = (_____ + _____) x

_____ = (_____ x _____) +(_____ x _____)

_____ = _____ + _____

_____ = _____ _____

Area = _____ square units.

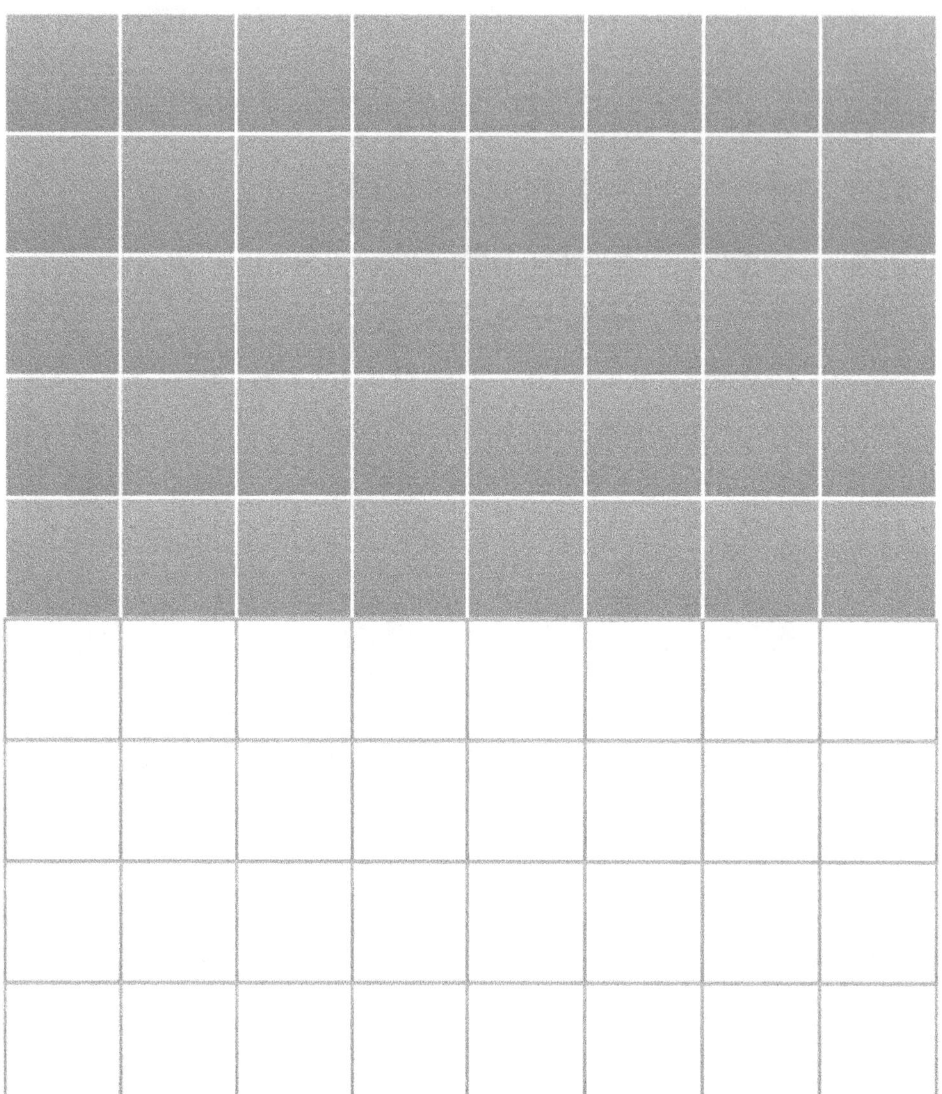

d.

9 x 8 = (____ + ____) x ____

____ = (____ x ____) + (____ x ____)

____ = ____ + ____

____ = ____

Area = ____ square units.

18. Use the centimeter grid to draw the following shape.

a. A square with an area of 32 square centimeters

b. A rectangle with an area of 15 square centimeters

c. A rectangle with 4 square centimeters by 2 square centimeters

19. Divide the shape into two shapes (shapes can be rectangles or squares) to find the area of the shape. Write multiplication statements for each shape to find the total area.

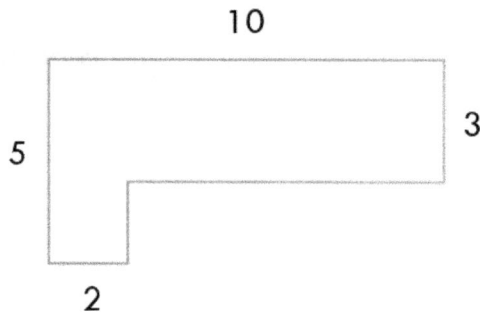

10

3

5

2

20. Shade an area to break the 16 x 4 grid. Then, find the sum of the areas of the smaller rectangles to find the total area.

Geometric Measurement - Perimeter

Perimeter is the length of the boundary that surrounds the shape.

Example

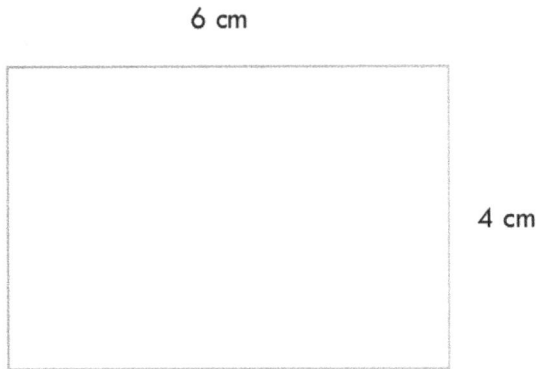

Perimeter of the rectangle is 6 + 4 + 6 + 4 = 20 cm

Let's practice

1. Outline the perimeter of these shapes with a red crayon.

a.

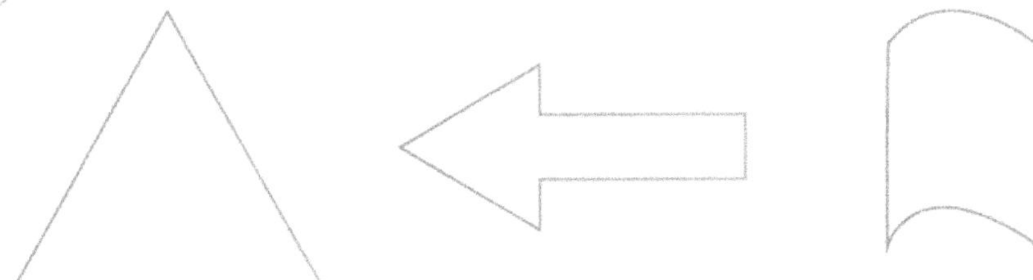

b. Explain how you know you outlined the perimeter of the shape.

____

____

2. Find the perimeter for each of these shapes given.

a.

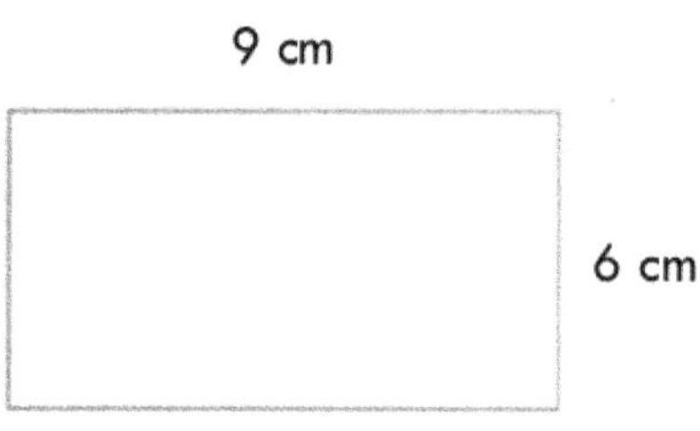

Perimeter = ____

b.

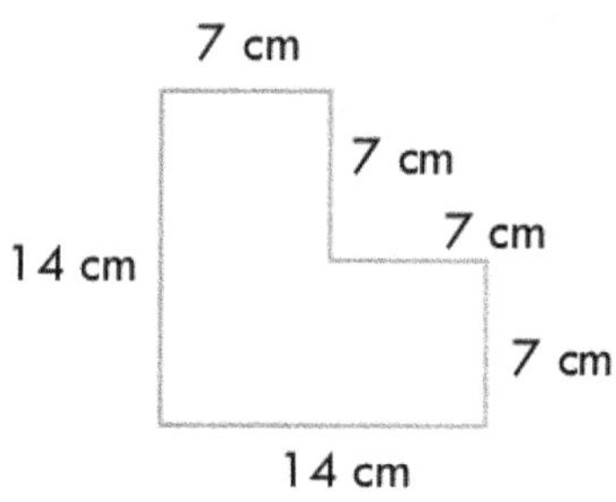

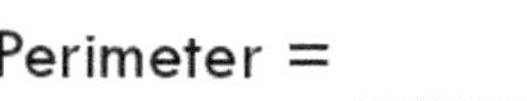
Perimeter = ____

c.

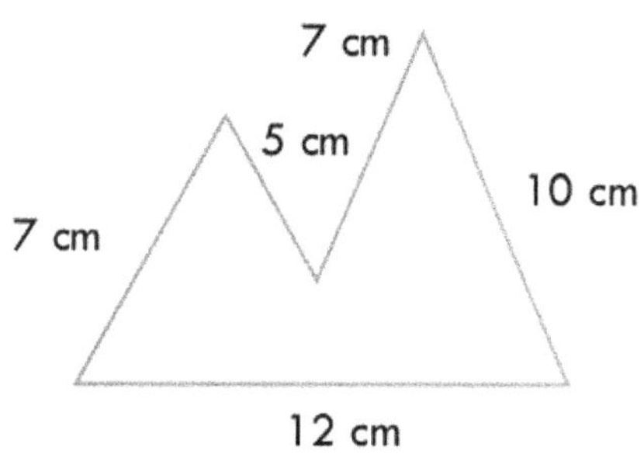

Perimeter = ____

d.

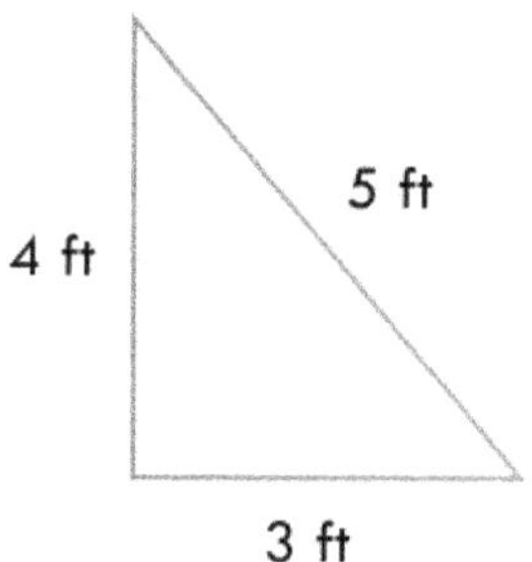

Perimeter = ____

e.

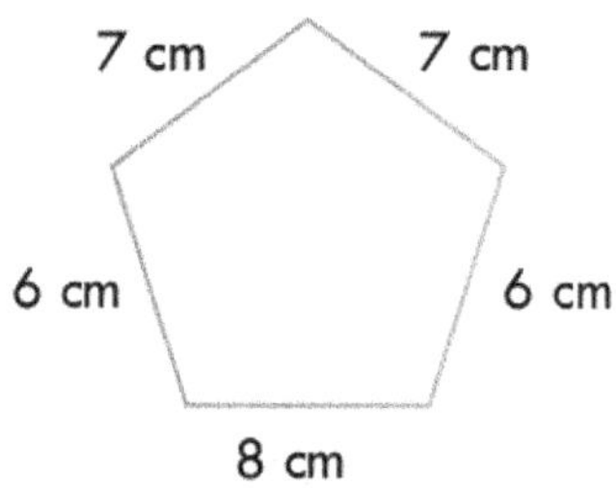

Perimeter = ____

f.

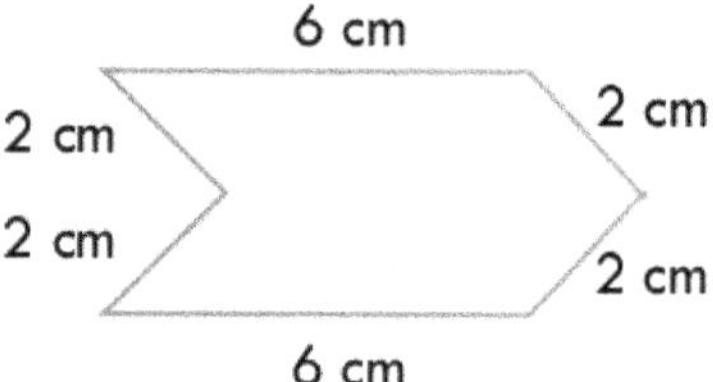

Perimeter = ____

3. Which shape has a greater perimeter? Write it in the box provided.

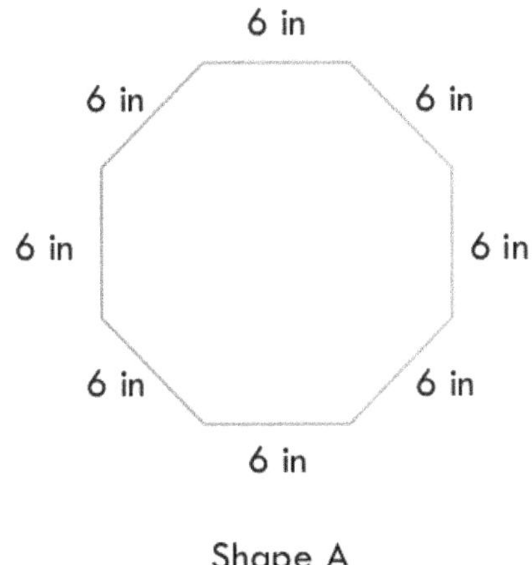

Shape A

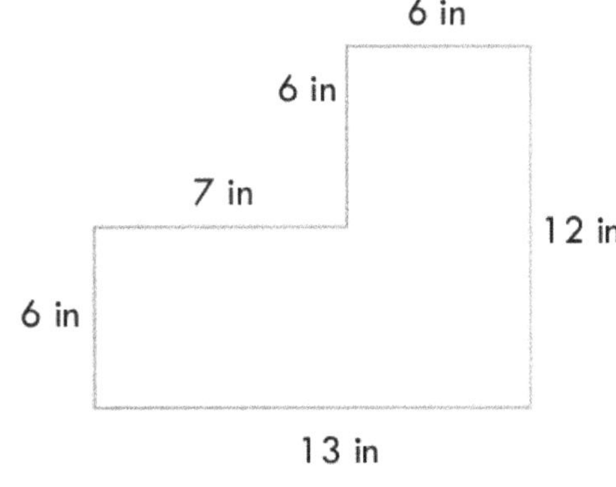

Shape B

4. Measure and label the side lengths of the shapes below in centimeters. Then, find the perimeter of each shape.

a.

Perimeter = ____ cm + ____ cm + ____ cm + ____ cm

= ____ cm

b.

Perimeter = _____ cm + _____ cm + _____ cm + _____ cm + _____ cm+ _____ cm

= _____ cm

c.

Perimeter = _____ cm

d.

Perimeter = ____ cm

5. Eric and Victor draw the shapes shown below. Eric says his shape has a greater perimeter since it has 4 sides. Is Eric correct? Explain your answer.

Eric's shape

Victor's shape

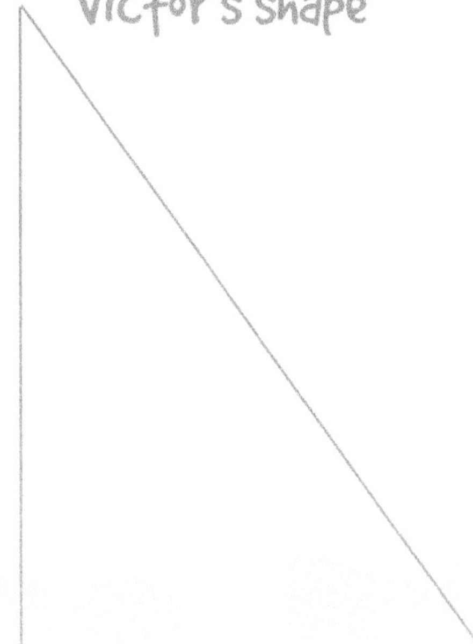

Explanation - ______________________

____

6. Label the unknown sides of these regular shapes and then, find the perimeter of each.

a.

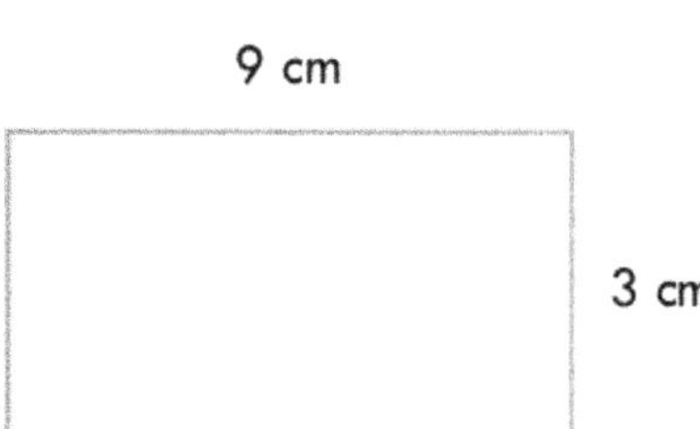

Perimeter = ____

b.

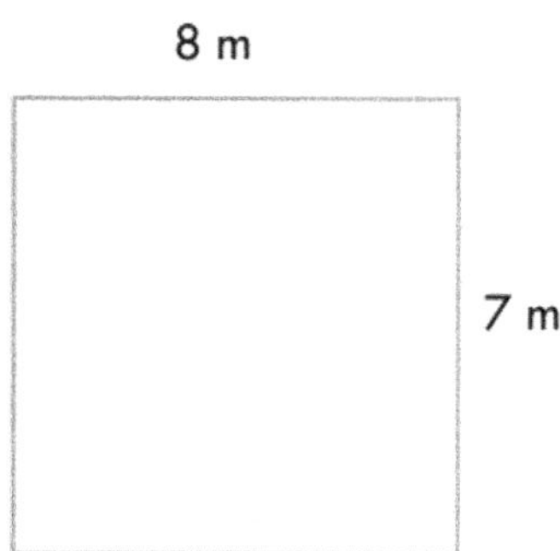

Perimeter = ____

c.

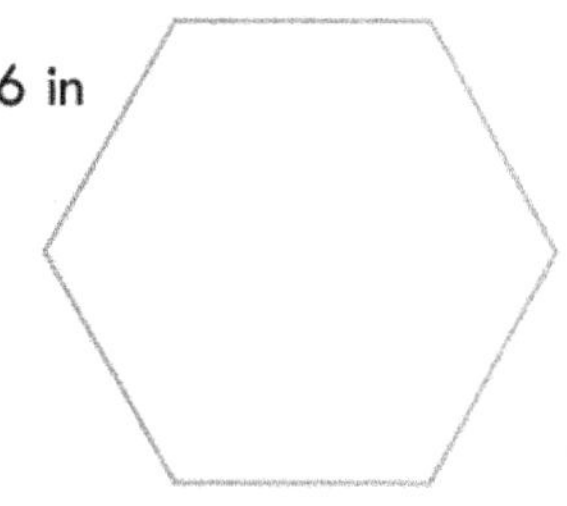

Perimeter = ____

d.

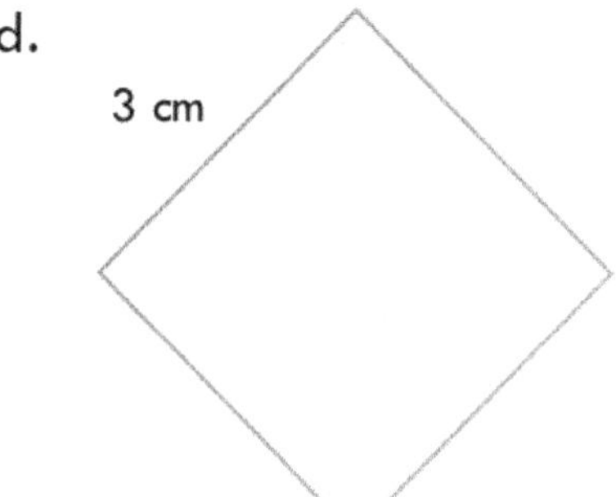

Perimeter = ____

The football field problem

7. Frank measures a football field and notes them as 45 m wide and 90 m long. What is the perimeter of the football field?

Perimeter = ______

8. Maggie makes a greeting card for her mother using an 8" by 4" rectangle chart paper. What length of ribbon would she need to decorate the borders of the card?

9. Tylor used 6 craft sticks to make a hexagon. Each stick is 8 cm each. What is the perimeter of his craft stick?

10. Each side of a square book measures 11 cm. What would be the perimeter of the book?

11. Paige drew a regular rectangle and Maize drew a regular hexagon as shown below. Whose shape has a greater perimeter? Write the name of the person in the empty box.

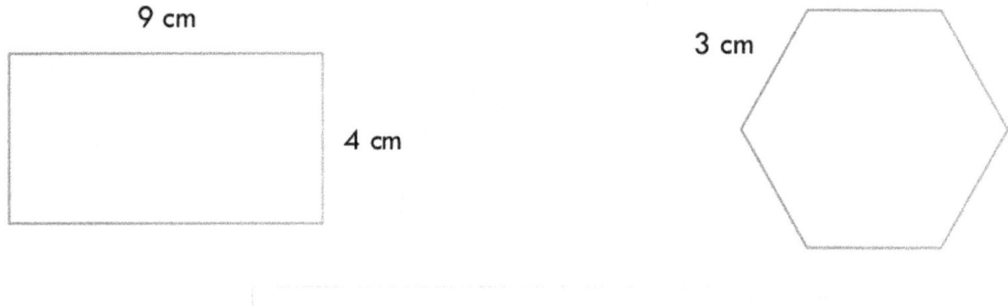

12. A regular pentagon has 4cm as one of its sides. Mary and Ann calculate the perimeter in two different ways. Whose work is correct? Explain your answer.

Mary's work

Perimeter = 4cm + 4cm + 4cm + 4cm + 4cm

= 20 cm

Ann's work

Perimeter = 5 x 4cm

= 20 cm

Explanation - ______________________________

13. Alice has a square piece that has 4 cm as one of its sides.

a. What will be the perimeter of the square?

____

b. She then placed another square with the same perimeter as shown below.

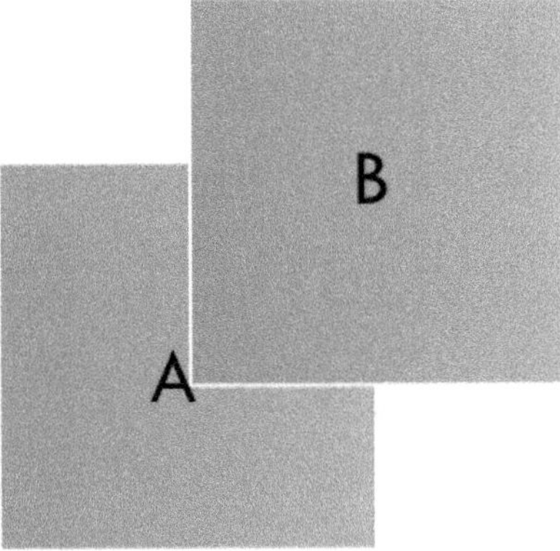

Will the perimeter now be Shape A + Shape B? Tick your answer.

Yes No

14. Draw a square that measures 3 cm for each side. Find the perimeter of this square.

15. Use this grid to draw:

a. a square with a perimeter of 36 units. Colour the perimeter yellow.

b. two different rectangles with a perimeter of 10 units each such that the areas of each are different from the other. Colour the perimeter of each rectangle in green.

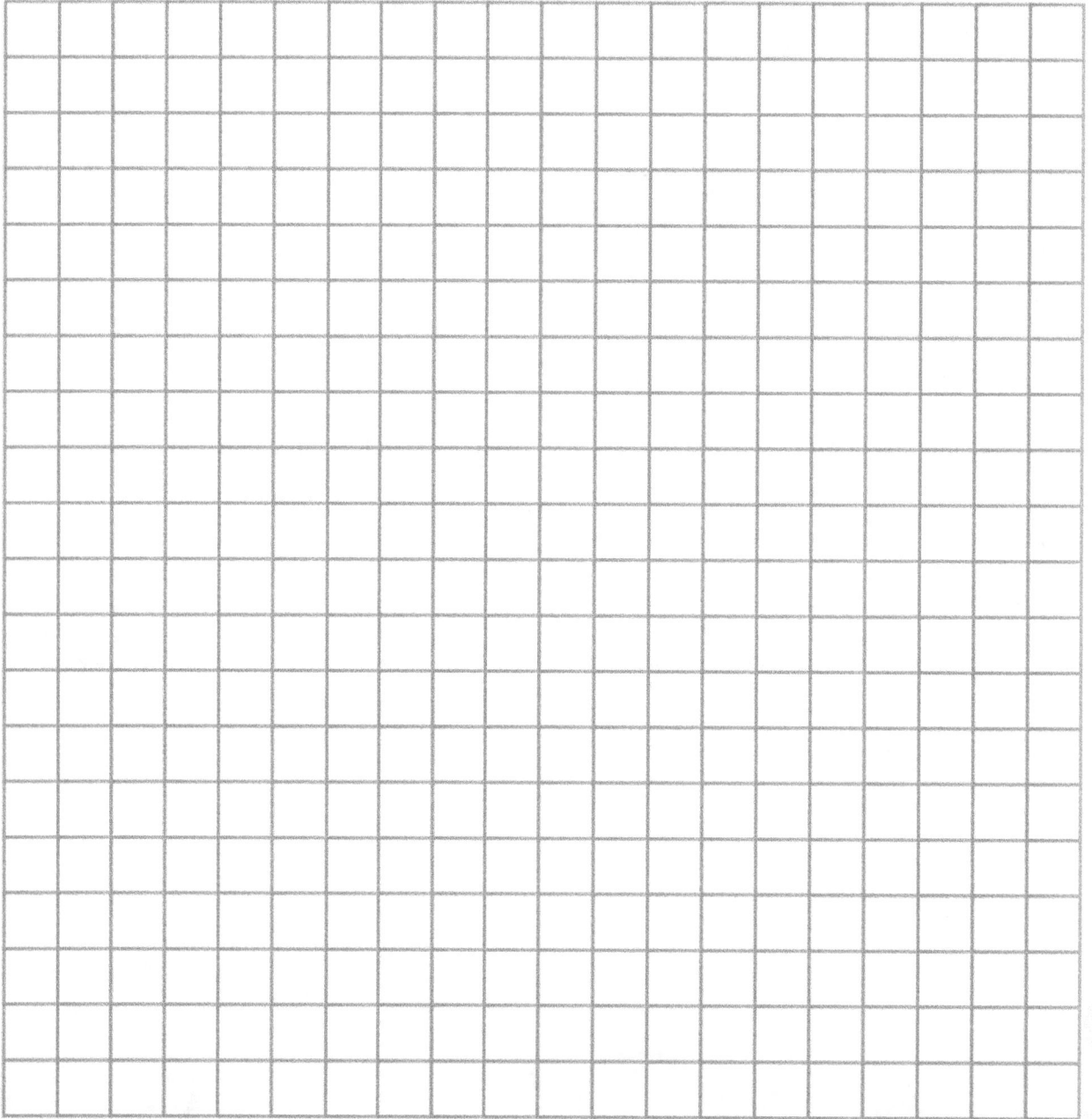

16. Find the perimeter of this hexagon.

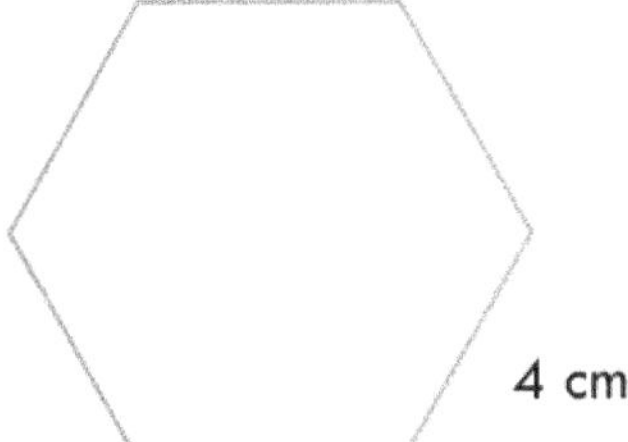

a. Perimeter = ____

b. Henry put a few of these shapes together as shown below. Find the perimeter of this new shape. [Hint: Outline the perimeter first]

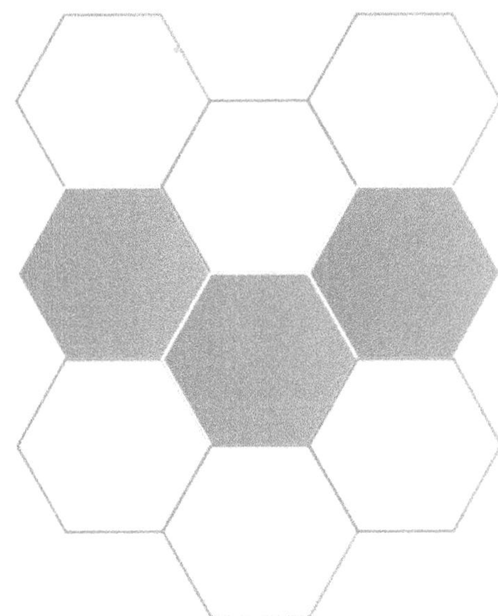

Perimeter = ____

c. Explain how you calculate the perimeter of the tessellation.

____

17. Find the perimeter of these shapes using a string.

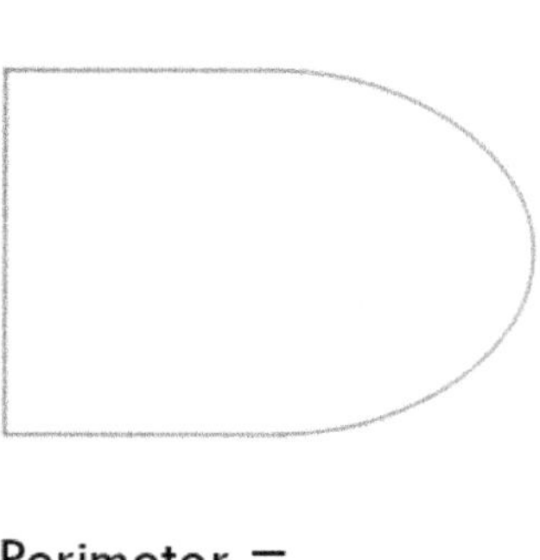

Perimeter = ___

Perimeter = ___

18. Label the unknown side lengths. Then, find its perimeter.

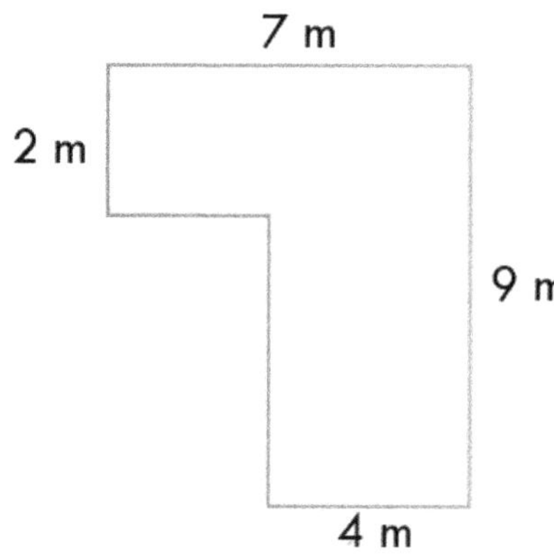

a. Perimeter = ___

19. Label the unknown side length and then find the perimeter of the shaded rectangle.

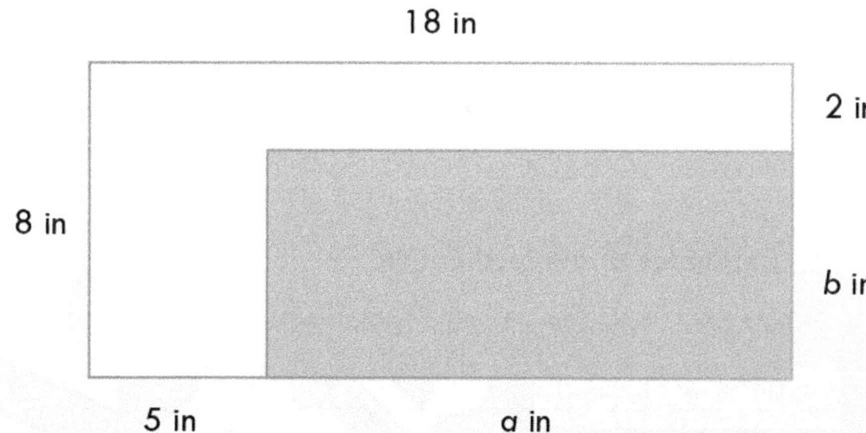

Perimeter = ___

Geometry

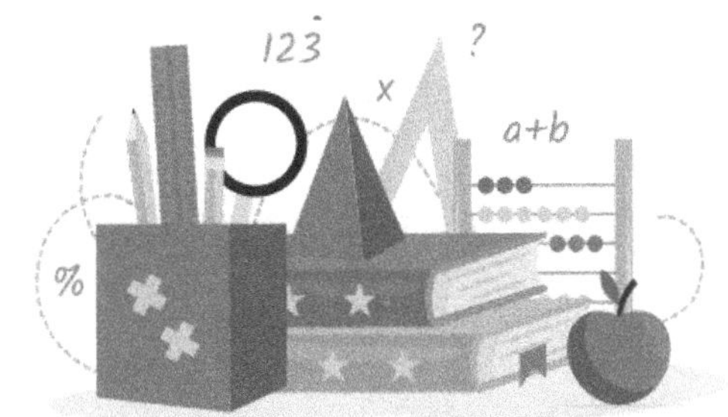

Angle	The point where two sides of a shape meet to make a corner is called an angle. Right angles have square corners.
Diagonal	A line that connects the opposite corners in a plane shape is called diagonal.
Regular polygon	A polygon with all equal sides and all equal angles is called a regular polygon.

Let's practice

1. Match the shapes to the correct attribute.

a. At least one set of parallel sides

b. 4 right angles

c. 4 right angles and 4 equal sides

d. Two sets of parallel sides

2. Tick the correct answer for each.

a. A polygon with four sides is called ________ .

- [ ] Triangle
- [ ] Hexagons
- [ ] Quadrilaterals
- [ ] Pentagons

b. A trapezium is also called a ________ .

- [ ] Trapezoid
- [ ] Rectangle
- [ ] Square
- [ ] Rhombus

c. ________ is also a rectangle.

- [ ] Trapezoid
- [ ] Rhombus
- [ ] Square
- [ ] parallelogram

3. Complete the table by writing 'true' or 'false'. One is done for you.

Attribute	Polygon	True or False
a. 2 sets of parallel sides	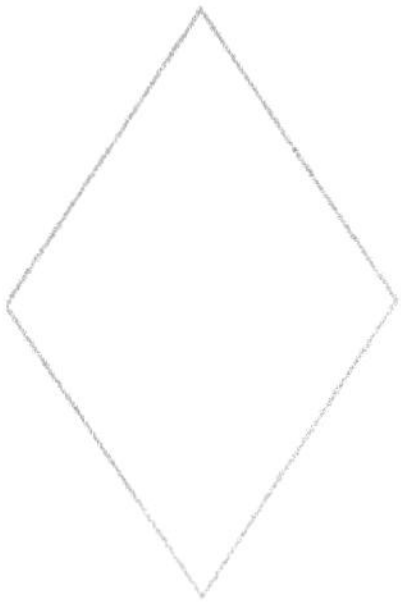	True
b. Quadrilateral		
c. 2 right angles		
d. 3 right angles		

4. Lucy drew these shapes. Circle the regular polygons among the given shapes.

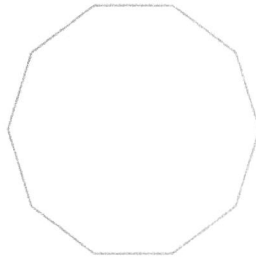

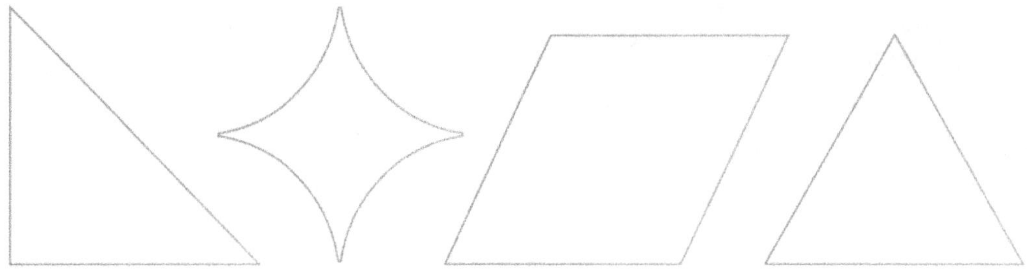

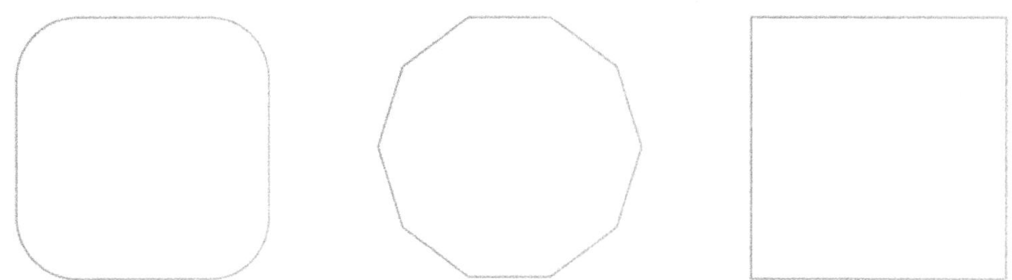

5. List as many attributes as possible for each of these polygons.

a.

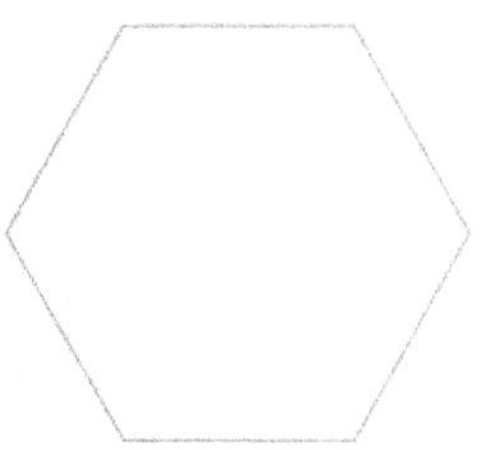

b.

c. Name at least one attribute that they both have in common.

6. Jenny drew a square but named it a rhombus.

a. Do you think Jenny is right? Explain your answer. Make a drawing if needed.

____

b. Do you think you can name a rhombus as a square? Explain your answer.

____

____

7. Fred used different shapes and made two different hexagons. Write the unit fraction for the shaded portion in each hexagon.

a. b.

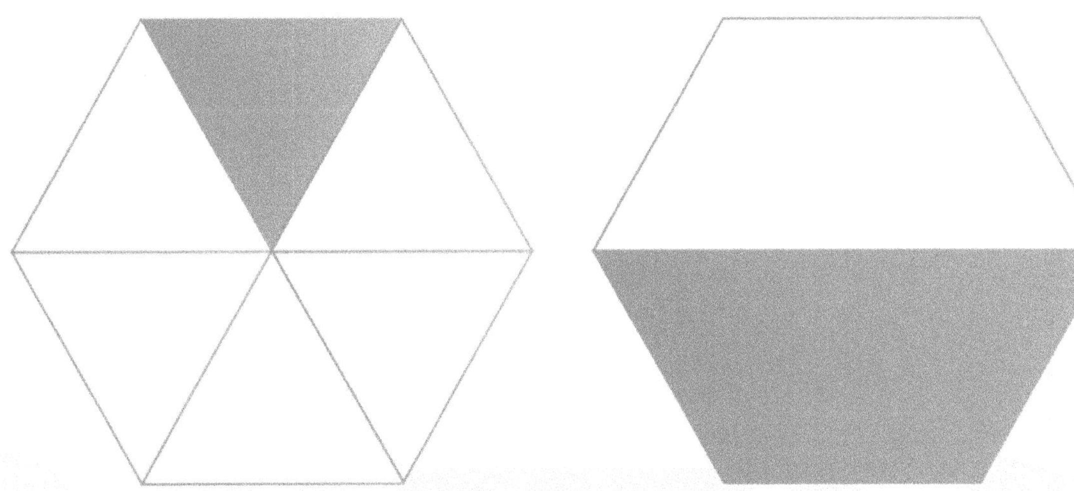

Fraction - ________ Fraction - ________

8. Which shapes did Fred use to form the hexagons in question 7. Write for both a and b.

a. ________

b. ________

9. Divide the below square in such a way that you get 4 triangles.

10. Use a ruler and a right angle tool to draw the following polygons.

a. Draw a quadrilateral with only one set of parallel sides. Colour the parallel sides green.

b. Draw a pentagon with at least two sides equal.

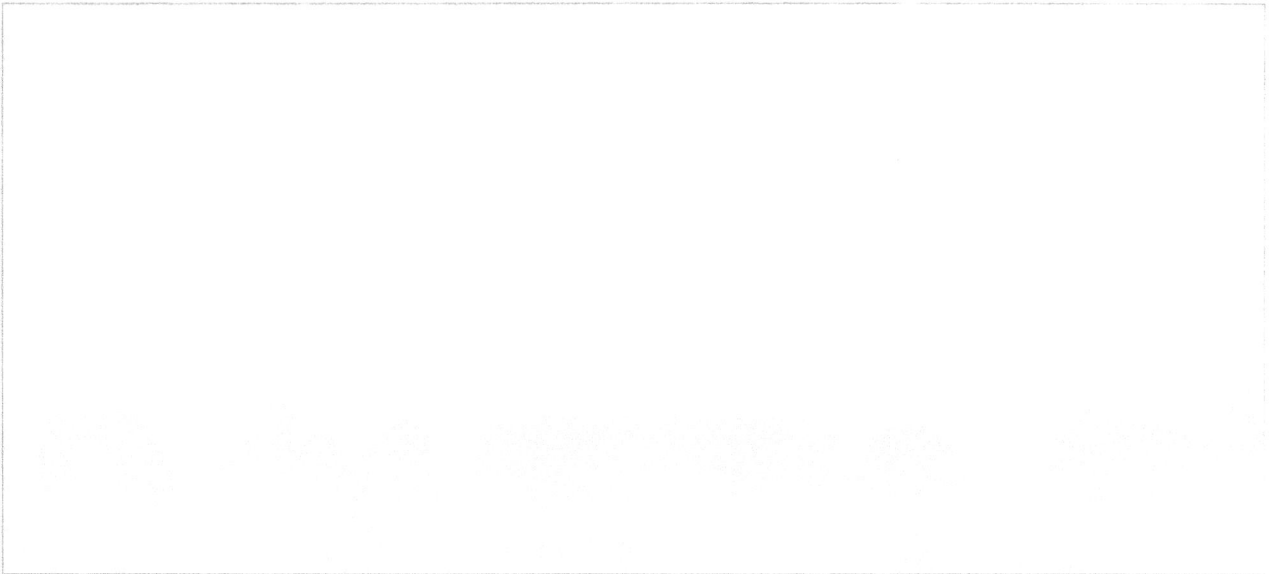

11. Draw a line to divide the below trapezoid into two equal trapezoids. Color one portion of the trapezoid and write its fraction.

Fraction: ______

12. Draw two lines to make 4 equal rectangles in the given square. Shade one portion and write a fraction for it.

Fraction: ______

13. How would you represent 1/8th of this parallelogram? Draw lines and shade to show your answer.

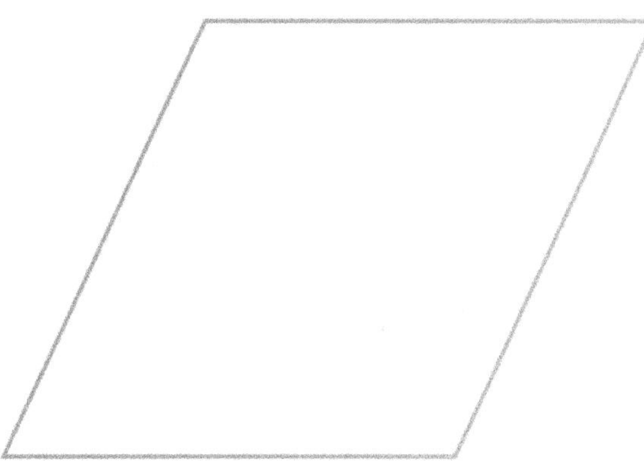

14. Eric covers this shape with triangles. How many triangles will it take to cover this shape?

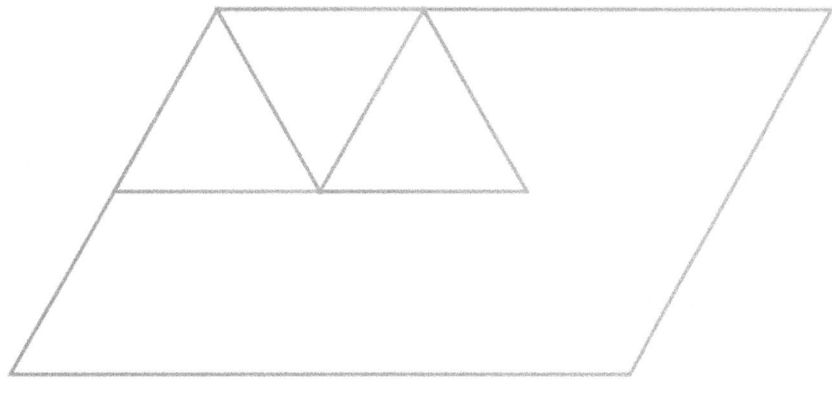

_______ triangles.

15. Sam says he drew a polygon with 2 sides and 2 angles. Is that possible? Explain your answer. Draw if needed.

16. Create a closed shape of your own using how many ever lines you wish. Write the attributes of your creation and give it a name.

17. Use various polygons and to draw a man. Write down the number of shapes used.

18. Each ☐ is one unit each. Are both the rectangles of the same size? Explain your answer.

____

____

19. There is a trapezoid and a triangle given. Which shape would you get if you combine both of them?

____

Draw and name the new shape.

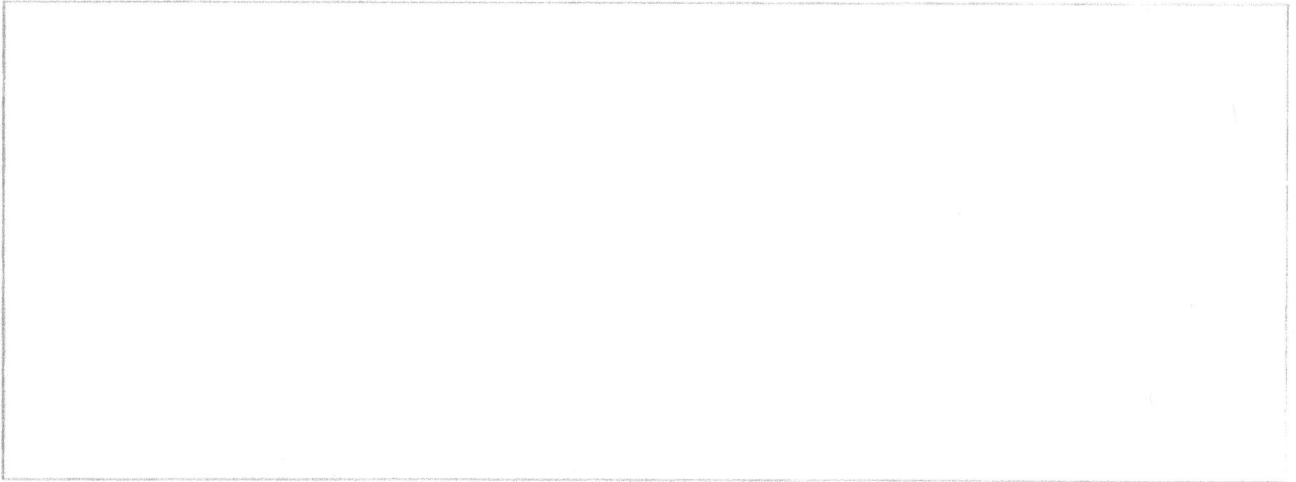

20. Draw a rhombus using two triangles. Use the geoboard if needed.

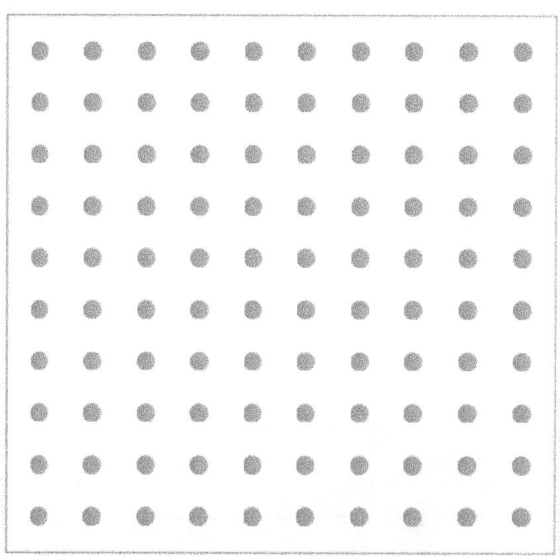

Science

Help your children learn and enjoy a wide range of information and fun facts that will surprise and amaze them. Find numerous Science experiments, cool facts, activities, and quizzes for the children to enjoy learning.

Physical Sciences

Energy

Energy is the ability to do work. It is all around us. There are different forms of energy. A few of them are listed here.

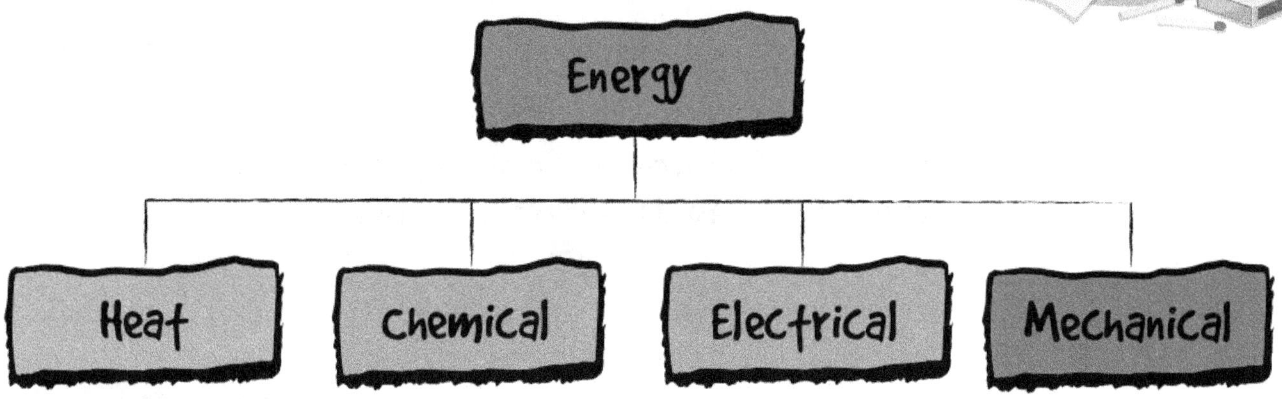

Humans have always been dependent on energy for many activities. Before electricity, humans were harnessing different natural sources of energy to complete their tasks.

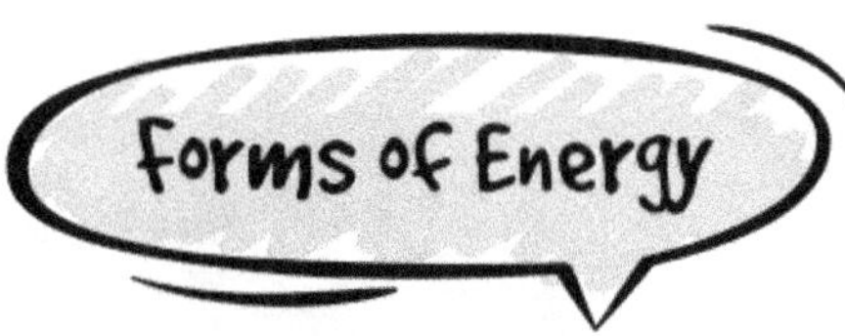

Identify and label one form of energy in each of these scenarios.

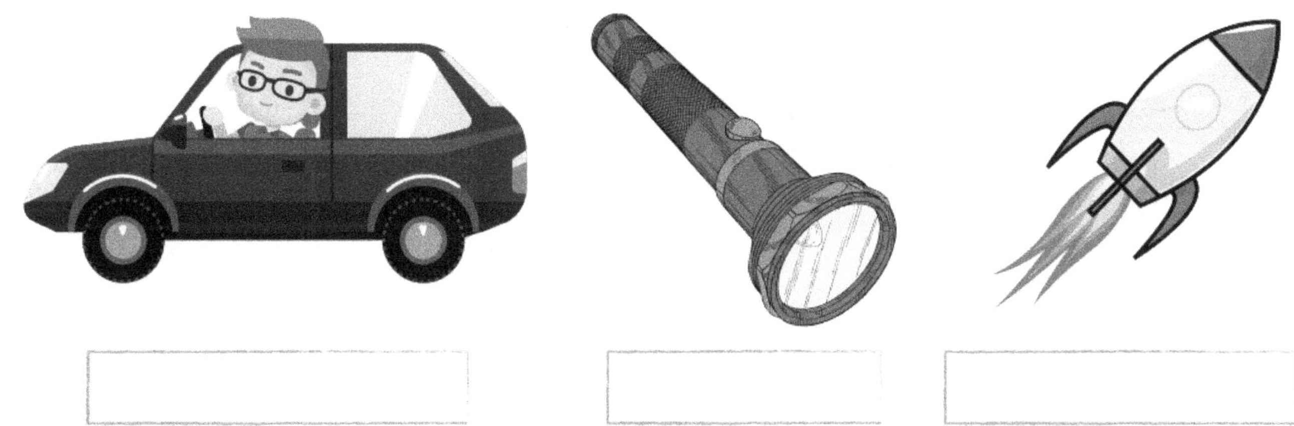

Types of Energy

There are two basic types of energy.

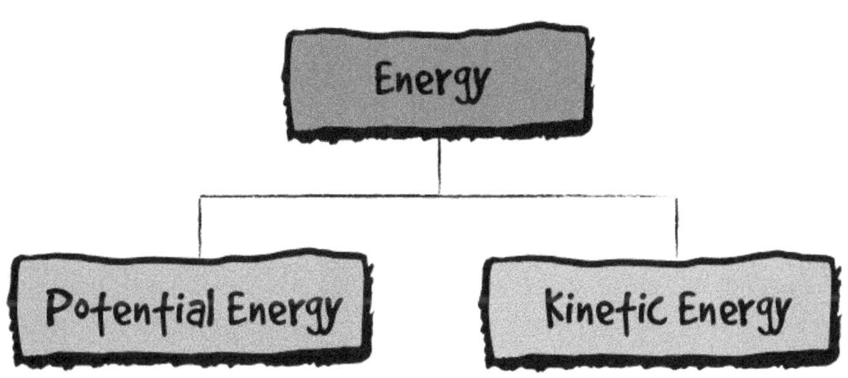

Potential energy	stored energy
Kinetic energy	energy in the form of motion

Identify the type of energy in each of these scenarios.

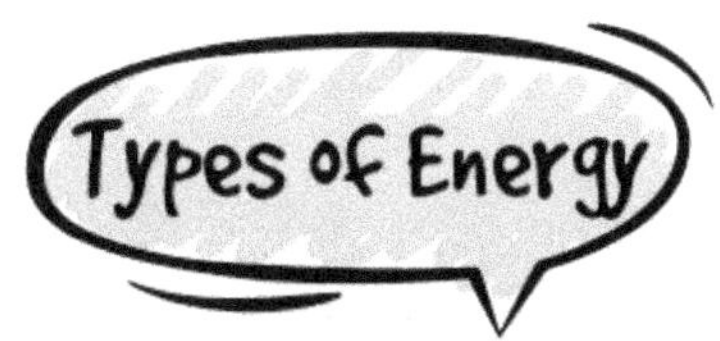

What type are these forms of energy? Place a tick in the appropriate field. Some forms of energies can be both types. Give one example for each.

Forms of energy	Example (for each type if both)	Potential Energy	Kinetic Energy
1. Sound energy			
2. Gravitational energy			
3. Electrical energy			
4. Mechanical energy			
5. Heat energy			
6. Wind energy			
7. Chemical energy			
8. Light energy			
9. Wave energy			

Match the different forms of energy with a medium or an appliance that is used to harness/use it.

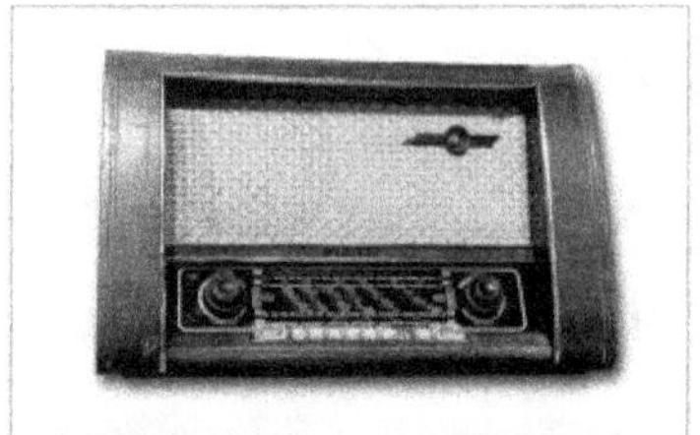

Wind energy

Electrical energy

Chemical energy

Sound energy

Gravitational energy

Light energy

The appliances listed here take electrical energy as input. Identify the output form of energy.

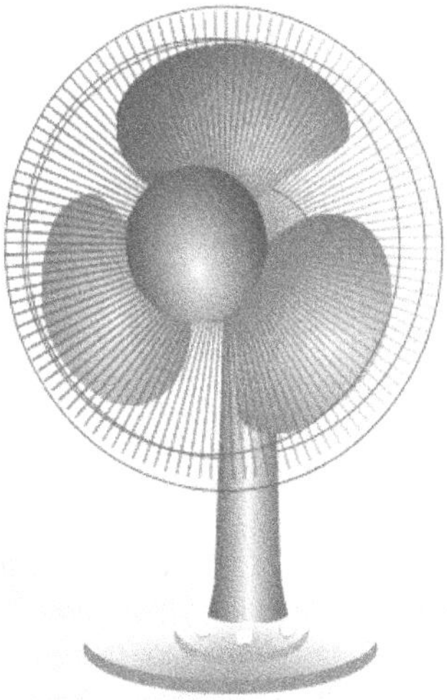

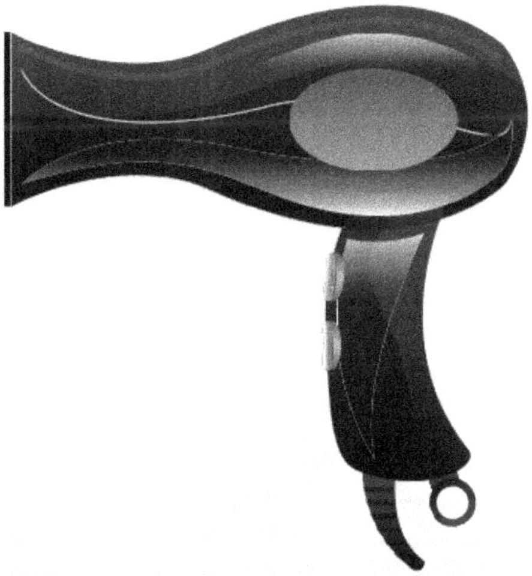

Matter and Its States

Matter	anything that occupies space
Mass	how much matter is present in an object

There are 3 states of matter as shown below.

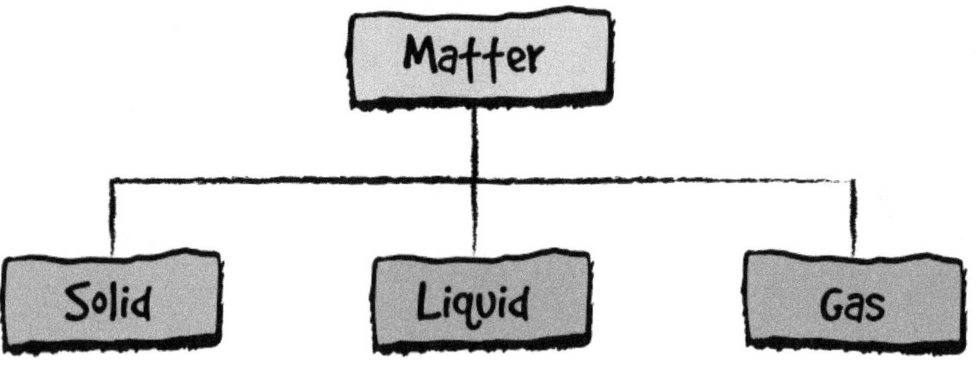

Complete the steps given below.

Step 1 Identify one of each solid, liquid and gas in your house.

Solid: ______________________________

Liquid: ______________________________

Gas: ______________________________

Draw the identified objects in the table given below.

Complete the table by placing a ✓ mark for the properties that are applicable to each object and a ✗ mark for those that are not applicable.

Name of the property	Solid	Liquid	Gas
Example			
Is rigid			
Has shape			
Can flow			
Spreads out evenly			
Is visible			
Can be felt			
Can be squished			
How many ticks?			

Changes in the States of Matter

Matter can change from one state to another when heat is added or removed from it. When matter changes from one state to another, its property also changes accordingly. The various processes involved in change in states of matter are shown below.

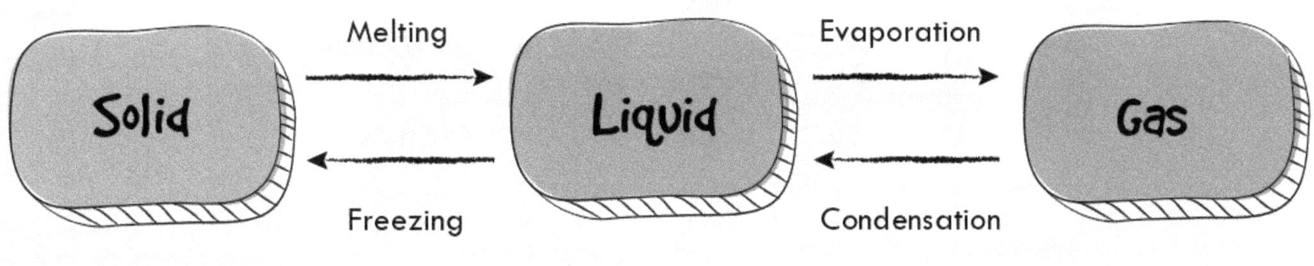

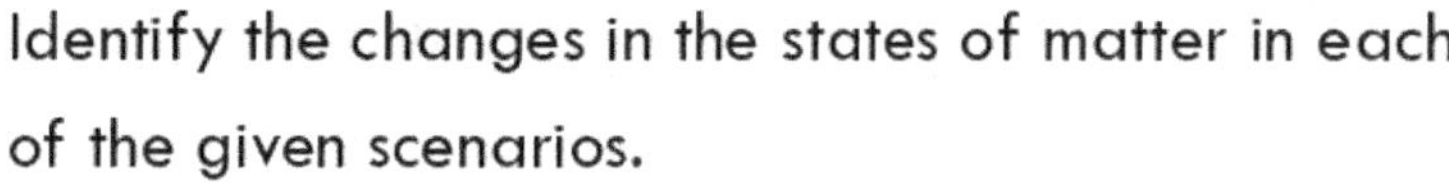

Identify the changes in the states of matter in each of the given scenarios.

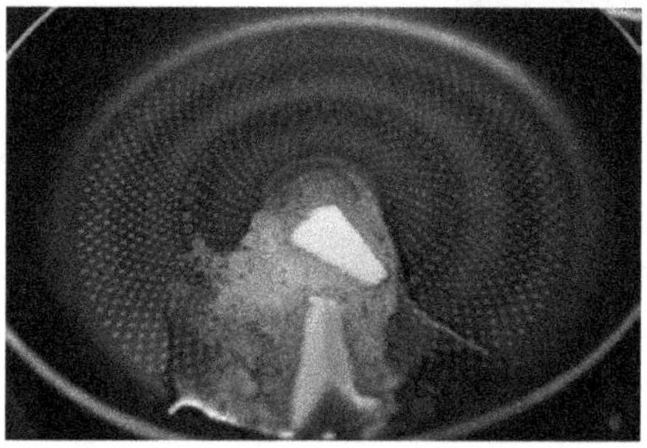

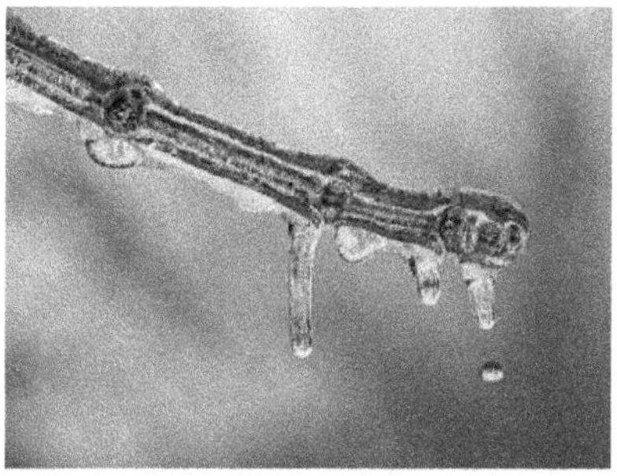

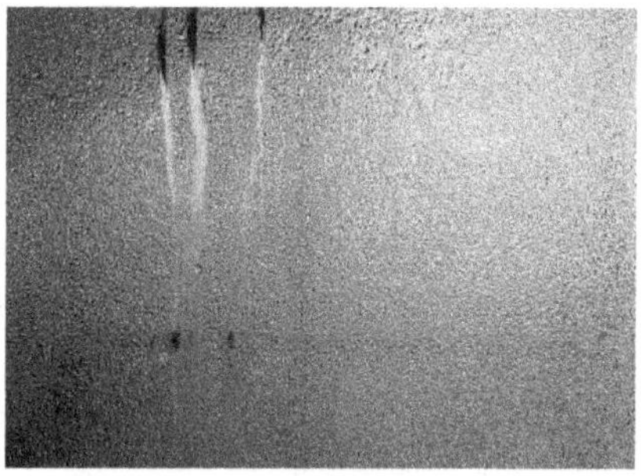

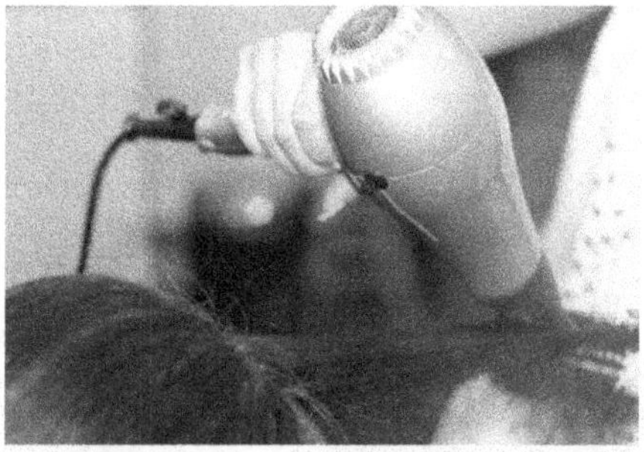

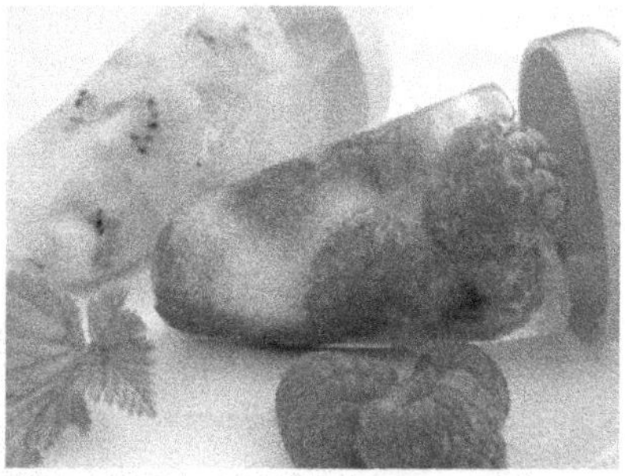

How do states of matter change?

Explain the changes in the states of matter in the given scenarios.

How does a runny egg become hard?

____

____

How does a candle melt when it is lit?

____

____

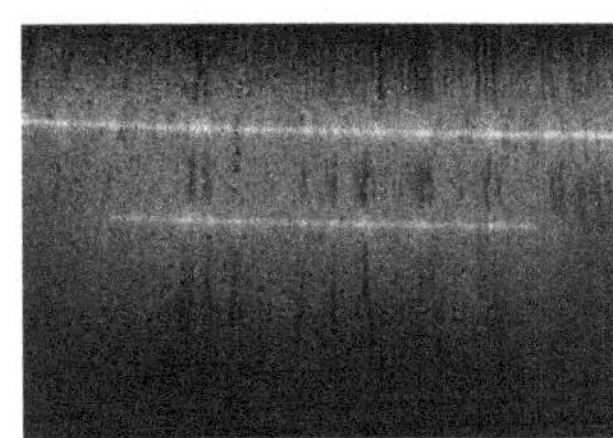

How does vapour form on a mirror?

____

____

How does water become ice?

____

____

How is a cloud formed from water vapour?

____

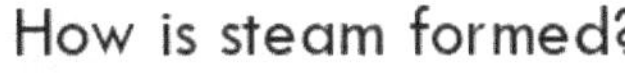

How is steam formed?

____

____

Types of Changes

Matter has 2 types of changes.

Physical Change	changes the shape of the matter but retains the properties
Chemical Change	the properties of the changed matter are very different from the original matter

Identify the type of change for each of the scenarios.

1. Bending a metal pipe	☐ Physical change	☐ Chemical change
2. Burning a paper	☐ Physical change	☐ Chemical change
3. Crushing a chalk	☐ Physical change	☐ Chemical change
4. Mashing a potato	☐ Physical change	☐ Chemical change
5. Adding lemon juice to water	☐ Physical change	☐ Chemical change
6. Baking a cookie dough	☐ Physical change	☐ Chemical change
7. Slicing cheese	☐ Physical change	☐ Chemical change
8. Burning sugar to make caramel	☐ Physical change	☐ Chemical change
9. Melting butter	☐ Physical change	☐ Chemical change
10. Condensation of water vapour on glass	☐ Physical change	☐ Chemical change
11. Metal spoon rusting	☐ Physical change	☐ Chemical change
12. Tearing a piece of paper	☐ Physical change	☐ Chemical change

Physical Change or Chemical Change?

Determine if the following processes are physical changes or chemical changes.

a. photosynthesis - ______________________________

b. explode - ______________________________

c. crush - ______________________________

d. ferment - ______________________________

e. boil - ______________________________

f. combustion - ______________________________

g. condensation - ______________________________

h. freeze - ______________________________

i. vaporize - ______________________________

j. rust - ______________________________

k. melt - ______________________________

l. grind - ______________________________

Atoms and Elements

Atom	the smallest particle of an element that has properties similar to that of the element
Element	a basic building block of matter

Physical Sciences - Light

objective

To understand light has a source and travels in a direction.

- Light is a form of energy.
- Some light waves are visible to naked eye. For example the colours on the rainbow.
- Light is a wave and travels in a straight line.
- The light waves bounce off an object causing reflection.
- Smooth surfaces bounce back light in one direction causing the formation of a clear image.
- Rough surfaces bounce back light in many different directions. Hence, the image thus formed is blurry.

Look at the list of sources of light. For natural sources of light, write an 'N' and for artificial sources of light, write an 'A'.

Passage of light through various materials

Not all materials allow the passage of light. While some materials allow partial passage, some completely block light. Hence, materials can be classified based on the property of light passage.

Materials that allow light to pass through them are called **transparent** materials. These allow you to see through clearly.

Materials that do not allow light to pass through them are called **opaque** materials. These do not allow you to see through.

Some materials that allow partial passage of light are called **translucent** materials. These do not let you see objects clearly.

Complete the table given below.

Material	Can you see through it?	Can you see a flashlight's light through it?	Type of the material
Cling film	Yes	Yes	
Polythene bag			Translucent
Tissue paper			Translucent
Aluminium foil	No		
Baking paper	No	Yes	
Cardboard	No	No	

Identify 5 more objects of each of these types of materials in and around your house.

Transparent objects	Translucent objects	opaque objects

Investigate

What do you think will happen to the transparency of water when it is freezed?

____

____

____

Take some transparent water (without impurities) in a cup and freeze it overnight. Check the frozen water the next day.

Is the ice that is formed transparent, translucent or opaque? Why?

____

____

____

Draw lines to match the organisms with their shadows.

Observe the shadow of each of these objects and draw a sun to denote the source of light in the appropriate position.

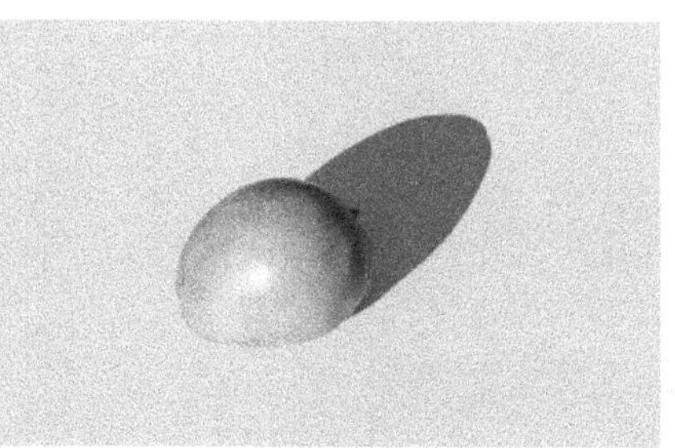

Where is the shadow cast?

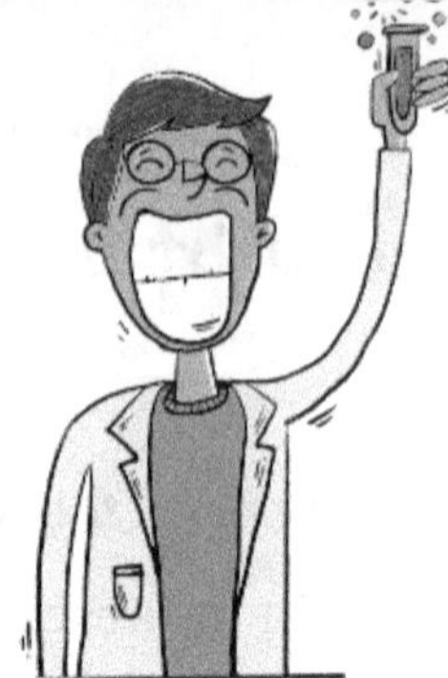

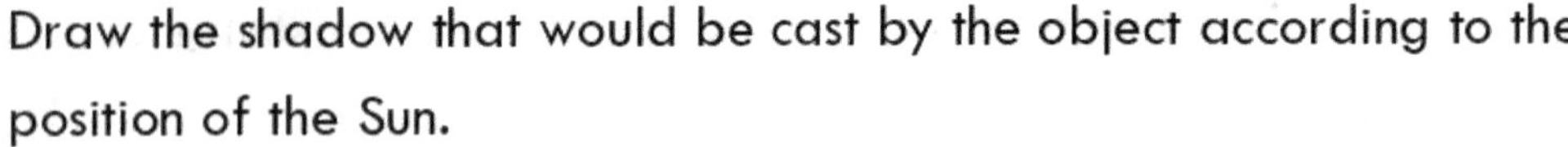

Draw the shadow that would be cast by the object according to the position of the Sun.

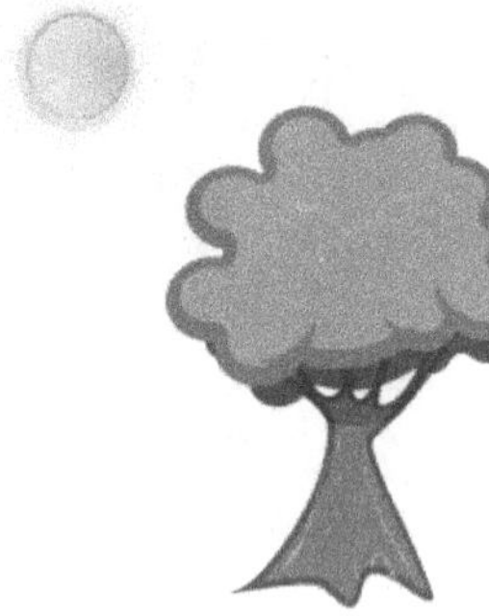

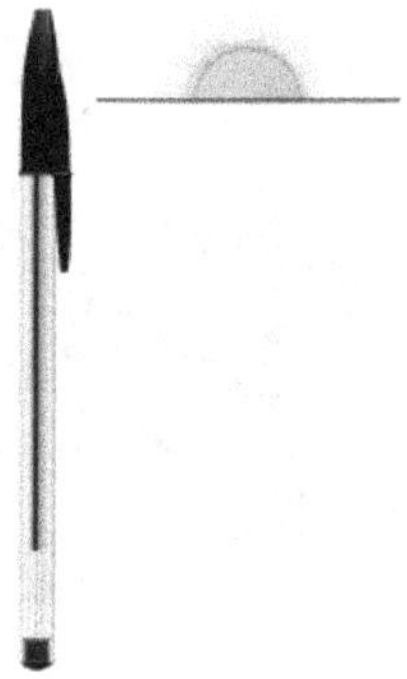

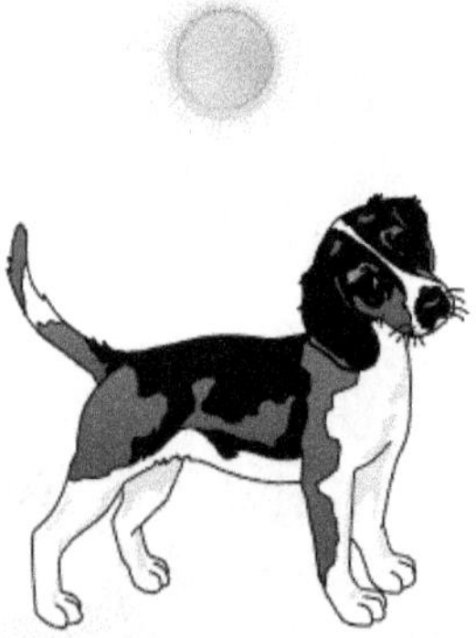

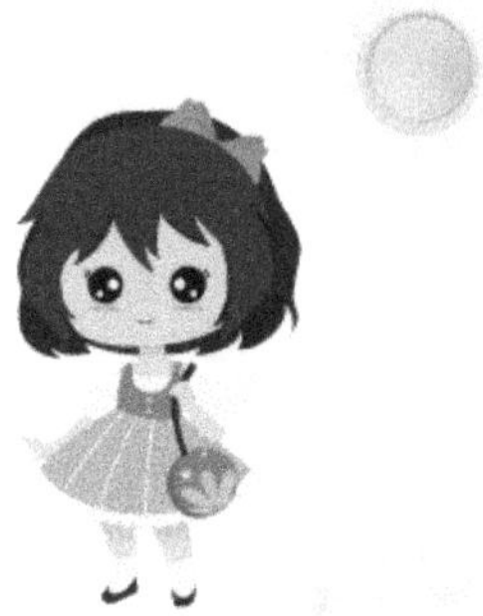

How do we see different colors?

Draw a light diagram to show how an object is seen in a particular color. Show all of the colors coming from the light source, and the colors that are reflected off the object.

Life Sciences

Adaptation

Adaptation	a characteristic feature of an organism that helps it survive in a specific environment
Biome	a community of plants and animals that are adapted to their environment

There are different types of biomes on Earth.
A few of them are given below.

Biomes

- Grassland
- Tundra
- ocean
- Desert
- Forest
- Wetland

organisms and their Adaptations

Complete the table given below.

organism	Biome	Adaptation and Survival
	Desert	
	Forest	

organism	Biome	Adaptation and Survival
	Temperate Forest	

	Wetlands	

Migration

Every year some animals move from one place to another, travelling thousands of miles in the spring and return thousands of miles in the fall. Such long trips the animals take are called **migrations.**

Migration is one of the behavioural adaptations of animals to the changing environment. They usually migrate to find warmer weather, better food supplies or a safe place to reproduce.

Write the names of 5 migratory birds and 5 migratory animals.

Birds	Animals

We know that animals migrate for various reasons. Do you think humans also migrate? Give 3 reasons for your answer.

Migratory Animals case Study

Read the information given in the table and answer the questions that follow.

Animal	Migrates from	Migrates to	Reason	Approximate distance in miles (to and fro)
	Brazil	Ascension Island	to lay eggs	2500
	the Arctic	Antarctica	to find food and a warmer weather	22000
	southeastern Serengeti	across Savannah to open woodlands	to find food and water during droughts	500

	United States and Canada	California, Florida, Mexico	to find warmer weather	4000
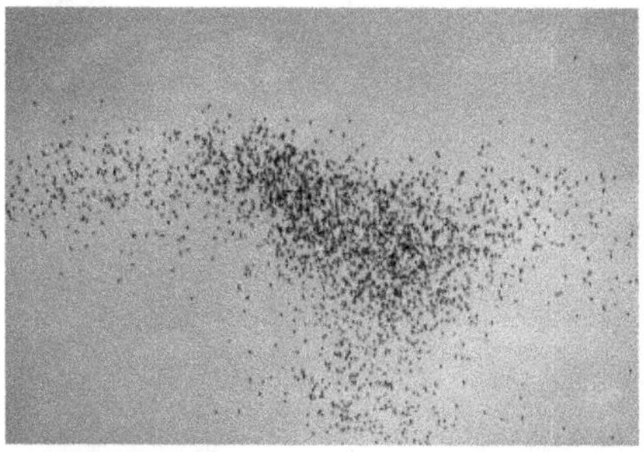	Texas caves	central Mexico	to find food and warmer weather	1600
	northern Pacific Ocean	off the coast of Baja California in Mexico	to find warmer waters and to give birth	10000
	Alaska	Argentina	to find warmer weather	16000
	Northern and central United States and Canada	central Brazil and Argentina	to find warmer weather	9000

1. Which of the animals migrate the farthest?

2. Which of the animals migrate the shortest?

3. Which animals migrate to Argentina?

4. Which animals migrate to Mexico?

5. Which animal migrates 800 miles, one way?

6. How many more miles does a monarch butterfly migrate than a female green turtle?

7. What is the most common reason for migration for the animals given in the table?

8. Why do gray whales migrate?

9. Why do you think animals migrate to Mexico?

10. What is the main reason for animals to migrate?

Extinct Animals and Fossils

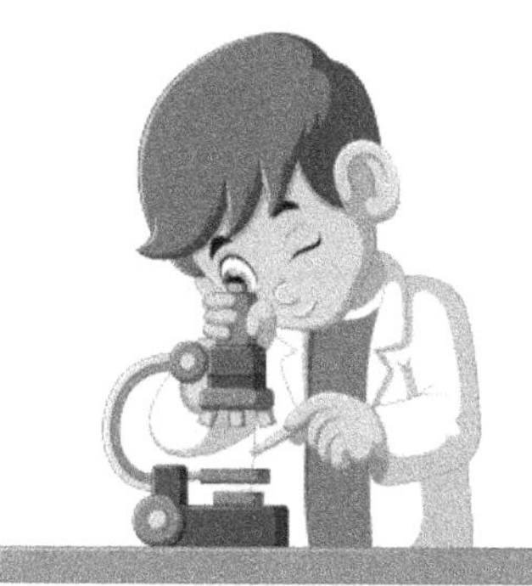

Find the given fossils and extinct animals in the word grid.

m	d	z	t	s	c	a	m	e	l	o	p	s
e	k	n	s	w	e	r	n	x	z	y	z	i
x	y	b	a	o	r	c	a	u	r	o	c	h
m	a	m	m	o	t	h	u	g	v	n	h	k
k	v	w	r	l	j	a	t	x	l	q	m	n
l	m	i	z	h	t	e	i	r	p	u	h	r
c	o	l	m	h	w	o	l	b	f	a	z	j
r	s	a	u	r	o	p	o	d	b	g	z	t
i	a	h	n	e	v	t	i	h	l	g	v	w
n	s	h	n	z	a	e	d	m	g	a	p	o
o	a	e	d	m	e	r	a	h	b	r	c	v
i	u	e	k	d	s	y	f	z	h	y	n	a
d	r	z	b	n	b	x	s	r	v	f	c	e

- sauropod
- auroch
- archaeopteryx
- mammoth
- camelops
- mosasaur
- quagga
- nautiloid
- crinoid

Real Life and Extinct Animals

Draw lines to match the living animals with their extinct counterparts.

Certain animals are said to be extinct because they are no longer living on the face of the planet. Endangered animals are those that are in danger of

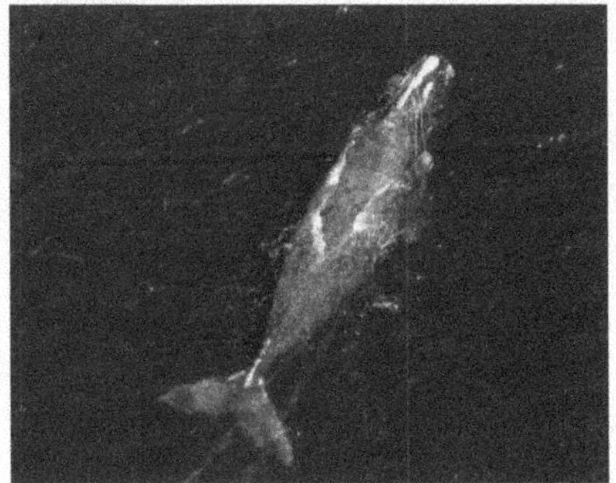

becoming extinct. An animal is considered to be endangered when there are only a few of them alive on Earth.For example: North Atlantic Whales are considered to be endangered as they are only about 350 in the world.

Endangered Animals

Use the clues to identify the endangered animals. Choose them from the given word box.

1. The "mane" reason that I am endangered is that I am hunted for sport.

2. When prairie dogs were poisoned, their homes were plowed, and I became endangered.

3. Hunting from aircrafts and motorboats is now banned in the Arctic Circle, where I am found.

4. Although I am the fastest land mammal, I am hunted and killed for my fur coat.

5. Poachers often hunt and kill me to sell my head, hands and feet as souvenirs.

6. When people started to clear bamboo forests, many of my species starved to death.

7. I am the largest living land mammal, and I am hunted for my tusks.

8. I am almost extinct because I am hunted and killed by people who are scared of my bark and bite.

9. I am under a great threat because the beaches I breed on are being developed for tourists.

10. I am critically endangered but poachers still hunt me for my horn.

- black rhinoceros
- giant panda
- African elephant
- mountain gorilla
- Mediterranean monk seal
- gray wolf
- cheetah
- Asiatic lion
- polar bear
- black-footed ferret

Imagine you had the power to save one of the world's endangered animals or plants, which one would you help, and why?

Complete the table and create a report on your favourite animal that is extinct.

Draw a picture of the animal here.	Name: ________ Habitat: ________ Size: ________ Lifespan: ________ Food habit: ________ Year of extinction: ________ Reason for extinction: ________

Report:

Read each scenario and predict if the organism is endangered or extinct. Write your answer in the space provided and give reasons.

The dodo bird used to live on an island where sailors landed in the 18th century. They killed many birds for food. Over time, the count of dodo birds got lesser and lesser.	
Deforestation is removing the homes and food of the Carolina northern flying squirrel.	
A dam is built in the area that usually has water. The water supply is cut in some areas. What will happen to the fish if this is their only home?	

Earth Sciences

Heavenly bodies

Solar system	the Sun, planets and other objects together
Planet	a large sphere that moves around the Sun
Star	hot, burning sphere of gases
Constellation	a group of stars
Moon	a natural satellite that orbits planets
Asteroid	a large rock or metal in space

Identify

Name the heavenly bodies.

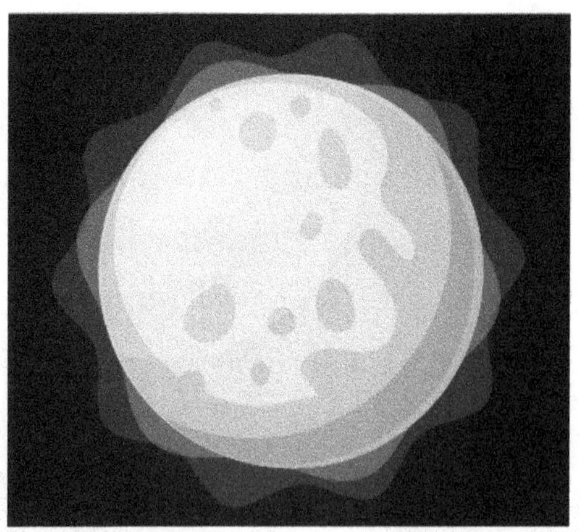

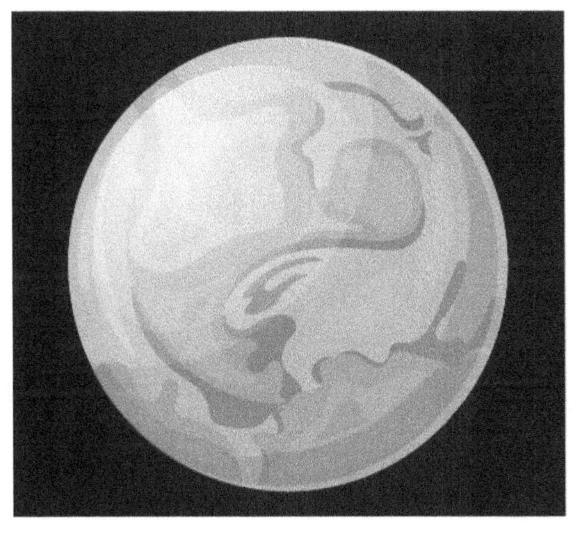

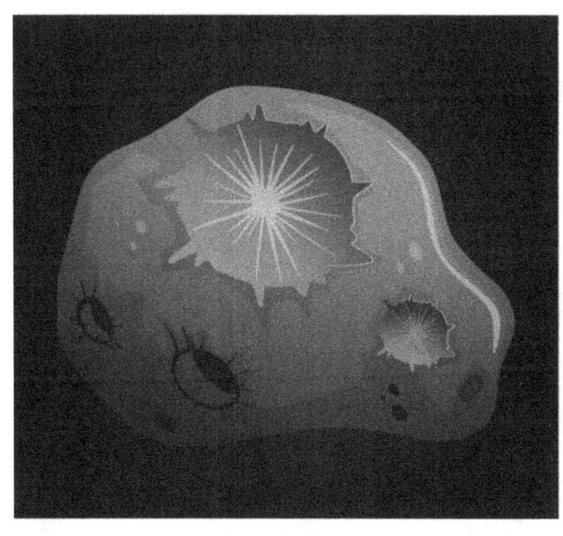

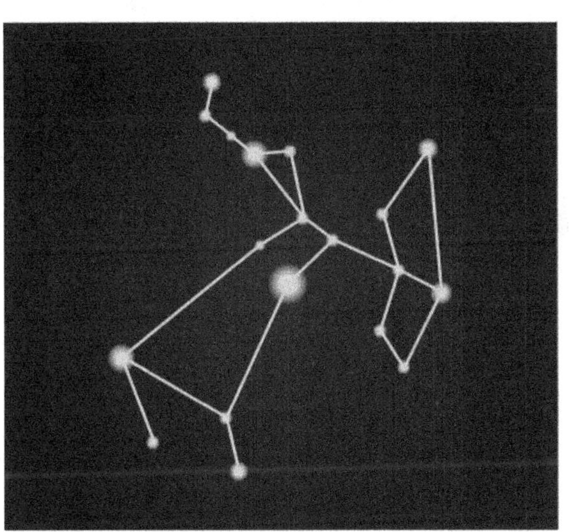

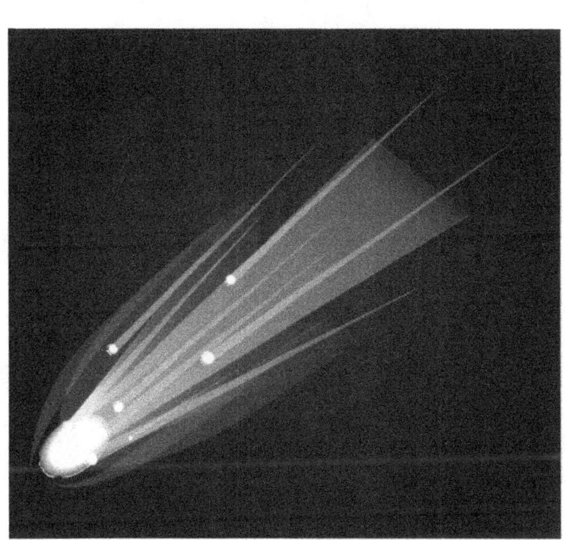

Label the Solar System

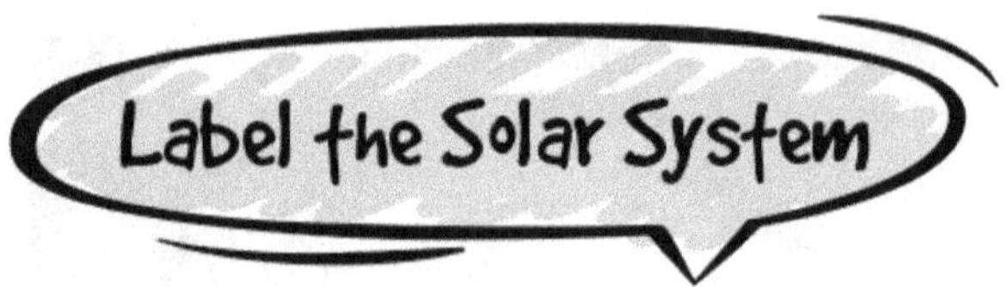

Label the heavenly bodies you are able to identify in the picture shown here.

Did You Know?

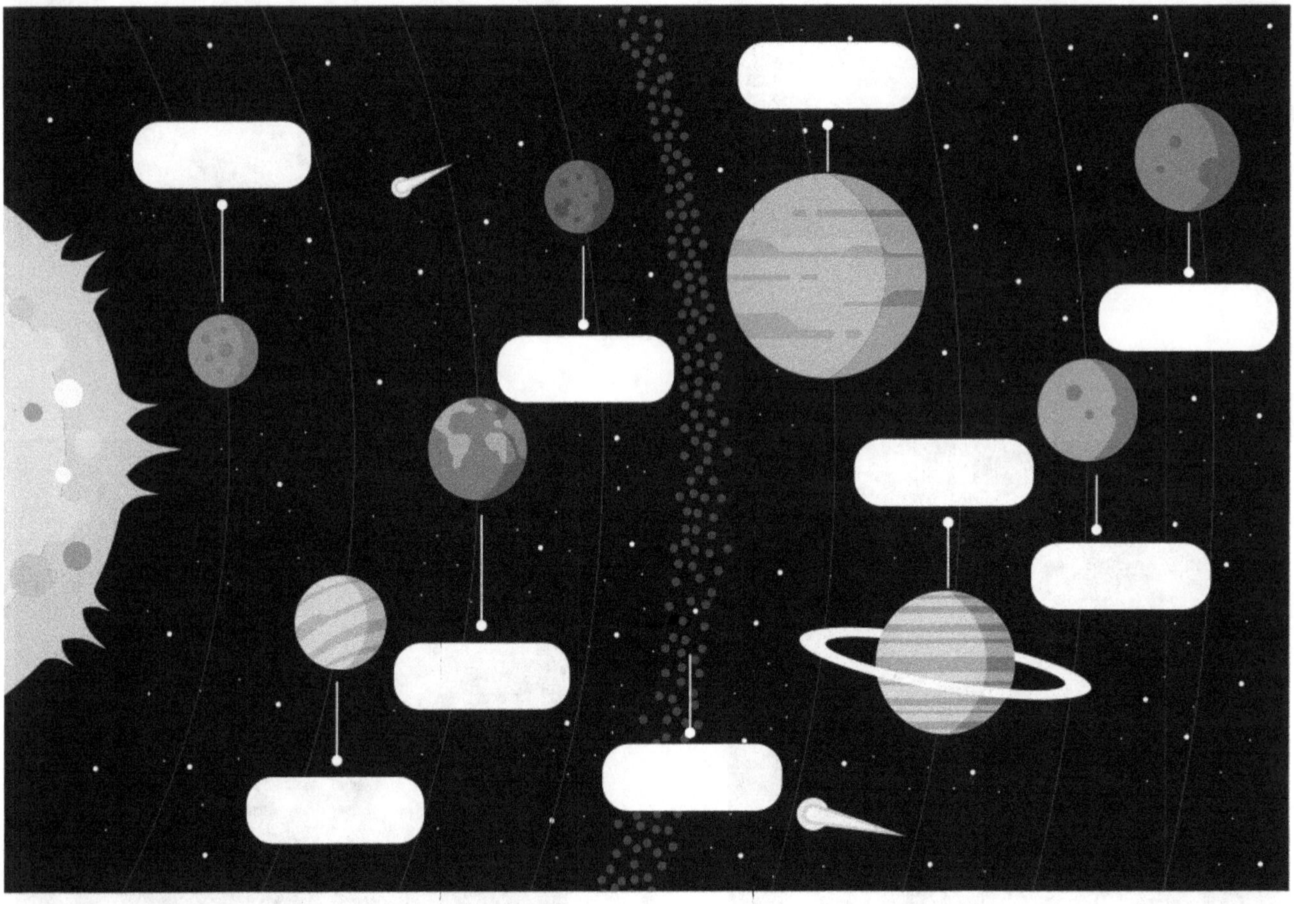

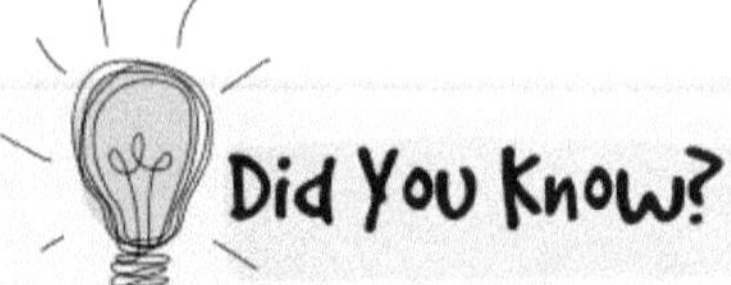

The region located between the orbits of the planets Jupiter and Mars, in the Solar System, is called the **Asteroid belt**, as it is occupied by a great many **asteroids**.

Identify the planets using the given clues. Who am I?

1. I am the red planet.
2. I am the hottest planet.
3. I am the largest planet.
4. I have beautiful rings around me.
5. I have oceans.
7. I am the smallest planet.
8. I am called the sideways planet.

Draw a picture of the solar system.

Discovery of a New Planet

You are the scientist who has just discovered a new planet. Draw a picture of it and list ways humans can live in harmony with the environment on this new planet.

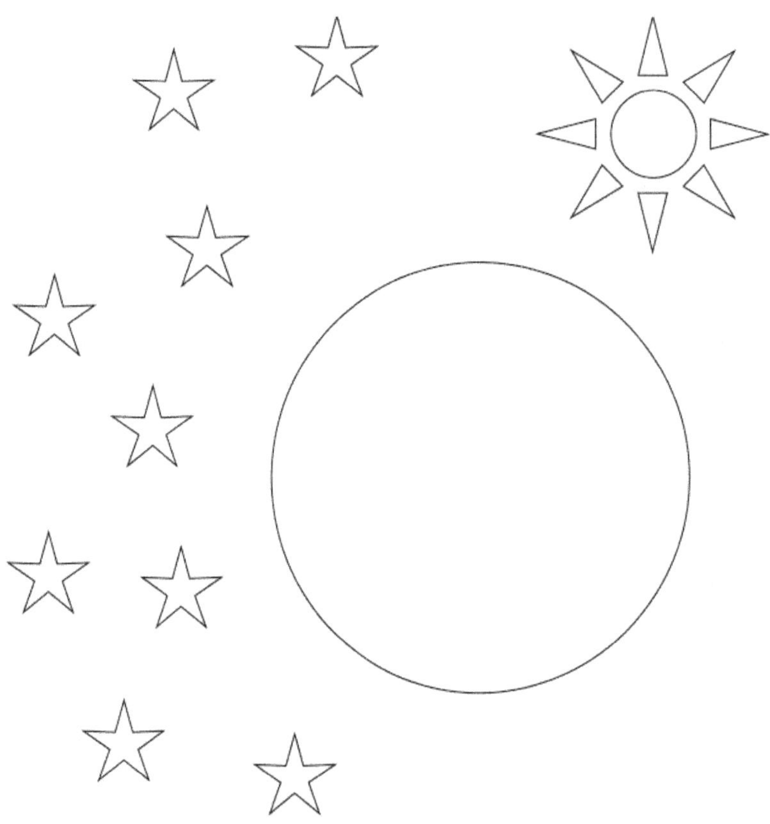

1. Name of your planet: ______________________________

2. How is this planet habitable for humans? ______________________________

____

3. What steps would you suggest people to take to protect the environment?

____

____

Let's do an activity to prove that the earth rotates.

What you need:

- A disposable plate
- Modelling clay
- A pen

How to do:

Step 1 Take a lump of the modelling clay and fix it on the plate.

Step 2 Insert the pen vertically, on the clay, such that it stands upright as shown in the figure.

Step 3 Place this setup in a sunny spot in the morning.

Step 4 The pen's shadow is cast on the plate. Mark the spot of the shadow with a pencil.

Step 5 Leave the setup in the sun undisturbed.

Step 6 Every one hour, check and mark the spot of the shadow, until it gets dark.

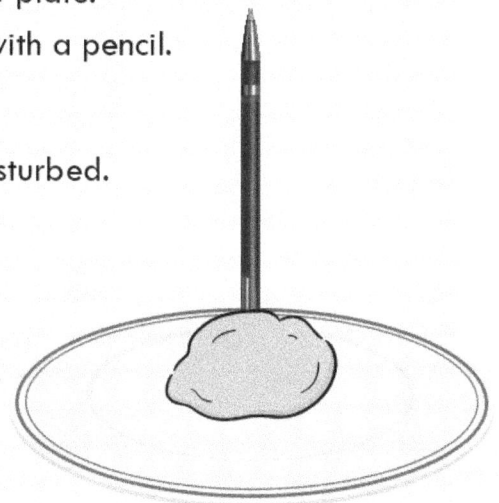

Observation:

The shadow moved and covered ____________ (more than/less than/almost) half the plate.

Inference:

____

____

____

____

Complete the crossword using the given hints.

Across:

3. planet closest to the Sun
7. planet with a great red spot
9. to turn about one's axis
10. star closest to Earth
12. the Sun, planets and other bodies together
15. cloudy planet
16. a space traveller
17. number of stars in our solar system
19. dwarf planet with two moons
20. a place where astronauts live in space

Down:

1. humans have sent robots to this red planet

2. furthest planet from the Sun

4. natural satellite

5. a force that pulls things towards each other

6. planet with the brightest rings

8. instruments used for having a closer look at the stars

11. the 'ice giant' planet

13. Jupiter, Saturn, Uranus, and Neptune have ________________

14. only planet that has humans

17. Earth moves on a fixed path called

18. number of planets in our solar system __________

Imagine you are a pirate sailing in the sea through the night. What would you see through your telescope? Draw it here.

Make a waning moon cookie model.

What you need:

- Disposable plate
- 8 Oreo biscuits
- Pen
- A spoon

What to do:

- Use a spoon to scrape the cream of the biscuits to make it resemble the different phases of the moon.
- Place them on the plate and label the phases.
- A sample is shown below.

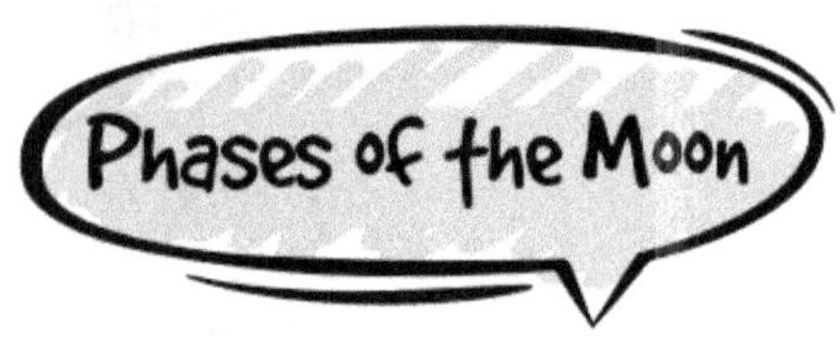

Complete the table below on the different phases of the moon.

Moon Phase	Picture of what the Moon looks like from Earth	Positions of the Sun, Moon and the Earth
New moon		Sun
		Sun
1st quarter		Sun

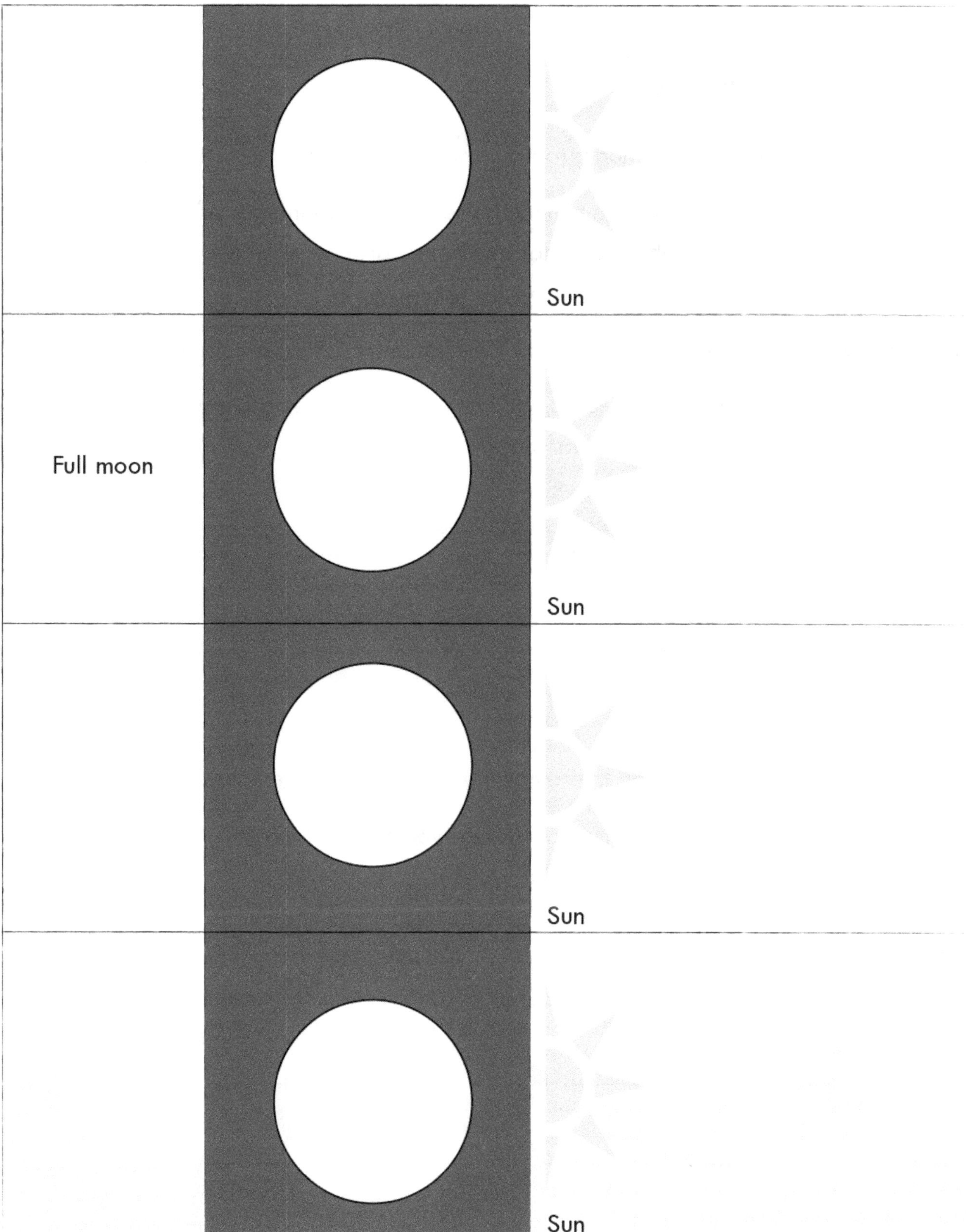
Full moon
Sun
Sun
Sun
Sun

Did You Know?

Most other planets have moons too!

The word 'moon' is a common noun. It is used to denote the moons of other planets too. However, the moon that orbits the Earth is called the **Moon,** while the moons of other planets have specific names.

For example, Mars has 2 moons and their names are **Phobos** and **Deimos.**

Also, Jupiter has about 79 moons, the largest of them being **Ganymede.** It is also the largest moon in our solar system.

Naming the moon

Jupiter has 53 named moons and the remaining 26 are yet to be named.

If you can name one of those moons, what would you name it? Why?

Observe the given image of seasons caused by the Earth's revolution and answer the questions that follow.

March 20
Spring
Autumn
June 20/21
Summer
Winter
December 21/22
Winter
Summer
September 22/23
Autumn
Spring

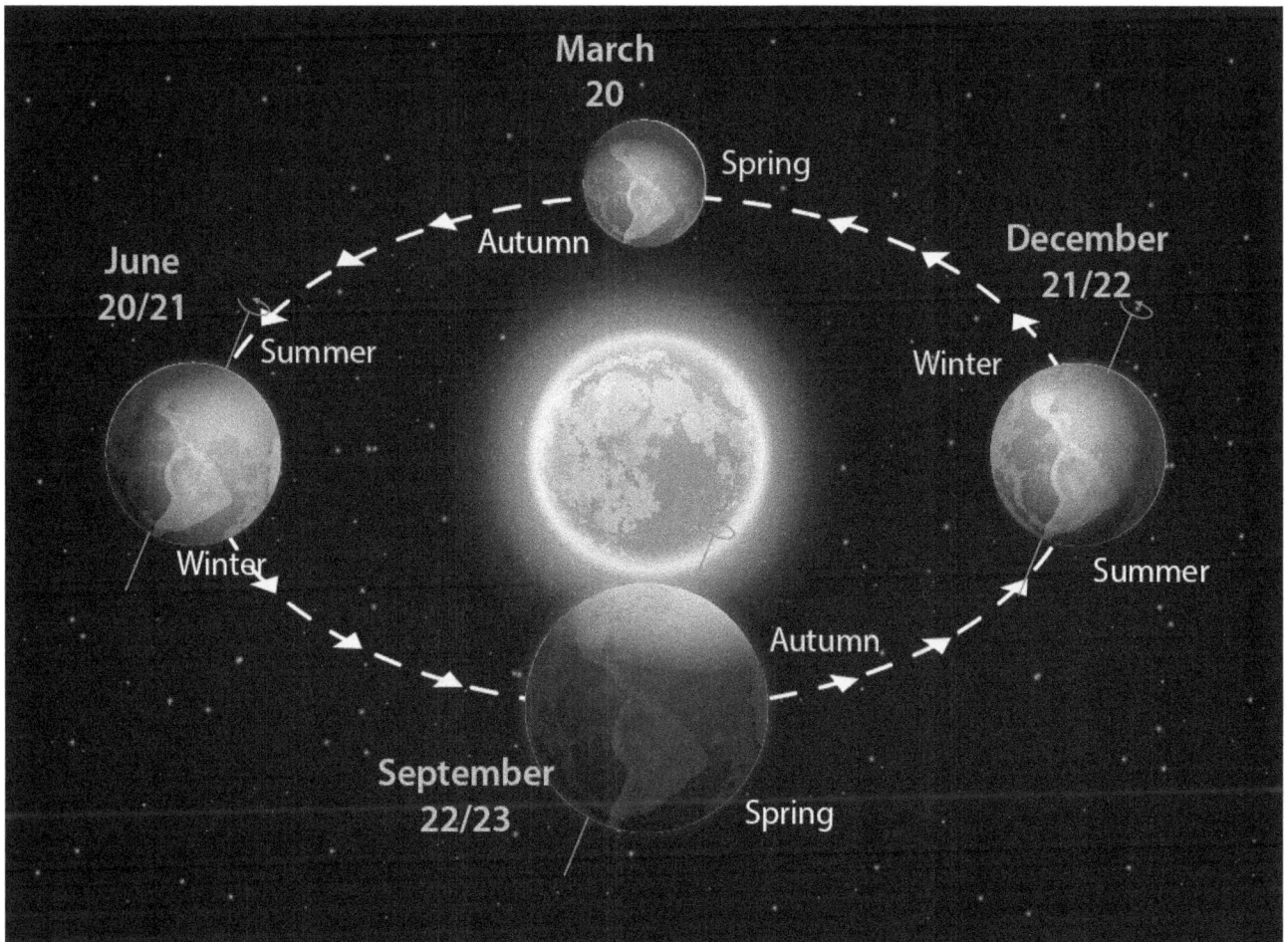

1. Do both the hemispheres have the same season through the year?

___

2. Why is it that the northern and southern hemisphere have different seasons at any given time?

3. Complete the table.

Month	Season in Northern Hemisphere	Season in Southern Hemisphere

4. Which month are you in now?

5. What season is it in your place?

Complete the table by placing an 'X' in the appropriate boxes to indicate the characteristics of asteroids, comets and meteors. A characteristic may fall into more than one category.

	Asteroid	Comet	Meteor
often called 'Shooting stars'			
is visible in our sky			
made up of rock			
orbits the Sun			
frozen ball of dust			
orbits between Mars and Jupiter			
usually burns up as it nears the Earth			
appears as a streak in the sky			
called 'dirty snowball'			

Answers

English Answer Key

Plural Nouns

churches
babies
fingers
people
feet
wolves
oxen
media
butterflies
sheep

Abstract Nouns

(faith)	(silence)	(lie)
lock	(delay)	pear
book	shirt	(joy)
(nap)	(wisdom)	chair

Find Me

1. childhood
2. luck
3. ideas
4. truth
5. pain
6. internet
7. education
8. dream
9. Beauty
10. imagination

Complete Me

1. pleasure
2. anger
3. kindness
4. happiness
5. honesty
6. loyalty
7. Curiosity
8. enjoyment
9. love
10. fear

Noun	**Pronoun**
Elsa	we
A bus	he
You and bill	I
That boy	they
The girls	it
____________ (Your name)	you
You and I	she

1. they
2. he
3. mine
4. any
5. she
6. their
7. both
8. it

Present tense: awake, tell, scurry, become, see

Past tense: sold, heard, took, wore, threw

Nouns (singular): egg, bottle, mirror, battery

Nouns (plural): cars, pens, lids, walls .

Verbs (singular): am, pushes, sleeps, rises

Verbs (plural): snore, think, wash, panic

1. Y - the subject “they” and the verb “were” are both plural.
2. N - the subject “singer” is singular, but the verb “play” is plural.
3. N - the subject “people” is plural, but the verb “is” is singular.
4. N - the subject “baby” is singular, but the verb “are” is plural.
5. Y - the subject “trees” and the verb “look” are both plural.
6. N - the subject “he or she” is singular as the conjunction “or” connects the subject, but the verb “are” is plural.
7. Y- the subject “parrot” and the verb “does” are both singular.
8. N - the subject “I” is singular, but the verb “were” is plural.

1. its
2. them
3. its
4. his or her
5. their
6. their

Adjective	Pronoun
smelly	street
noisy	hot dogs
clear	neighbor
scary	pumpkin
creamy	nails
crooked	socks
friendly	glass
spicy	children
sharp	yogurt
large	costume

What Do I Modify?

1. divided
2. practice
3. opened
4. looked
5. cheered

File Away

Nouns	pond, frogs, woods, trees (saw can be here as well)	**Explanation:** names of places and animal
Verbs	decided, cheering, jumping, saw	**Explanation:** action words
Adjectives	valuable, dry, two, famous	**Explanation:** describe the nouns: lesson, field, frogs
Adverbs	between, higher, relentlessly, quickly	**Explanation:** describe the verbs: landed, jumping, tried

Adjective	C / S	Explanation
older	C	Superlative is oldest.
darkest	S	Comparative is darker.
prettiest	S	Comparative is prettier.
cheaper	C	Superlative is cheapest.
wisest	S	Comparative is wiser.
easier	C	Superlative is easiest.
taller	C	Superlative is tallest.
deeper	C	Superlative is deepest.

Adjective	Comparative form	Superlative form
angry	angrier	angriest
bright	brighter	brightest
good	better	best
dull	duller	dullest
soft	softer	softest
lovely	lovelier	loveliest
quick	quicker	quickest
easy	easier	easiest
heavy	heavier	heaviest
bad	worse	worst

1. fiercer
2. quietest
3. more colorful
4. sweeter
5. fastest
6. bigger
7. funniest
8. longest
9. more expensive
10. silliest

1. louder
2. farther
3. more often
4. harder
5. better
6. latest
7. nearest
8. most frequently

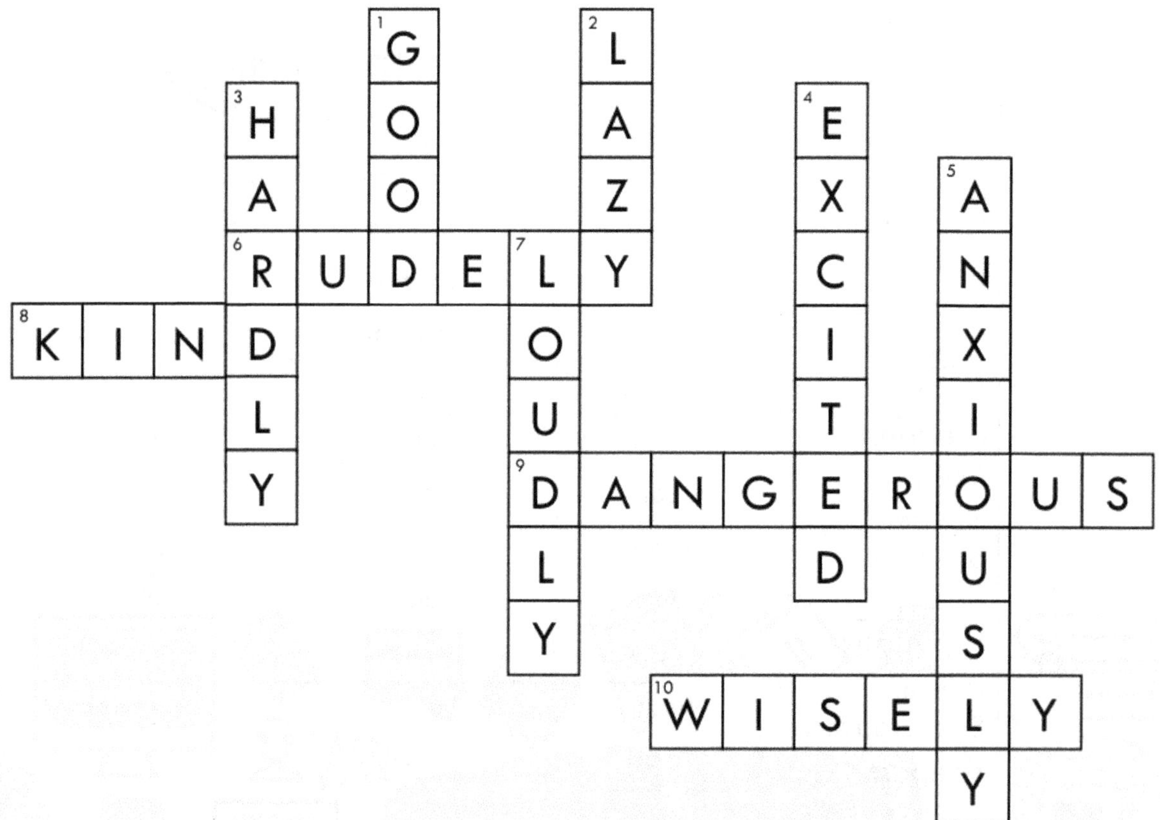

ACROSS	DOWN
2. while	1. because
5. though	3. before
6. after	4. yet
7. whenever	

I ran. - Independent

Explanation: Though the sentence has only a subject and a verb, it is a complete sentence.

After they arrived. - Dependent

Explanation: This is a dependent clause as the writer has not included what happened after they arrived.

Though she was working. - Dependent

Explanation: The part that answers "what happened despite her working" is missing, so this is a dependent clause.

He likes tea. - Independent

Explanation: Though the sentence is short, it is a complete sentence.

They, in the middle of the room, made the announcement. - Independent

Explanation: The sentence has a complete subject and predicate; hence it is complete.

Whenever I see someone sad and in need. - Dependent

Explanation: The part that answers "what you do on seeing someone sad and in need" is missing, so this is a dependent clause.

The classroom is bright. - Independent

Explanation: The sentence has a complete subject and predicate; hence it is complete.

Because she was in the house. - Dependent

Explanation: The part that answers "what happened as she was in the house" is missing, so this is a dependent clause.

Answer may vary

Capitalization

1. The museum opens at 9 am.
2. Sydney is in Australia.
3. I take guitar lessons from Mr. Immanuel.
4. I have to attend Manny's birthday party on Sunday.
5. Easter usually falls in April.
6. Uncle Bernie will celebrate Christmas with us this year.
7. Mona and Mini are at the library.
8. President Clinton is from the state of Arkansas.

1. The mother asked the doctor, "Will he be alright?"
2. Kate said quickly, "I know the answer."
3. Sally told her friends, "Please be careful."
4. "Is dinner ready?" asked Father.
5. "I love the gift," she said.
6. "We need to fill gas," Phil said as he got out of the car.
7. Remo said, "I would like another piece."
8. The student asked the teacher, "May I leave early today?"

The letter M!

Answer may vary

1. own: known, thrown, grown
2. ake: take, bake, lake
3. ight: eight, fight, light
4. eel: feel, reel, kneel
5. ink: blink, think, sink

Unscramble the Words

CIRCUS, FUNNY, FOOD, KNOW, SPEAK, TURN, AUGUST, WALK

GIRAFFE

CALENDAR

POTATOES

WRITING

JEWELRY

FURNITURE

Revised spelling: irritate, library, lettuce, purpose, grammar, effect, assist, occur

Multiple Meaning Words

Show the Difference

Answers may vary

rest	inactive
rest	left over
saw	tool to cut wood or metal
saw	past tense of see
trunk	the bark of a tree
trunk	a storage area in a car
fell	cut down a tree
fell	past tense of fall

1. healthy and strong

Explanation: The clue words are "very active all day."

2. decrease

Explanation: The clue words are "lose interest" and "but."

3. rarely

Explanation: The clue word is "never."

4. persuasive

Explanation: The clue words are "convinces people to do what she wants."

5. large amount

Explanation: The clue words are "whereas Henry gave away very less."

Root Words and Affixes

Split It Up

Word	Prefix	Suffix	Possible answers
asleep	a		aside, anew,
grandson	grand		grandfather, grandchild
colorful		ful	helpful, careful
leader		er	caterer, heater
disbelief	dis		disappear, disagree
return	re		redo, replay, rewrite

Hyperbole

Yes or No?

1. Y
2. N
3. Y
4. Y
5. N
6. N
7. Y
8. N

Create Hyperbole

Answers may vary

Connotation and Denotation

Positive, Negative, or Neutral?

1. negative
2. positive
3. positive
4. negative
5. neutral

Color Time!

positive: excited, ask, help

negative: peculiar, disappoint, picky

neutral: bought, thing, piece, project, wheels, arm

Note: The words ask and help can be neutral/positive

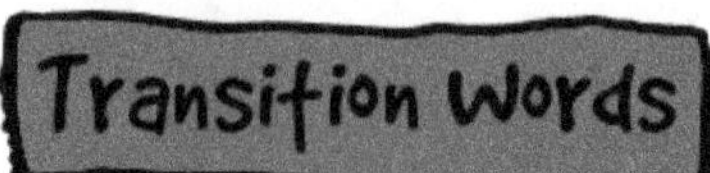

Answer: no other word in English ends with -gry.

1. however
2. In fact
3. As a result
4. Although
5. yet
6. Likewise
7. even though
8. meanwhile

P	U	G	V	P	H	D	B	A	S
S	S	E	L	E	U	L	C	P	O
D	E	S	I	R	P	R	U	S	T
I	G	P	Z	O	F	H	H	V	H
E	L	I	H	W	N	A	E	M	E
T	M	T	Z	G	W	C	E	V	R
Z	T	C	G	W	P	R	D	U	W
K	Y	L	L	A	N	I	F	W	I
G	F	A	M	C	T	J	R	K	S
V	S	O	O	N	W	J	S	O	E

SO MEANWHILE SOON
FINALLY CLUELESS SURPRISED
OTHERWISE

Missing Words

one of the

but/whereas

but/whereas

hence

Originally

Later

In some instances

In short

The Power of Words

1. The village where the frogs lived was hit by a drought. So they were looking for a new home.
2. The frogs had to travel through dry fields and woods in search of water.
3. Glen and Gina fell into a deep pit.
4. Glen heard the other frogs say that the pit was too deep to climb out of. He lost hope and stopped jumping. He fell into the pit and died.
5. The other frogs learned that one should never give up whatever the odds.
6. The other moral I learned is that always encourage people when they are in trouble. It matters what you say to them.

My Lost Puppy

1. The puppy's name was Cookie.
2. Cookie, chasing a dragonfly, bounded into the woods and got lost.
3. The author went home to bring his parents and the three went in search of Cookie. When they did not find her, they made 'Missing Dog' flyers.
4. Mrs. James' cat Smokey found Cookie. Cookie walked back home with him. When Mrs. James saw Cookie and called the number on the flyer to notify the owner of the dog.
5. Yes. Cookie walked home calmly alongside the author even without a leash.
6. Answer may vary.

1. following passion
2. robotics - home, mom; woodworking - school, Mr. Carmen.
3. by practice
4. building and creating new things
5. to share her experience/to entertain the readers

Answers may vary

music

painting

cooking

gardening

fishing

Evening Ditty

1. an evening song

Explanation: Evening Ditty is a song as it does not have a plotline or follow any structure of a story.

2. the author

Explanation: The author Joseph Ritson is the narrator as he uses the pronouns "you" and "us" in the song.

3. first person

Explanation: The pronoun "us" shows that the song is in first person point of view.

4. play - day; call - all

Explanation: These words have the similar ending sound.

5. A penny loaf will serve us all.

Explanation: A penny loaf is a small bun, which is exaggerated to be able to serve all the children for supper.

Are you asleep yet?

1. north
2. west
3. south east
4. east
5. west
6. east
7. south
8. north

Interpret Data

According to this survey:

1. Surfing is the least favorite sport.

2. Basketball is the most favorite sport.

3. Baseball and beach volleyball earned the same number of votes.

4. Answers may vary.

How to Make a Paper Fish?

Illustrations in Text

1. paper, scissor, and markers

2. Things You Need and Steps in the Process

3. Pictures act as a reference point to check if we are on track and to simplify any difficult instruction.

4. 8 steps

5. Answers will vary.

1. Mexico, North America

2. Brazil, South America

3. Spain

4. Saudi Arabia

5. Russia

6. Australia

Text Features

1. Table of contents

2. Illustration

3. Glossary

1. Lesson 1: 3 sections; Lesson 2: 4 sections

2. lesson 2, section 1

3. subsection 2 of lesson 2 section 3

4. section 4

5. The picture explains the stages of metamorphosis of a frog.

6. Glossary can be found at the end of a lesson or a poem/passage to explain difficult or technical words.

1. The arrows helped to understand where to begin and end

2. No.

can

Explanation: All others make another word when read backwards.

Math Answer Key

1. a. 4 + 4 + 4 = 12

Three groups of four = twelve 3 x 4 = 12

b. 5 + 5 = 10

Two groups of five = ten 2 x 5 = 10

c. 3 + 3 + 3 + 3 + 3 + 3 + 3 + 3 = 24

Eight groups of three = twenty-four 8 x 3 = 24

2. The picture shows 2 groups of 3 doughnuts.

3. 4 groups of 4 oranges can be represented as given.
As addition sentence - 4 + 4 + 4 + 4 = 16

As multiplication sentence - 4 x 4 = 16

4. Four times five is twenty which is represented in the multiplication sentence as 4 x 5 = 20.

5. a. i) 3 rows ii) 2 objects in each row.

b. i) 3 rows ii) 3 objects in each row.

c. i) 5 rows ii) 2 objects in each row.

d. i) 4 rows ii) 2 objects in each row.

6. a.

b. The answer may vary. Dots are grouped in 3s in both the arrays. In the given image the dots are not arranged in an array.

  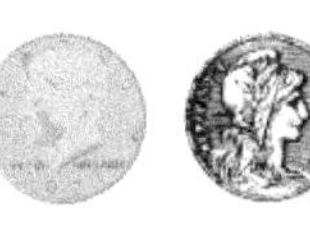   

  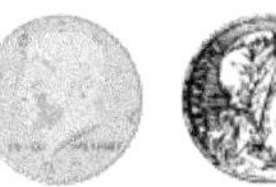  

7. 5 rows of 6 coins.

Multiplication sentence: 5 x 6 = 30

8. a. 6 threes

b. 3 x 7

c. 8 x 7

d. 8 x 9 = 9 x 8

e. 3 x 2

9. a. 20 = 5 x 4

20 = 4 x 5

b. 10 = 2 x 5

10 = 5 x 2

c. 15 = 3 × 5

15 = 5 × 3

d. 42 = 7 x 6

42 = 6 x 7

10. a. Unit form: 4 nines

4 x 9 = 9 x 4

Total: 36

b. Unit form: 5 eights + 1 eight

= 40 + 8

= 48

Facts: 6 x 8 = 48

8 x 6 = 48

c. Unit form: 5 sixes

5 x 6 = 6 x 5

Total: 30

d. Unit form: 7 sevens + 3 sevens

= 49 + 21

= 70

Facts: 10 x 7 = 70

7 x 10 = 70

11. 9, 18, 27, 36, 45, 54, 63, 72, 81, 90

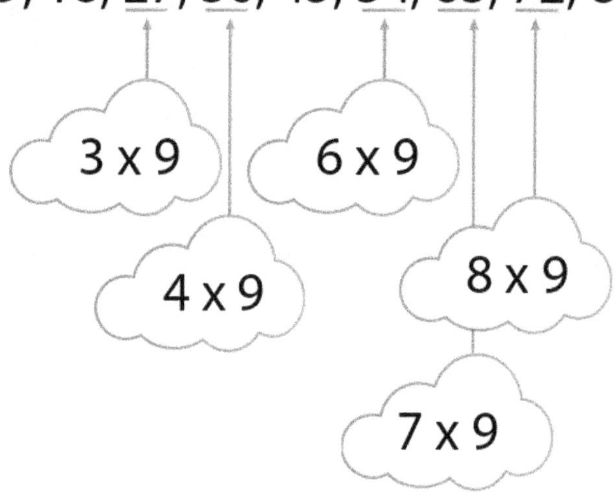

12. Picture:          

Words: Nine fives is forty-five

Numbers: $9 \times 5 = 45$

13.

a. $32 \div 8 = 4$ plants

b. $35 \div 5 = 7$ magazines

c. $30 \div 5 = 6$ smoothies

14.

b. $m = 5 \times 7$; $m = \$35$, thus Mia spends $35.

c. $c = 32 \div 8$; $c = 4$, thus Mr. Micheal buys 4 kg of wheat.

d. $4 \times 3 = 12$; $12 \div 6 = c$, thus each boy will get 2 football cards.

15.

b. $28 \div 4 = 7$

c. $54 \div 6 = 9$

d. $99 \div 9 = 11$

Properties of Multiplication and Division

1.

a. 5 x 3 = 15

15 ÷ 3 = 5

b. 4 x 4 = 16

16 ÷ 4 = 4

c. 2 x 4 = 8

8 ÷ 4 = 2

d. 2 x 12 = 24

24 ÷ 12 = 2

Relationship between division and Multiplication

2.

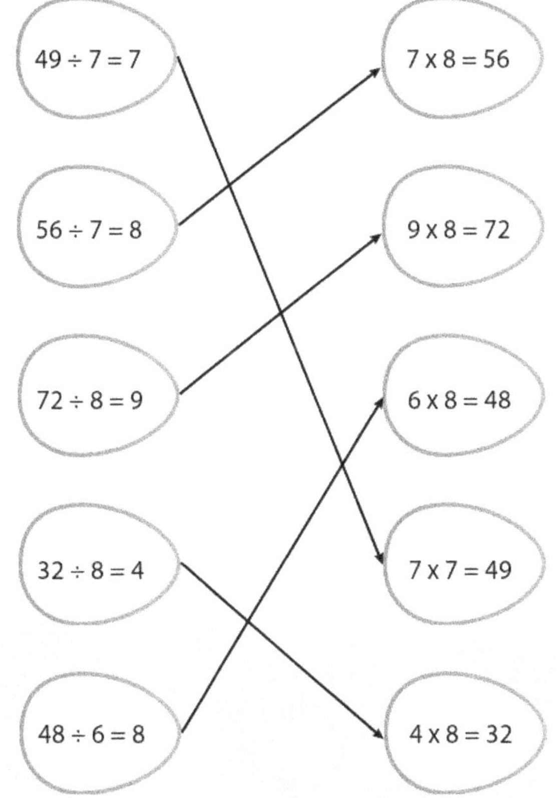

3. Answers may vary

Arrays and division

4. a) 15 ÷ 3 = 5

There are 5 packets of strawberries.

b) 24 ÷ 6 = 4

There are 4 bowls of fish.

5. a. 8 x 9 = 72

9 x 8 = 72

72 ÷ 8 = 9

72 ÷ 9 = 8

b. 7 x 9 = 63

9 x 7 = 63

63 ÷ 7 = 9

63 ÷ 9 = 7

c. 7 x 8 = 56

8 x 7 = 56

56 ÷ 8 = 7

56 ÷ 7 = 8

d. 8 x 6 = 48

6 x 8 = 48

48 ÷ 8 = 6

48 ÷ 6 = 8

Let us understand - Tape diagrams

6. 15 ÷ 3 = 5

There are 5 shirts on each rack.

7. 21 ÷ 7 = 3

Each piece is 3 meters long.

8. 30 ÷ 5 = 6

There are 6 boxes.

9. a. 10 ÷ 2 = 5

There are 5 baskets.

b.

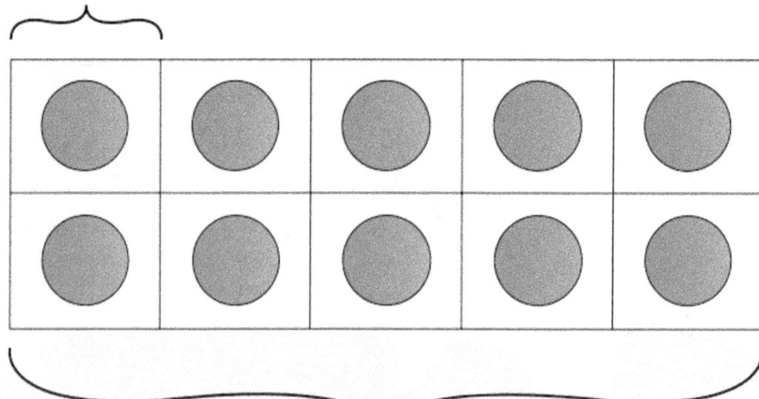

10. 72 ÷ 6 = 12

There are 12 stamps on each page.

Number Search

11. Possible fact families:

4 , 28, 7 → 28 ÷ 7 = 4
3, 11, 33 → 33 ÷ 3 = 11
3 , 8, 24 → 24 ÷ 8 = 3
8 , 9, 72 → 72 ÷ 9 = 8
4, 16, 4 → 16 ÷ 4 = 4
4, 5, 20 → 20 ÷ 5 = 4
8, 6, 48 → 48 ÷ 6 = 8
7, 8, 56 → 56 ÷ 7 = 8
5, 6, 30 → 30 ÷ 5 = 6
8, 32, 4 → 32 ÷ 8 = 4

12. a. 18 ÷ 2 = 9, Ricky pays $9.

b. 30 ÷ 6 = 5, There are 5 rows.

If 6 more tomato plants are added, 36 ÷ 6 = 6. Thus, there will be 6 rows.

c. 14 stones + 2 stones = 16 stones

16 ÷ 4 = 4, thus there are 4 rows in the box.

d. 48 ÷ 6 = 8, thus Daniel worked for eight hours.

Multi-Digit Arithmetic

1. a. 35 c. 1125 e. 1385 g. 1285 i. 1455

b. 295 d. 275 f. 65 h. 205 j. 525

2.

The object measures between (which two tens)	Length rounded to the nearest 10 cm
20 cm to 30 cm	20
90 cm to 100 cm	100
10 cm to 20 cm	20
10 cm to 20 cm	20
90 cm to 100 cm	90

3.

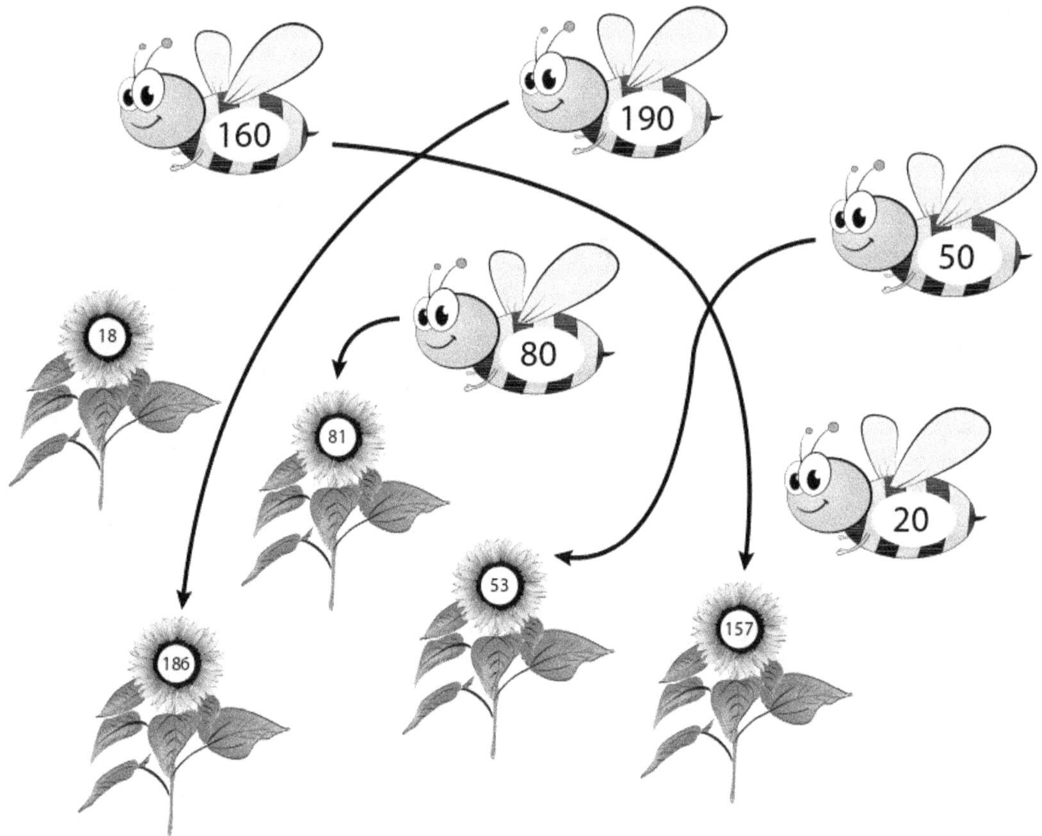

4. a. 130 milliliters

b. 300 grams

c. 200 grams

d. 8:10 in the morning

e. 6:00 in the evening

f. 100 km

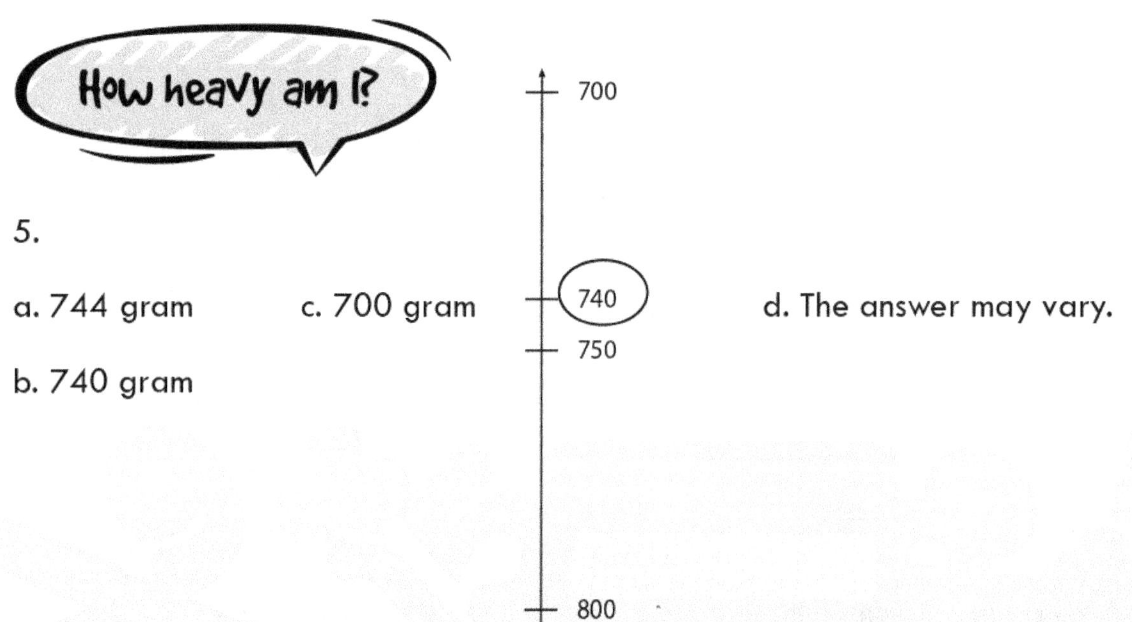

5.

a. 744 gram

b. 740 gram

c. 700 gram

d. The answer may vary.

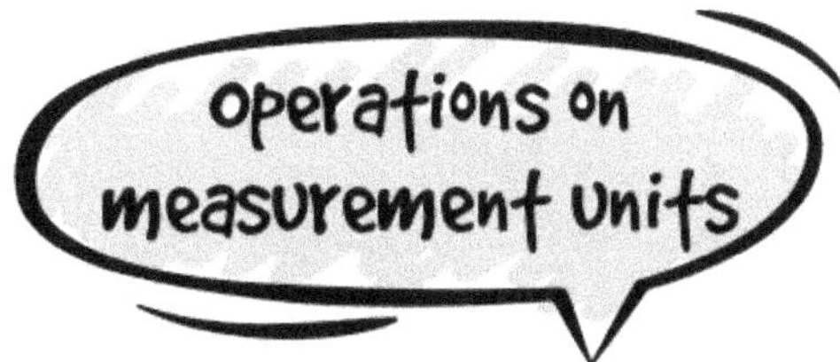

6. b. 90 m

c. 157 mL

d. 279 g

e. 4 kg 465 g

f. 6 L 682 mL

7. a. 56 + 74 = 130 rocks

b. 330 + 220 = 550 mL; 550 + 220 = 770 mL

c. 28 + 12 = 40 minutes

d. 22 + 13 = 35 minutes; 35 + 22 = 57 minutes

8. c, c

9. On rounding to the nearest ten,

Saturday	Sunday	Monday
240 km	250 km	200 km

Saturday + Sunday = 240 + 250 = 490 km

Saturday + Monday = 240 + 200 = 240 km

Sunday + Monday = 250 + 200 = 450 km

Thus, Sunday and Monday are the two days.

10. a. 244 g b. 317 cm c. 675 km d. 405 kg e. 3 L 159 mL f. 5 L 446 mL

11. 750 g - 550 g = 200 g

12. a. 9 ones, 9 b. 6 tens, 60 c. 12 ones, 12 d. 12 tens, 120

13. a. 20 x 4 = 80, thus 4 minibus can carry 80 passengers.

b. 9 x 30 = 270, thus 270 desks in all.

c. 20 x 5 = 100, thus 100 beds can be placed.

d. 6 x 60 = 360. 360 + 10 = 370, thus there will be 370 seconds.

14. $20 x 6 = $120

The sewing box cost $135.

She does not have enough money to buy the sewing kit box.

135 - 120 = 15. She is short of $15.

15. Lucas works for 8 + 8 = 16 hours.

1 hour = $10

16 hours = $10 x 16 = $160, thus Lucas earns $160.

16. 32 x 2 = 64

64 rounded to nearest 10 is 60.

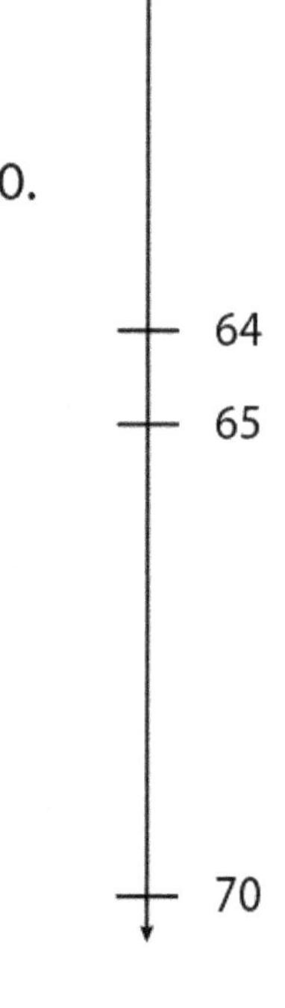

Round off to 100

17. The four numbers are,

102 96

101 98

18. Rocky = 137 marbles

Jason = Rocky's marbles + 73 marbles = 137 + 73 = 210 marbles

Rocky's marbles + Jason's marbles = 137 + 210 = 347 marbles in all.

19. a. Daniel drinks 196 + 242 = 438 mL

b. Jacob drinks 248 + 285 = 533 mL

c. Volume of mango and apple juice =
135 +248 = 383 mL

20. a. 389 Pomeranians

b. 143 more Pomeranians

1. The shapes a and d are shaded 1/8th.

2. The shapes b, c, e, f are divided into equal parts.

3. a. One-third

b. Two- fourths

4.

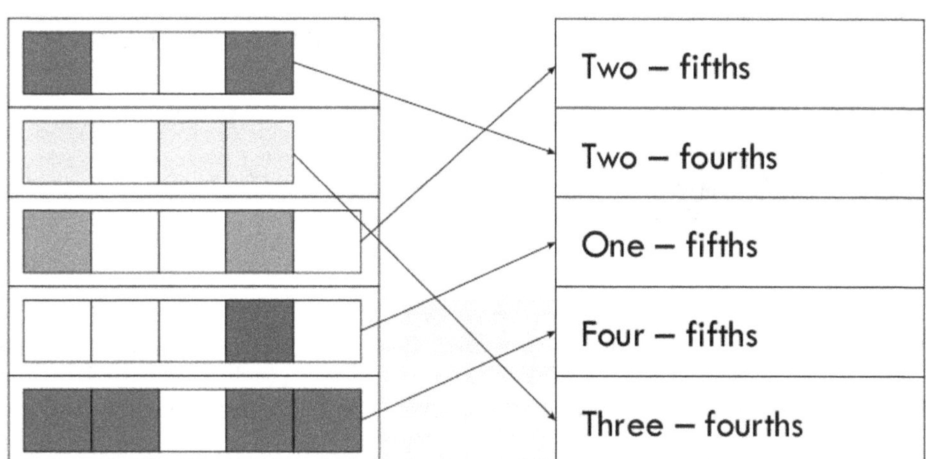

5. a. The number line in option i.

b. Three - fifths

6. a.

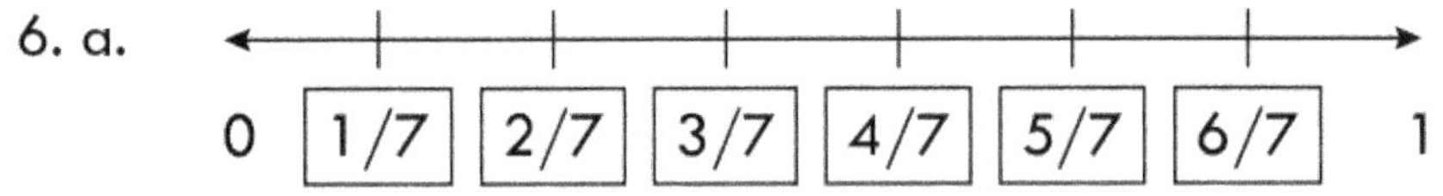

b.

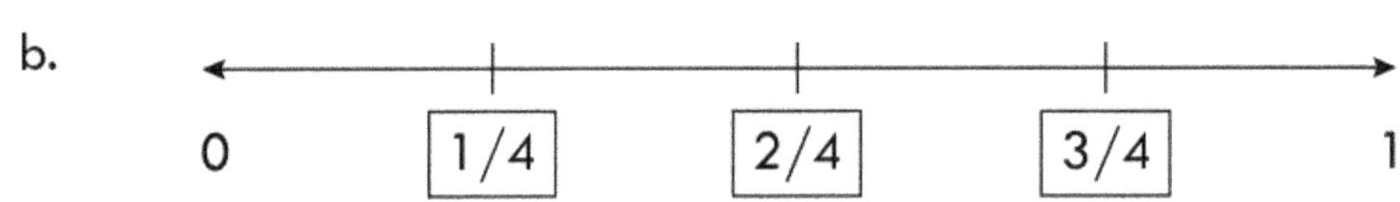

c.

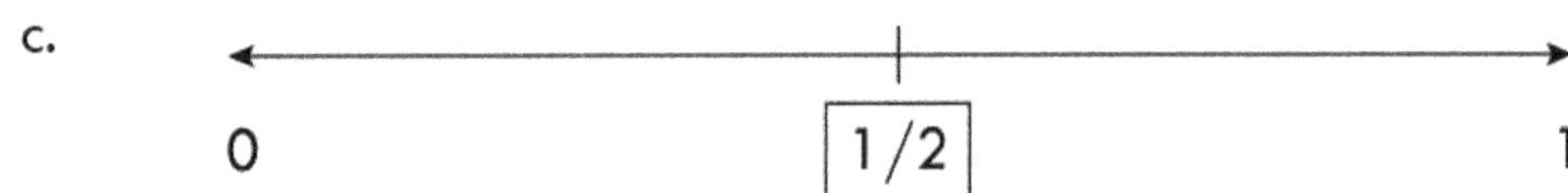

7. a. 9 equal parts

b.

1/9	2/9	3/9	4/9	1/9	1/9	1/9	1/9	1/9

c. 4/9

d. 5/9

8. a. Ron. Because 1 part of 3 parts is bigger in size than 1 part of 4 parts.

b. George. Because 1 part of 5 equal parts is more than 1 part of 8 equal parts.

9. a. Ava is right 1/3 is the same as two 1/6 as shown in the figure below.

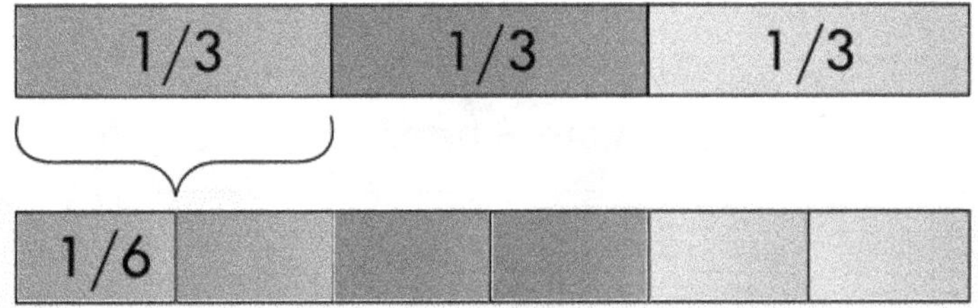

b. Bret is right. Dividing a cake into 4 parts gives 4 parts. Each of the 4 parts will be bigger than one of the 6 parts of the cake.

10. a.

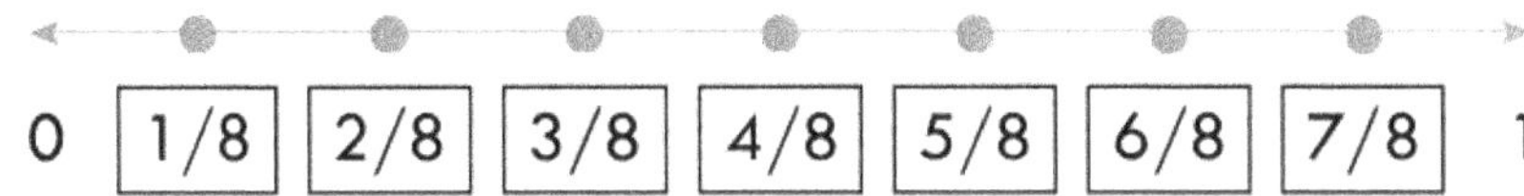

b. 4/8

c. 3/8

11.

a. <

b. >

c. <

d. >

e. >

12. a. Emma's sports kit is taller because 1/3 rd of the wardrobe is taller than 1/3rd of the study table.

b. Steve's sister is taller than him.

13.

a. 5/8

b. 2/5

14.

a. 5/7

b. 2/5

c. 5/10

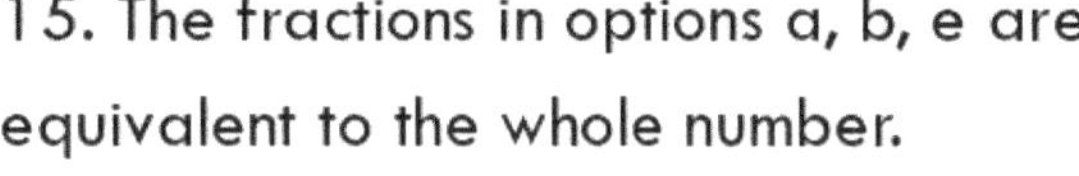

15. The fractions in options a, b, e are equivalent to the whole number.

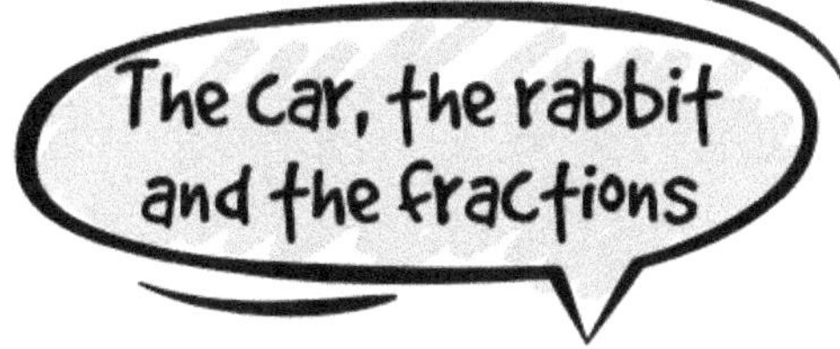

16. a. i. The car has traveled 2/5.

ii. The car should travel 3/5.

b. i. The rabbit hopped 9/10.

ii. The rabbit should hop 1/10.

17. a. 1/5. 15 divided by 3 = 5. He has cut it into 5 parts of 3 feet each. So each part represents 1/5.

b. Each piece represents 1/6. If she loses two pieces, she will be left with 4/6.

18.

a. ¼

b. 2/4

c. 1/8

19.

one-fourth

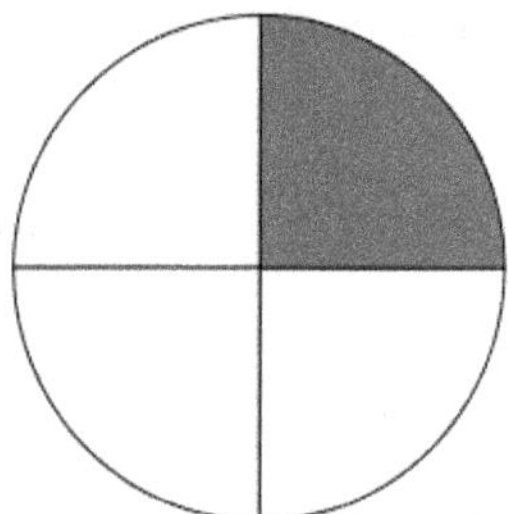

one-half

one-fifth

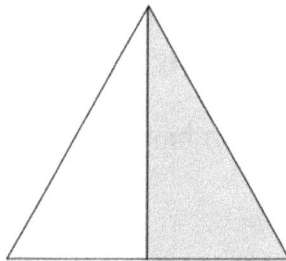

one-fourth

two-sixths

three-fourths

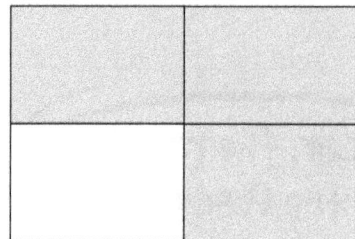

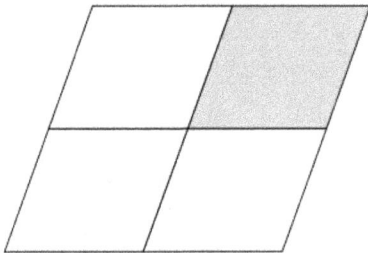

20. a. No, they are not fourths because they are of unequal sizes.

b.

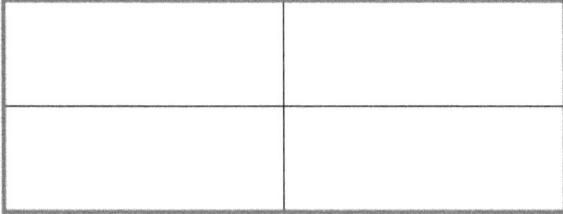

c. 1/4

1.

a. 2.40 pm

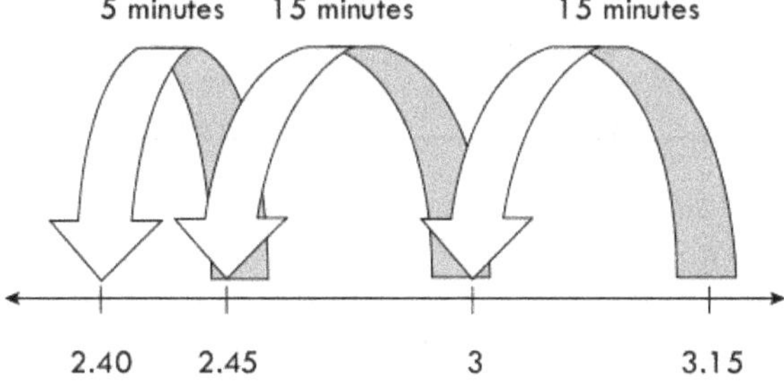

b. 58 minutes

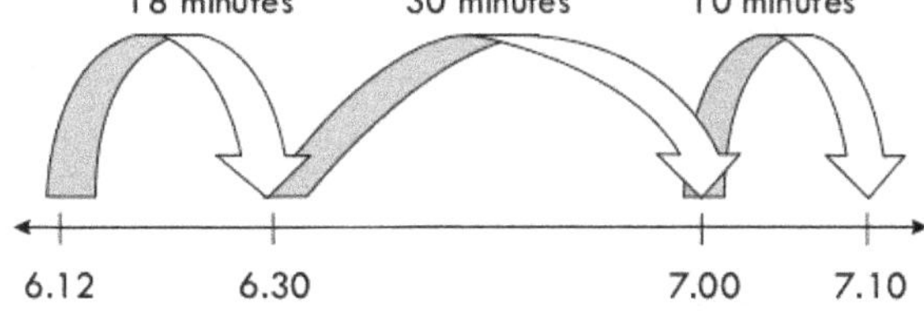

c. 3.57 pm

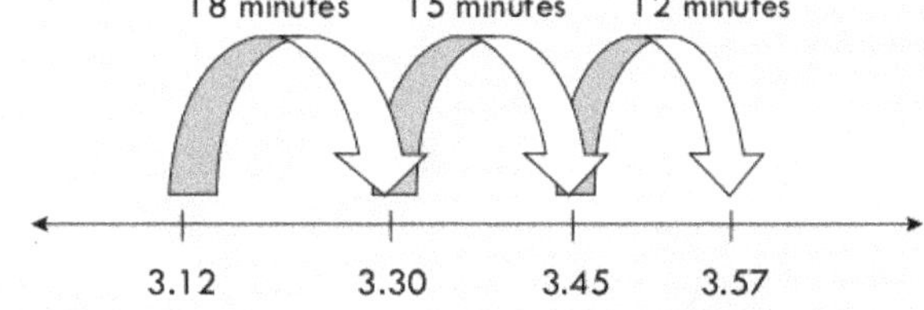

2. a. 27 minutes

b.

3. a. 5.23 pm

b. 7.34 pm

c. 1.02 pm

4.

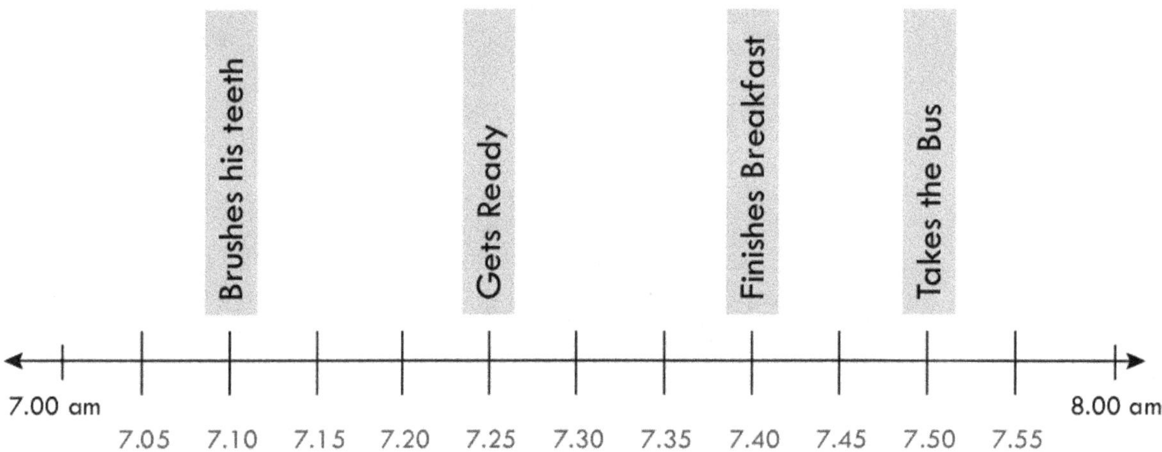

5.

a.

Player's name	Time arrived for practice
Joe	10.10 am
Peter	10.25 am
Johnny	10.40 am
Sam	10.50 am

b. Sam is the last to arrive for practice.

c. On skip counting by 5 minutes, from 10:25 to 10:40, the difference is 15 minutes.

6.

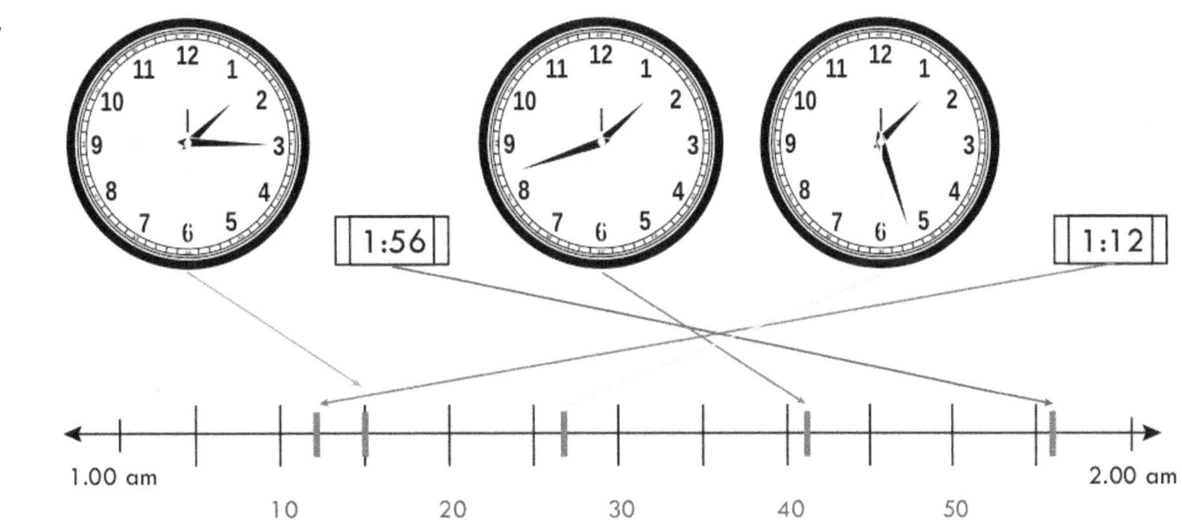

7. 28 minutes

8. a. 3 milliliters

b. 5 liters

c. 20 liters

d. 1 liter

e. 500 milliliters

9. a. 12 liters

b. 10 liters

c. 12 times

d. 205 milliliters

10. a. 300 milliliters

b. 400 milliliters

c. Sugar solution

d. 300 + 323 = 623 milliliters

11. a. Tank A has more capacity.

b. Tank C has the least capacity.

c. 63 + 24 = 87 liters

12. a. 36 kilograms

b. 90 packets

c. 1043 grams

d. 980 grams

13. a. Rice. The weight of the other objects will be in grams.

b. Spoon. The capacity of the spoon can only be measured in milliliters but the capacity of the other objects can also be measured in liters.

14. a. 1 kilogram = 1 bottle. 9 bottles will weigh 9 kilograms. Hence his bike weighs 9 kilograms

b. He is right. 1 kilogram = 1000 grams. 1000 grams can also be written as 10 x 100

15. a. Joshua

b. Ava

c. 23 seconds

d. 134 seconds

e. 56 - 45 = 11

1. a. 105 kids

b. Chips

c. Popcorn

d. 31-10 = 21, 21 kids preferred chips more than popcorn.

e. Apples

2. a. 2 x 5 = 10 cupcakes

b. 2 x 6 = 12 cupcakes

c. George sold 12 cupcakes.

d. Jack. He sold 2 cupcakes more than Stella.

e. Stella sold the least number of cupcakes.

3.

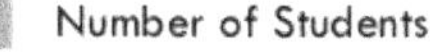

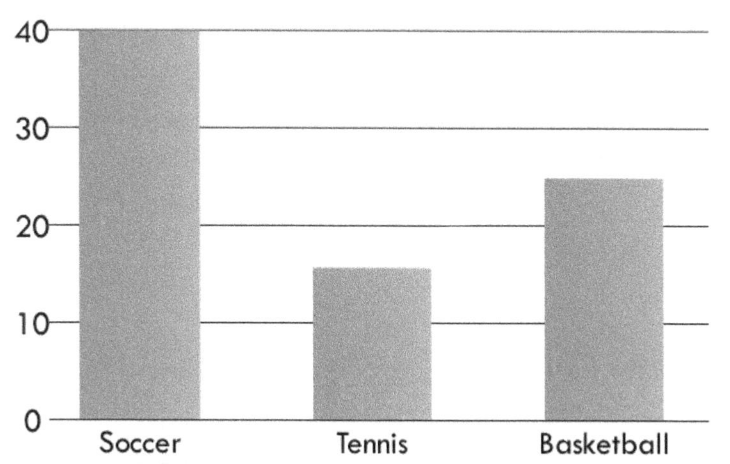

4. a. 17

b. Mint and Mango

c. 49

Ice cream Flavor	Number of Votes
Vanilla	
Chocolate	
Strawberry	
Mango	
Mint	

5. a. Mon: 24

Tue: 36

Wed: 12

Thu: 38

Fri: 15

b. Thursday

c. Wednesday

6.

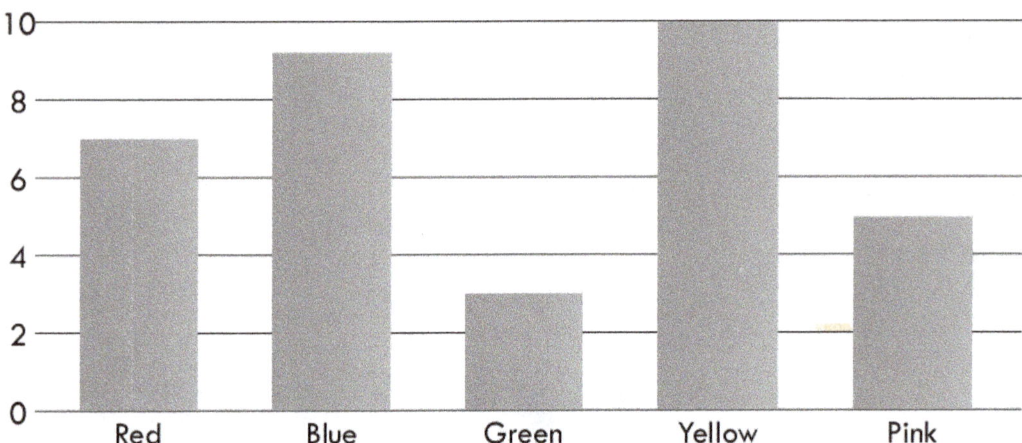

7.

a. 275

b. Arts

c. English and Science

d. English and Science

8. a. 9 days

b. December

c. 6 days

d. 18 days

How long am I?

9.

a. 4 inches

b. 2 and half inches

c. 3 and quarter inches

10. Option c - 9.5 inches

11.

a. 3 frogs

b. 1 frog

12.

a. 6 crayons

b. 3 crayons

13. a. Rod D

b. 2 ¾ miles

14. a. 61 - (12 + 15 + 21) = 13 apples.

b. The answer may vary.

Let's play a math game.

15. Answer may vary

16. a. 30

b. Wednesday

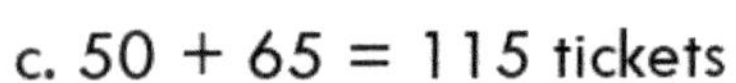

c. 50 + 65 = 115 tickets

d. 55 + 30 = 85 tickets

e. 50 - 40 = 10 tickets

f. 265 tickets

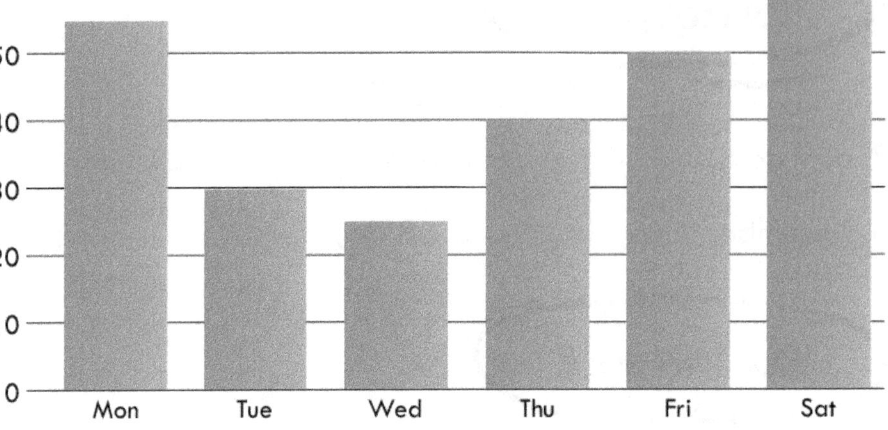

17.

a. 32 students

b. 19 students

c. 10

d. 8 students

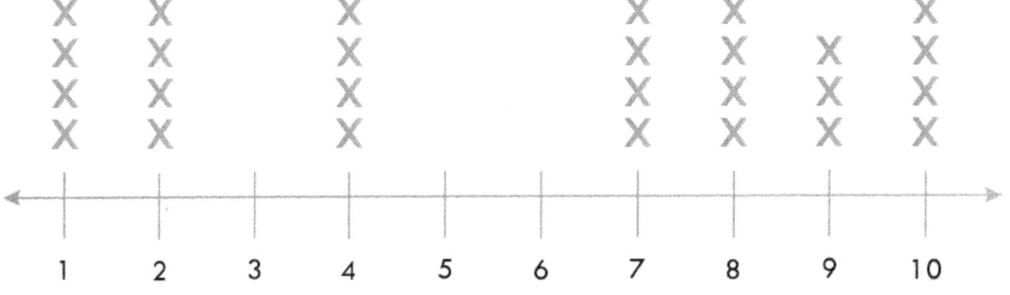

18. a. Oak - 16 trees

b. Answer may vary

19. 1 inch is made up of 2 half inches.

So, 3 inches = 3 x 2 = 6 half inches

1 inch	1 inch	1 inch

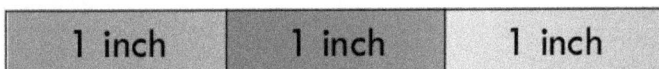

Half inch

20. a. 34 students

b. 10 students

c. Because 10 students measure 52 inches which is more than any other height measure.

d. 12 students

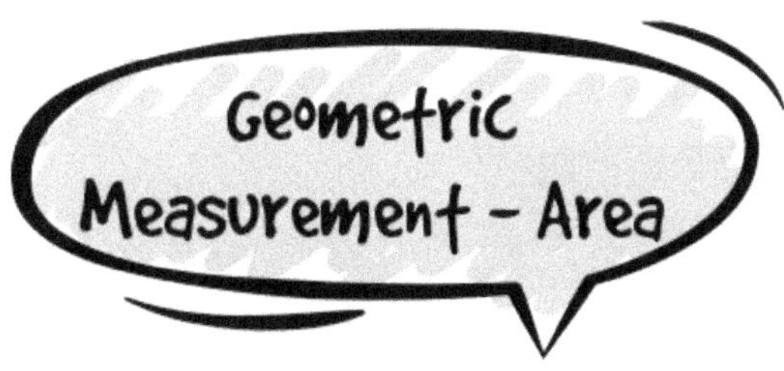

1.

2.

12 triangles 6 triangles 8 triangles.

3. Yes, both the shapes have the same area since they each have 8 square units.

4. a. 14 square units b. 16 square units c. 8 square units d. 4 square units

5. Rectangle A = 18 units

Rectangle B = 8 units

Rectangle C = 10 units

Thus, Rectangle A has the largest area.

6. 10 square units

a.

b.

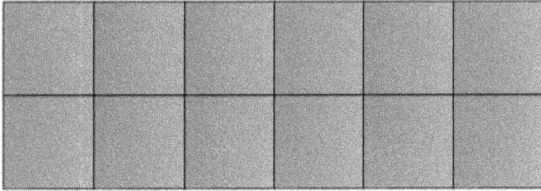

7. No, Hilda's square will have a bigger area since an inch is bigger than a centimeter.

8. A - 6 square units B - 12 square units C - 12 square units D - 24 square units

9. a. 25 square units b. 18 square units

10. A. 12 square units B.12 square units C. 6 square units D. 21 square units

11. A. 3 x 6 = 18 b. 3 x 8 =24 c. 5 x 3 = 15 d. 3 x 3 = 9

12. 8 square cm. By multiplying the length of the sides.

13. Area of the rectangle = 6 x 6 = 36

14.a. 3 x 6 = 18 tiles

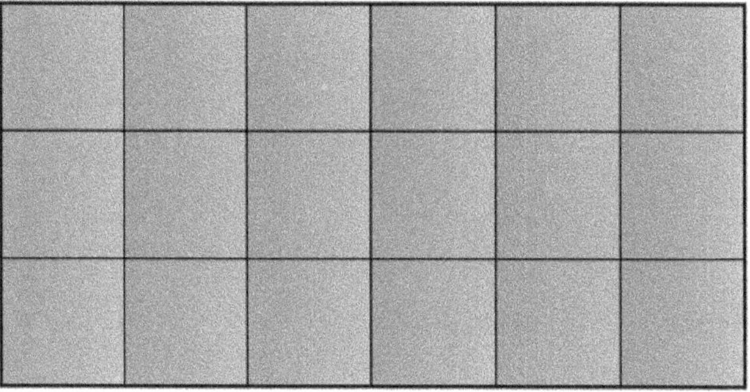

b. 3 x 3 = 9 tiles

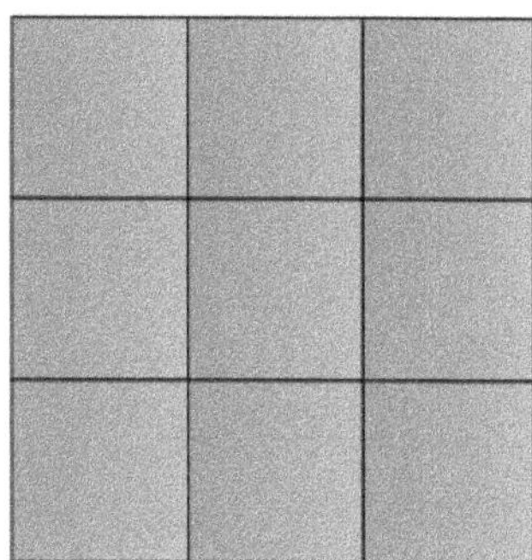

15. Nish's bedroom has an area of 42 square feet whereas her brother's room has an area of 45 square feet. Hence her brother's room is bigger.

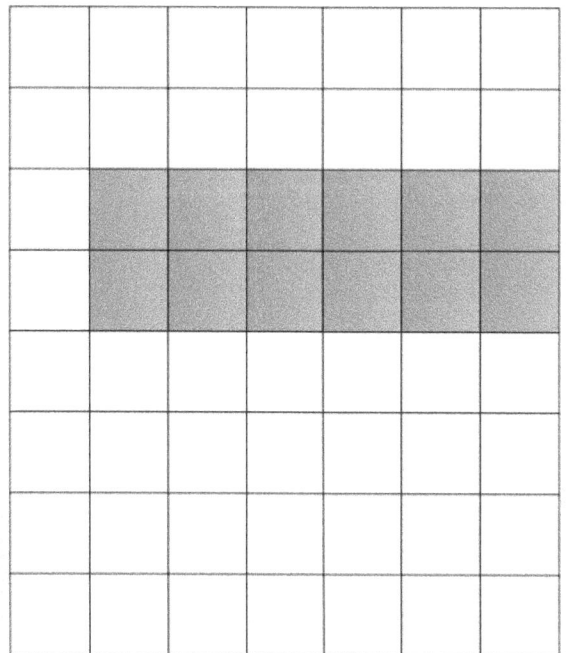

16.

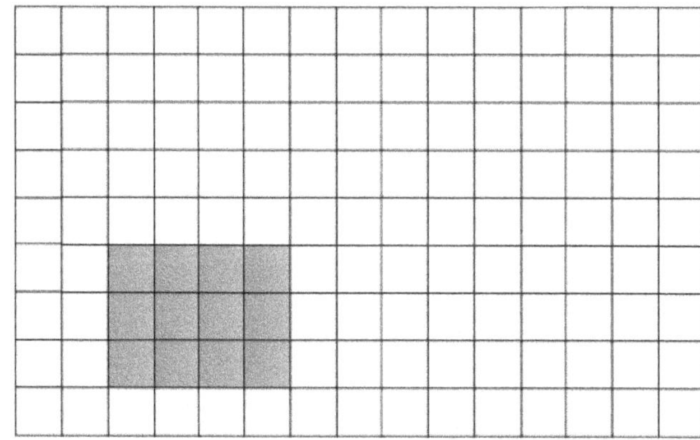

17. a. 8 x 7 = 35 + 21

= 56 square units

Area = 56 square units.

b. 12 x 4 = (10+ 2) x 4

= (10 x 4) +(2 x 4)

= 40 + 8

= 48

Area = 48 square units

c. 8 x 7 = (5 + 2) x 8

= (5 x 8) +(2 x 8)

= 40 + 16

= 56

Area = 56 square units

d. 9 x 8 = (5 + 4) x 8

= (5 x 8) +(4 x 8)

= 40 + 32

= 72

Area = 72 square units.

18. Answers may vary.

19. (2 x 2) + (3 x 10)

= 4 + 30

= 34

Area = 34 square units

20. Answers may vary.

Dave gets ready for school

1. b. By marking the covering of each shape.

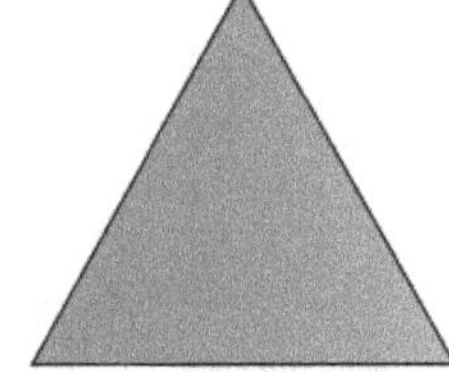

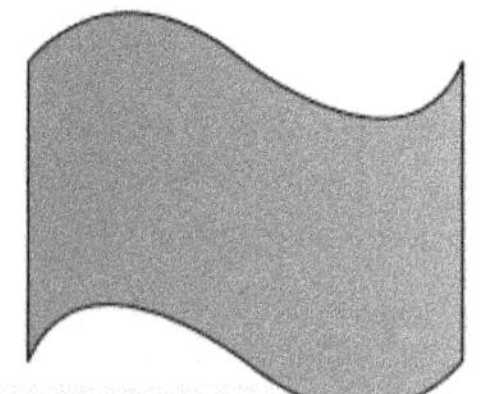

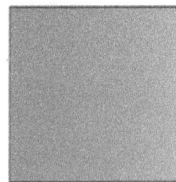

2. a. 30 cm b. 56 cm c. 41 cm d. 12 ft e. 34 cm f. 20 m

The greatest perimeter

3. Shape B

4. a. 4 + 4 + 4 + 4 = 16 cm

b. 5 + 5 + 5 + 5 + 5 + 5 = 30 cm

c. 4 + 5 + 4 + 5 = 18 cm

d. 7 + 3 + 3 + 2 + 4 + 1 = 20 cm

5. Eric's shape - 12 cm   Victor's shape - 24 cm

Eric is wrong since Victor's shape has a greater perimeter.

6. a. 24 cm   b. 30 m   c. 36 in   d. 12 cm

The football field problem

7. 270 m

Art, craft and math

8. 24"

9. 48 cm

10. 44 cm

11. Paige

12. Both methods are correct. Mary has used repeated addition whereas Ann has used multiplication to find the perimeter.

13. a. 16 cm b. No

14. Perimeter = 12 cm

15.

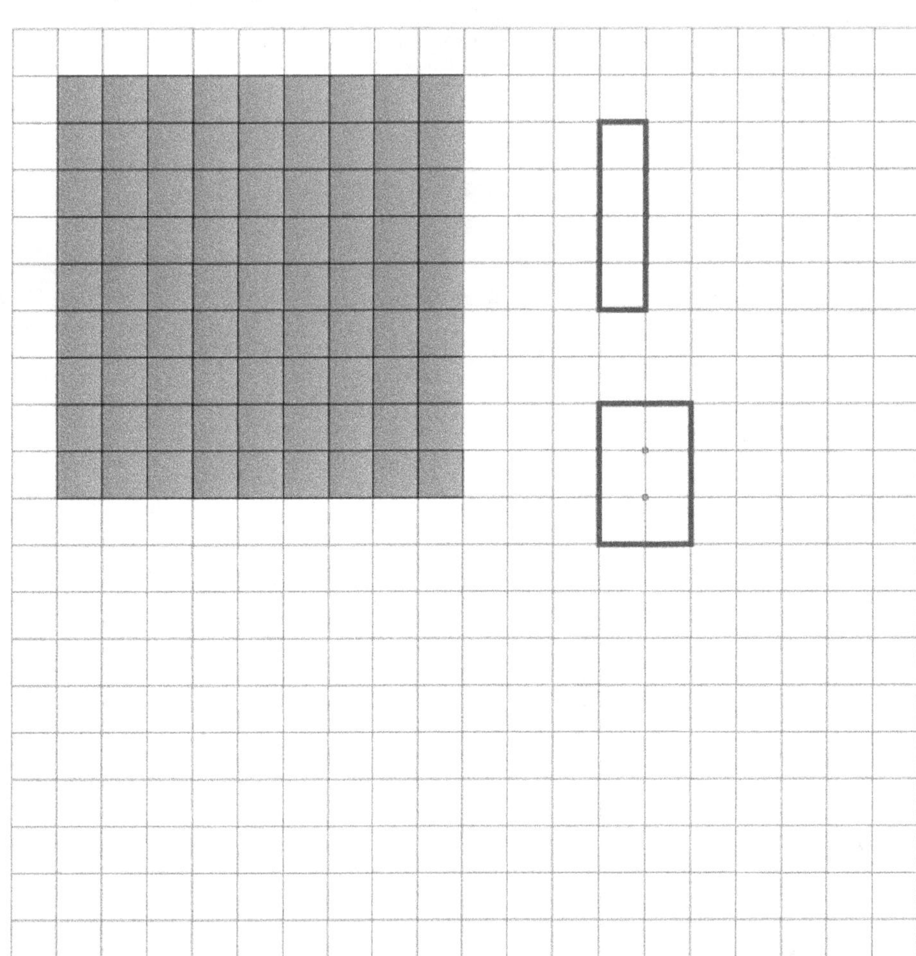

16.a. 24 cm

b. 88 cm

c. Counted the number of sides and multiplied it with the length of the sides.

17. Answers may vary.

18. 2 + 7 + 9 + 4 + 3 + x = 25 + x

x = 9 - 2 = 7

25 + 7 = 32 m

19. 38 in

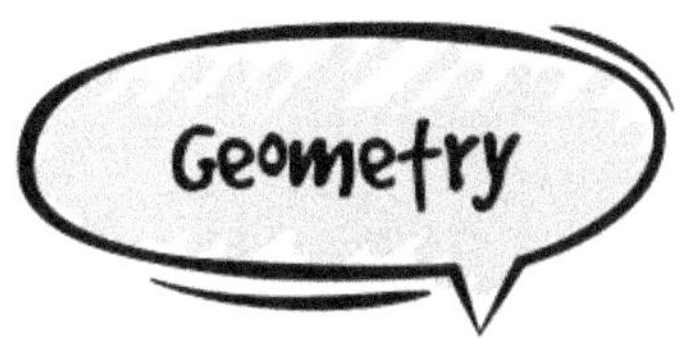

1.

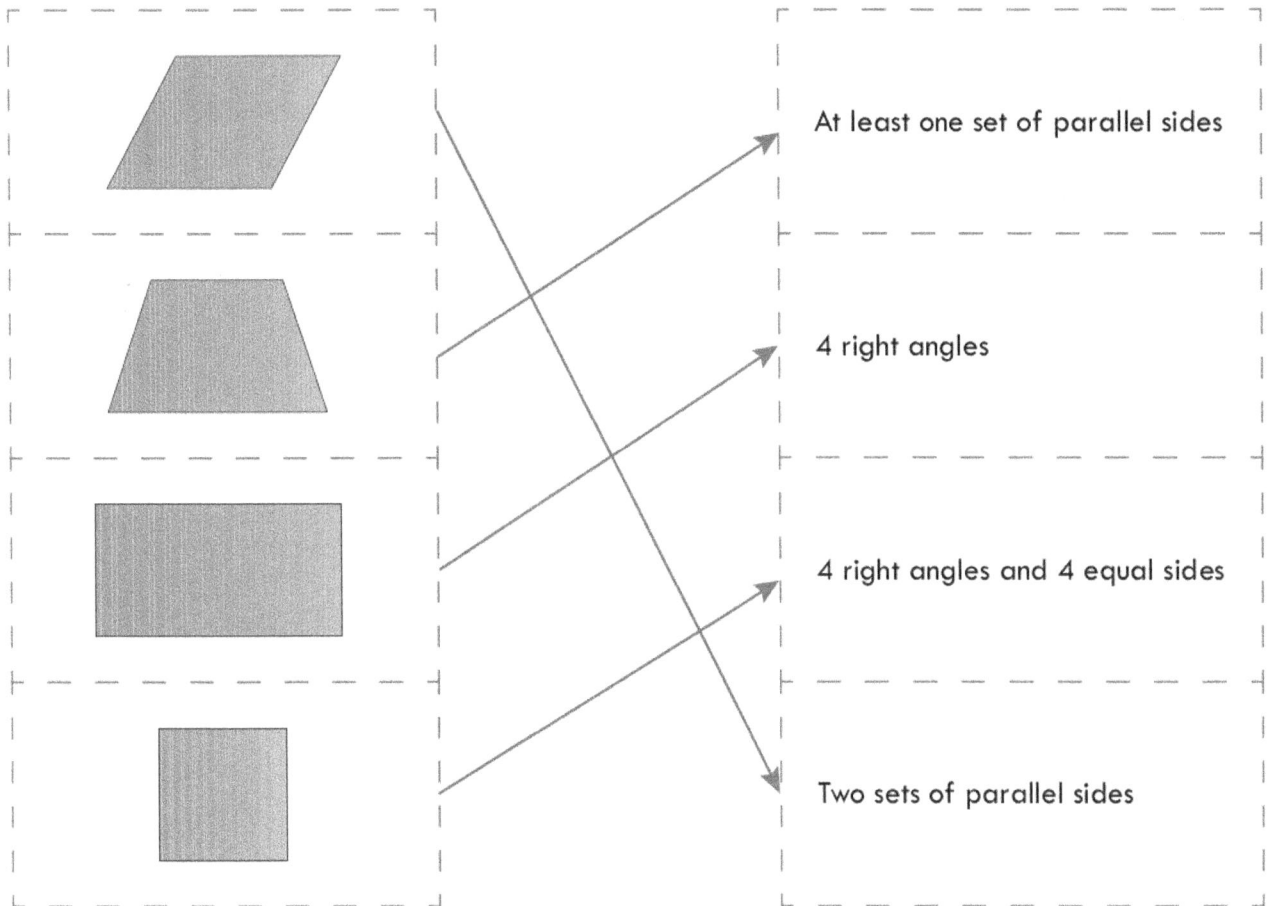

At least one set of parallel sides

4 right angles

4 right angles and 4 equal sides

Two sets of parallel sides

2. a. Quadrilaterals b. Trapezoid c. square

3. b. False c. True d. False

4.

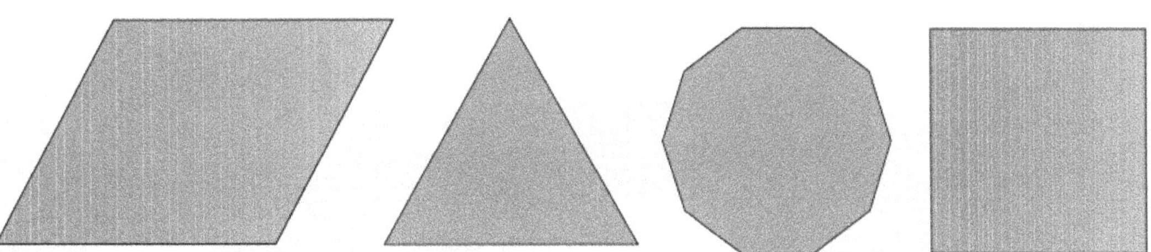

5. a. 6 sided shape. All sides and angles are equal. It is a regular polygon. 3 pairs of parallel sides.

b. It has 4 sides. It has equal sides and angles. It is a regular polygon. 2 pairs of parallel sides. Angles formed are 90 degrees.

c. All sides are equal, all angles are equal, it is a regular polygon.

6. a. Yes is it because a square satisfies all the properties of a rhombus.

b. A rhombus cannot be called a square if the angles are not 90 degrees. If the angles are 90 degrees, then that rhombus can be called a square.

7. a. 1/6 b. 1/2

8. a. Triangles b. Trapezoid

9.

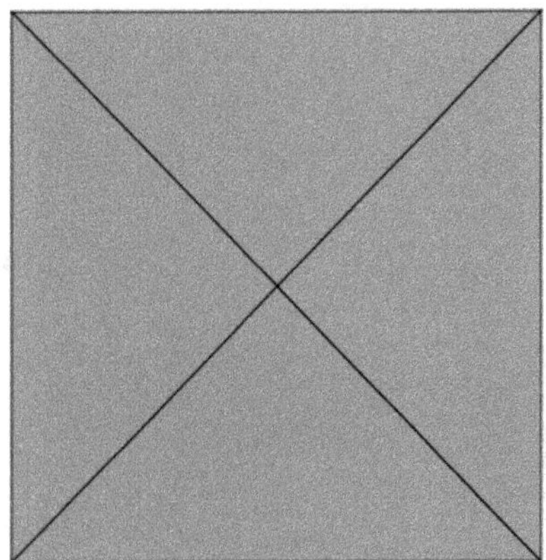

10. a.

b.

11. 1/2

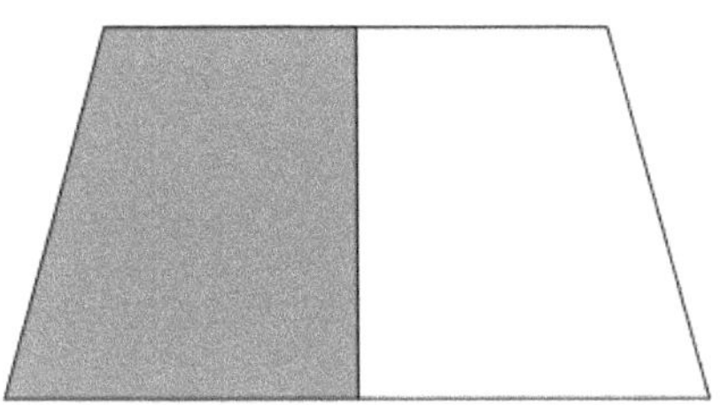

12. 1/4

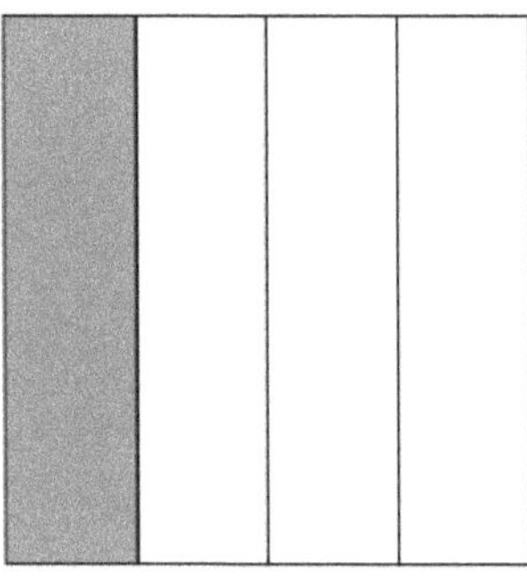

13.

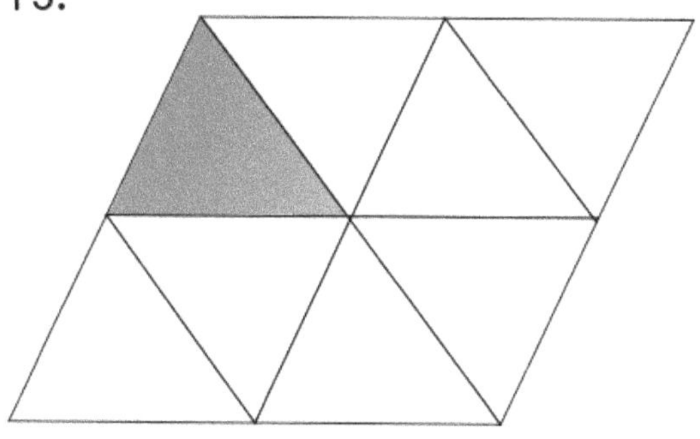

14. 12 triangles

15. No it's not possible. We need a closed figure to get more than 1 angle.

16. As per students drawing

17. As per students drawing

18. Yes both are of the same size since they both have 12 square units also of the same size.

19. A parallelogram

20.

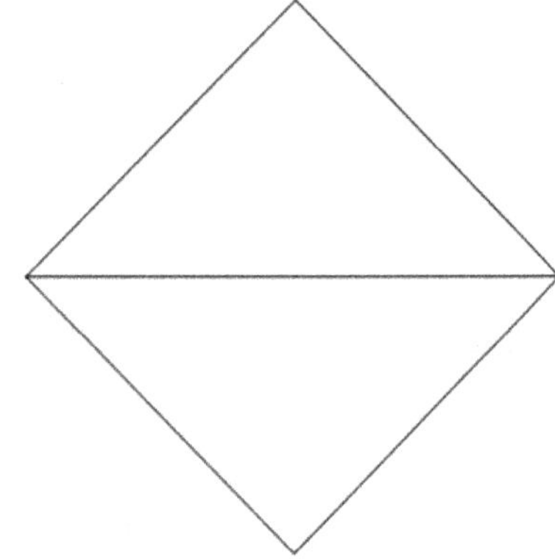

Science Answer Key

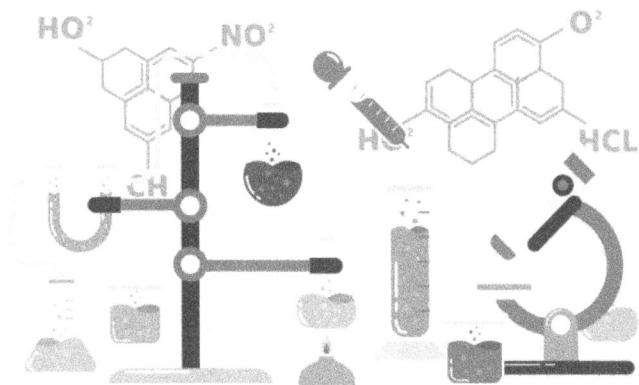

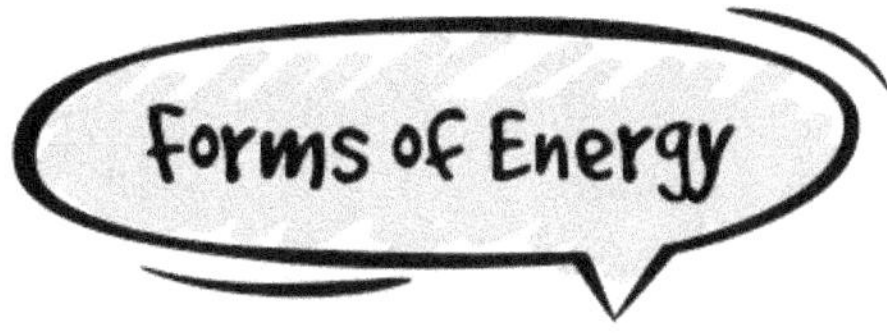

Heat energy

Solar energy

Electrical energy

Fuel or Chemical energy

Light energy

Fuel or Chemical energy

Kinetic energy Potential energy Kinetic energy

Kinetic energy Potential energy Potential energy

1. Kinetic Energy
2. Potential Energy
3. Potential Energy, Kinetic Energy
4. Potential Energy, Kinetic Energy
5. Kinetic Energy
6. Kinetic Energy
7. Potential Energy
8. Kinetic Energy
9. Kinetic Energy

Appliances

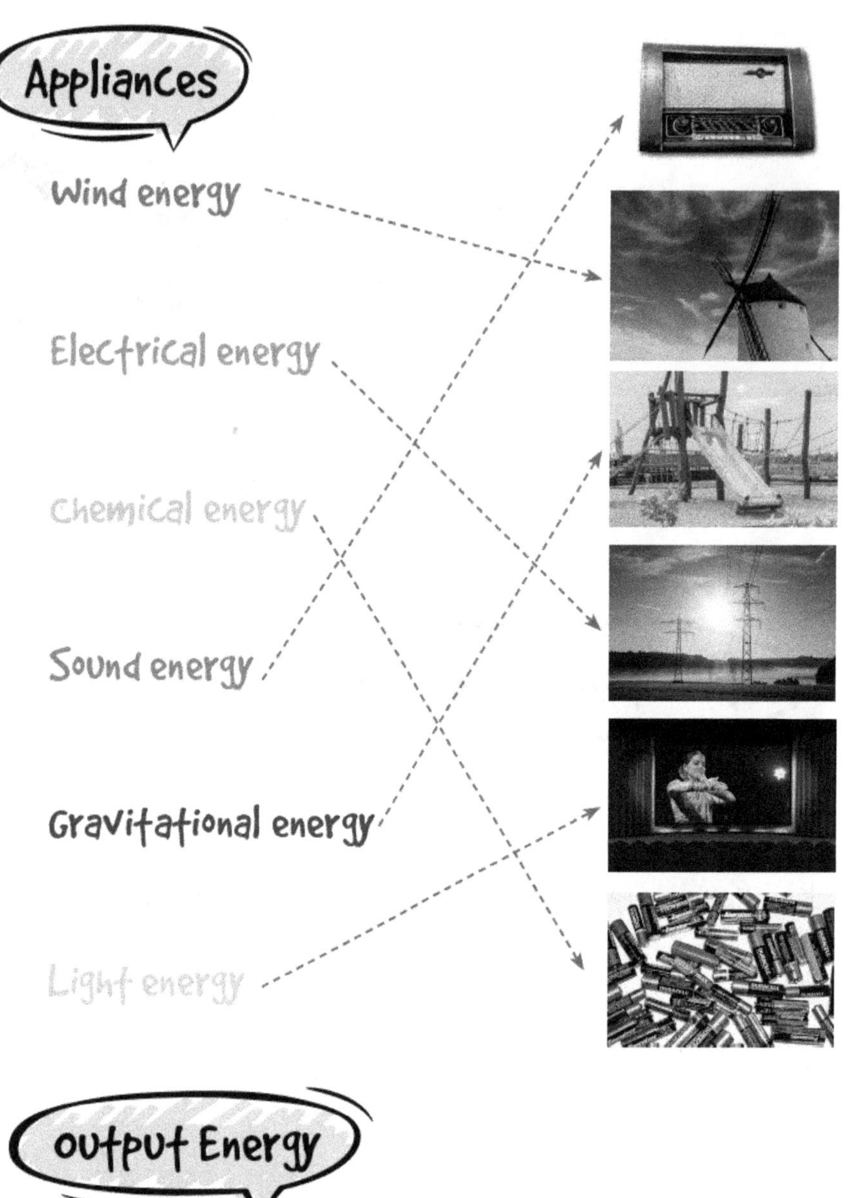

output Energy

Mechanical energy, because the blades in the mixie rotate

Light energy

Heat energy, because the heat in the oven helps us cook food

Mechanical energy or wind energy, as the blades of the fan rotate

Heat energy or wind energy, that helps us dry wet hair

Sound energy, that we hear as music

Evaporation, as water evaporates from wet clothes and dries them

Melting

Freezing

Condensation, water vapour condenses on the surface of the glass to form water droplets

Evaporation, water evaporates from wet hair to make it dry

Freezing, fruit juice freezes to form popsicles

1. Physical change, as only the shape of the pipe changes

2. Chemical change, burning paper forms ash thus changing the properties of the paper

3. Physical change, as the shape and of the chalk changes but it is still remains to be chalk

4. Physical change, as only the shape of the potato changes

5. Chemical change, as lemon juice changes the characteristics of water

6. Chemical change, because baking changes the characteristics of the dough

7. Physical change, as cheese slices are still cheese in a different shape and size

8. Chemical change, as sugar and caramel have different properties

9. Physical change, as the molten butter changes state and shape but with same characteristics

10. Physical change, as vapour condenses to form water droplets the properties are retained

11. Chemical change, as rust has different properties than a metal spoon

12. Physical change, as only the shape of the paper changes

Physical change or chemical change?

a. chemical change

b. chemical change

c. physical change

d. chemical change

e. physical change

f. chemical change

g. physical change

h. physical change

i. physical change

j. chemical change

k. physical change

l. physical change

Sources of Light

1. Natural
2. Artificial
3. Artificial
4. Natural
5. Natural
6. Artificial

Animals and their Shadows

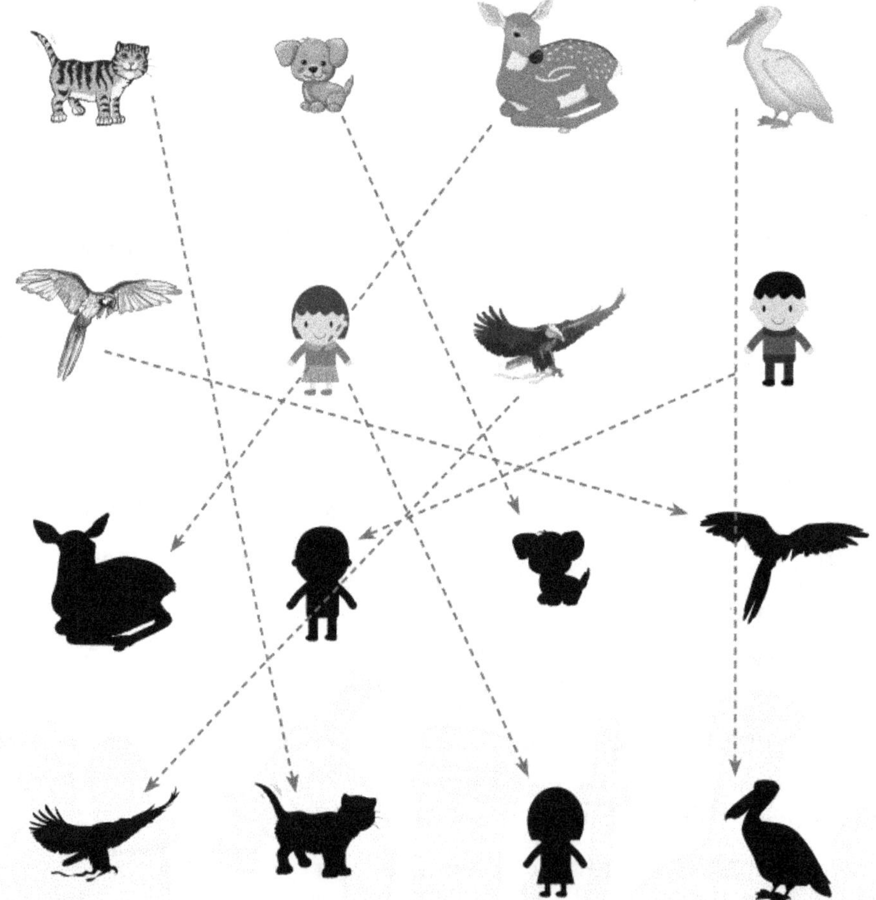

Light and Shadow

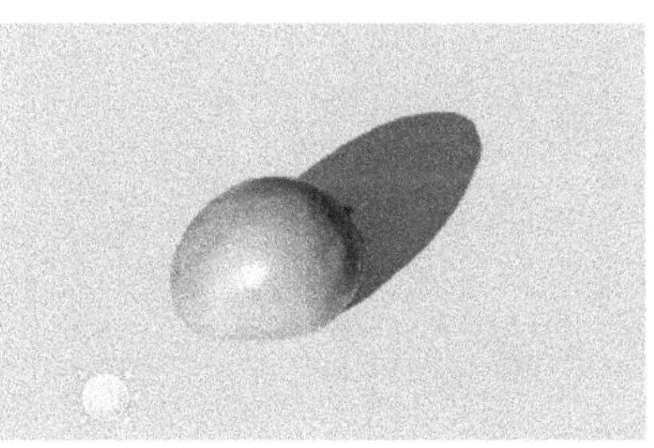

How do we see different colors?

m	d	z	t	s	c	a	m	e	l	o	p	s
e	k	n	s	w	e	r	n	x	z	y	z	i
x	y	b	a	o	r	c	a	u	r	o	c	h
m	a	m	m	o	t	h	u	g	v	n	h	k
k	v	w	r	l	j	a	t	x	l	q	m	n
l	m	i	z	h	t	e	i	r	p	u	h	r
c	o	l	m	h	w	o	l	b	f	a	z	j
r	s	a	u	r	o	p	o	d	b	g	z	t
i	a	h	n	e	v	t	i	h	l	g	v	w
n	s	h	n	z	a	e	d	m	g	a	p	o
o	a	e	d	m	e	r	a	h	b	r	c	v
i	u	e	k	d	s	y	f	z	h	y	n	a
d	r	z	b	n	b	x	s	r	v	f	c	e

Living Animals

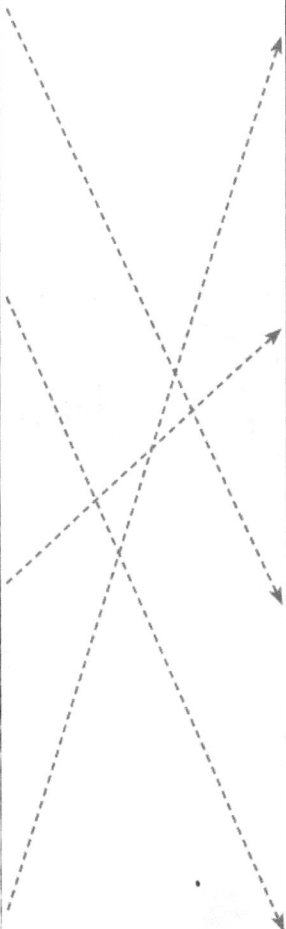

1. Asiatic lion
2. Black-footed ferret
3. Polar bear
4. Cheetah
5. Mountain gorilla
6. Giant panda
7. African elephant
8. Gray wolf
9. Mediterranean monk seal
10. Black rhinoceros

Solar system, Sun, Earth, Asteroid, Constellation, Stars and Comet

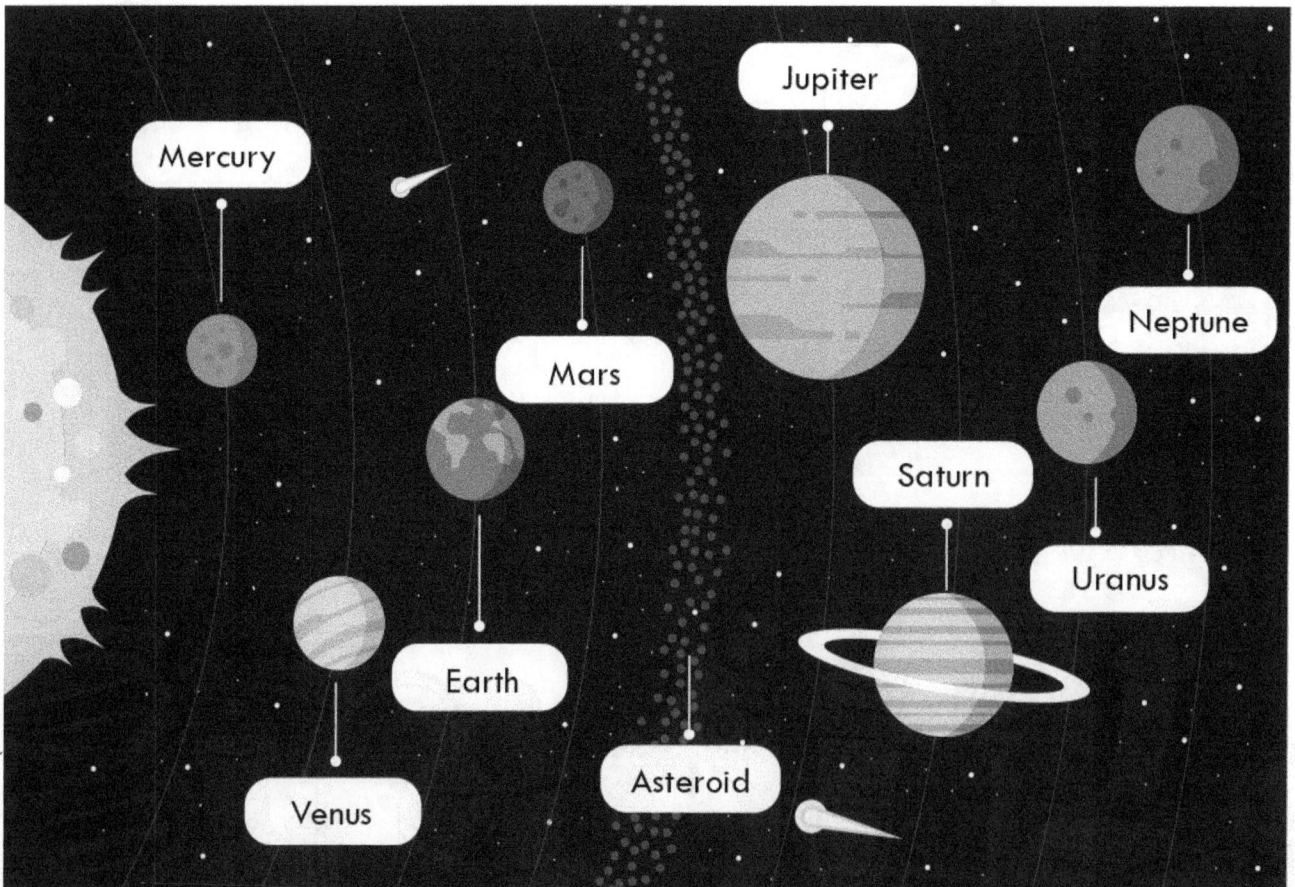

Jupiter
Mercury
Neptune
Mars
Saturn
Uranus
Earth
Asteroid
Venus

Across:
3. Mercury
7. Jupiter
9. Rotate
10. Sun
12. Solar system
15. Venus
16. Astronaut
17. One
19. Pluto
20. Space station

Down:
1. Mars
2. Neptune
4. Moon
5. Gravity
6. Saturn
8. Telescope
11. Uranus
13. Rings
14. Earth
17. Orbit
18. Eight

1. No, because of the Earth's tilted axis and revolution around the Sun.

2. The hemispheres have different seasons because the Earth's axis is tilted during its revolution around the sun this changes the exposure area of Earth to the Sun which causes the seasons.

3.

Month	Season in Northern Hemisphere	Season in Southern Hemisphere
March	Spring	Autumn
June	Summer	Winter
September	Autumn	Spring
December	Winter	Summer

Asteroid, Comet, and Meteor

	Asteroid	Comet	Meteor
often called 'Shooting stars'			X
is visible in our sky			X
made up of rock	X		X
orbits the Sun	X	X	
frozen ball of dust		X	
orbits between Mars and Jupiter	X		
usually burns up as it nears the Earth			X
appears as a streak in the sky			X
called 'dirty snowball'		X	

www.aceacademicpublishing.com

THE ONE BIG BOOK

GRADE 3

For English, Math, and Science

www.ingramcontent.com/pod-product-compliance
Lightning Source LLC
Chambersburg PA
CBHW080526090426
42733CB00015B/2499

9781949383379